Posthumanism and the Digital University

Also Available from Bloomsbury

Posthumanism and the Digital University

Texts, Bodies and Materialities

Lesley Gourlay

BLOOMSBURY ACADEMIC
LONDON · NEW YORK · OXFORD · NEW DELHI · SYDNEY

BLOOMSBURY ACADEMIC
Bloomsbury Publishing Plc
50 Bedford Square, London, WC1B 3DP, UK
1385 Broadway, New York, NY 10018, USA
29 Earlsfort Terrace, Dublin 2, Ireland

BLOOMSBURY, BLOOMSBURY ACADEMIC and the Diana logo are trademarks
of Bloomsbury Publishing Plc

First published in Great Britain 2021
This paperback edition published in 2022

Cover design by Rebecca Heselton
Photograph © springtime78/iStock

A catalogue record for this book is available from the British Library.

Library of Congress Cataloging-in-Publication Data
Names: Gourlay, Lesley, author.
Title: Posthumanism and the digital university: texts, bodies and materialities / Lesley Gourlay.
Description: London; New York: Bloomsbury Academic, 2020. |
Includes bibliographical references and index.
Identifiers: LCCN 2020032053 (print) | LCCN 2020032054 (ebook) |
ISBN 9781350038172 (hardback) | ISBN 9781350194038 (paperback) |
ISBN 9781350038189 (epub) | ISBN 9781350038196 (ebook)
Subjects: LCSH: Education, Higher–Effect of technological innovations on. |
Knowledge, Theory of. | Electronic information resources. | Posthumanism.
Classification: LCC LB2395.7.G689 2020 (print) | LCC LB2395.7 (ebook) |
DDC 378.1/7344678–dc23
LC record available at https://lccn.loc.gov/2020032053
LC ebook record available at https://lccn.loc.gov/2020032054

ISBN: HB: 978-1-3500-3817-2
PB: 978-1-3501-9403-8
ePDF: 978-1-3500-3819-6
eBook: 978-1-3500-3818-9

Typeset by RefineCatch Limited, Bungay, Suffolk

To find out more about our authors and books visit www.bloomsbury.com
and sign up for our newsletters.

Contents

Introduction

It is a commonplace in educational policy and theory to claim that digital technology has 'transformed' the university, the nature of learning, and even the essence of what it means to be a scholar or a student. However, arguably, these claims have not always been based on strong research evidence, and have also not been subject to adequate scrutiny in terms of what exactly they are referring to. What is meant by learning? What are students and scholars actually *doing* in the day-to-day life of the digital university? The project of this book is to examine in detail how the world of the digital interacts with texts, artefacts, devices, and people, in the contemporary university setting. My focus will be on how knowledge practices intersect with the digital, and also on the nature of analogue and digital texts, how they emerge, how they move around, and how they act on the world.

My starting point is that mainstream ideas about *epistemic practices*, (teaching, reading, discussing, writing and so on), are dominated by an only partially-acknowledged set of assumptions about agency, which is derived from a deeply humanist worldview. My central argument throughout the book is that this worldview has led to a view of digital epistemic practices which is limited, restrictive, and fundamentally inaccurate. Weaving together ideas and perspectives from a range of thinkers and disciplinary sources, I draw on ideas from *posthuman* and *new materialist* theory in particular, to attempt to open up our understanding about how digital epistemic practices operate, making a case that agency and the ways in which knowledge emerges – both analogue and digital – should be more accurately regarded as *more-than-human*.

As argued throughout the chapters, the conventional notion of the human subject in higher education relies on the assumption of a clearly-bounded individual, often portrayed as in some sense sequestered from others, away from sociopolitical forces, and even from materiality itself. In this imaginary, the prototypical student (or academic), I argue, is conjured as an idealized neoliberal subject, free from the 'bounds' of context, the social, the material, and the body itself. Acts of engagement and meaning-making are assumed to flow straightforwardly from human agency alone, and are posited as conscious, observable and singular. I seek to challenge this notion of the stable, individual human subject, and contend that this notion cannot be maintained in contemporary digital higher education.

Arguably, how students and academics write, talk and communicate in the university is a question which has not occupied a great deal of attention in the mainstream of higher educational theory, research and policy. Instead, the tendency in the wider field has been to regard forms of communication as unproblematically transparent, neutral means by which to move 'fully-formed' ideas around. This elision, I would argue, stems, at least in part, from a profoundly humanist set of assumptions regarding the nature of education and knowledge, which underscore the notion of the human subject as a freefloating, autonomous, but bounded, individual. In this worldview, knowledge, ideas and texts are cast as abstract, disembodied and separate from the sociolinguistic and sociomaterial conditions of their arising, which serves to reinscribe implicit notions of the knowledge as a clearly delineated, separate and *a priori* entity – the persistence of this tendency is evinced in the parlance of 'teaching and learning', by expressions such as 'knowledge transfer'. This view of knowledge arguably renders the emergence and enactment of epistemic practices as invisible, which may lead to these being viewed as in some sense fixed or 'natural', as opposed to having arisen over centuries through complex and historically changing mediatic conditions.

Mainstream thinking regarding higher education pedagogies (in some contexts) has moved away from a strongly cognitivist emphasis of the individual student gaining knowledge in relative isolation, towards a favouring of 'active learning', derived from a social constructivist framing, which sees the site of education as primarily residing in interaction with others. Interactivity and interlocution are encouraged as key markers of 'student engagement', to the point – I suggest – where these forms of participation have arguably taken on the role of a new, and normative, orthodoxy. However, despite the strong emphasis placed on interaction in notions of what constitutes 'good' higher education pedagogic practice, there is remarkably little attention paid to the detail of *how* this interaction takes place, and the relationships between epistemic practices and knowledge itself, in face-to-face and digital settings. In this regard, it could be argued that mainstream higher education pedagogy is somewhat undertheorized and epistemologically underdeveloped, in terms of how we understand its relationships to speech, writing, media and textual practices.

Arguably, this elision can be observed in a more marked form in the educational literature concerning engagement with digital media in the university, where there is a tendency to rely on notions of the digital as a disembodied, context-free realm, which is in some sense 'magical' and nonmaterial. This is accompanied by a related tendency to collapse into either ideologically-freighted and utopian 'brave new world' discourses of educational 'transformation', or alternatively to reach for moral panic discourses of falling standards, distraction, or loss of human control to 'the machines'. In both cases, I would argue, an accurate focus on the materiality of practices is lost, alongside a recognition of the intertwined nature of analogue and digital literacy practices.

Throughout this book I will use a series of concepts to consider different aspects of how texts operate in the university, in particular looking at the digital. I will take theoretical frameworks and ideas taken from posthumanism, new materialism, cultural studies, human geography, literacy studies, media studies, anthropology, and library and information science, in order to re-examine the nature of the university in the contemporary digital period. In doing so, it will focus on a series of themes in theoretical terms, applying each concept to a particular example of digital epistemic practice in higher education, discussing and interrogating various uses of digital technology in a range of higher education settings, such as writing on a laptop, a Massive Open Online Course (MOOC), a virtual learning environment, a 'flipped classroom', 'hyperwriting', Open Educational Practices (OEPs) and learning analytics. My approach to each of these has been derived from Adams and Thompson's (2016) approach to 'researching a posthuman world', in which they 'interview' objects. Using this methodology, over several chapters, I 'interview' one of these digital epistemic practices, in order to form a deeper set of insights into their nature, how they emerge, and how a range of human and nonhuman actors entangle in that process.

I also discuss what are often described as 'traditional' campus-based, face-to-face educational practices, and the relationships they have to digital education. In this regard, this should not be regarded as a book on 'elearning', or one which is exclusively focused on digital education, assuming the digital to be a clearly separate realm to the 'face-to-face'. The overall goal is to work towards a deeper but also more practical understanding of how these areas of higher education research and practices are intertwined, both historically, and in terms of practices, and to offer what I hope will be a fresh set of critical perspectives which might enable us to have more nuanced, insightful, and accurate view of digital higher education. This, I propose, may allow researchers, policymakers and practitioners to move away from ideologically-derived constructs of educational practices, students and academic staff, towards a more complex, messy, but finer-grained understanding of how knowledge emerges in 'the digital age'.

Chapter 1: More than Human

This is an attempt to provide a sketch map of the theoretical territory I will be picking my way through in the book. I do not set out to achieve a comprehensive overview of this complex field, but instead highlight areas where I feel these ideas have something to offer this particular project of understanding texts, practices and student engagement in the university, both in the past, and in the contemporary digital period. I begin by providing an overview of the main assumptions of humanism, and go on to set out the effects these have on how we understand the nature of education, learning, meaning-making, and human subjects in education. I then go on to propose that *posthumanism* and related field of *new materialism* can offer an alternative set of understandings. These ideas will be developed and illustrated with examples from the digital university over the subsequent chapters.

Chapter 2: Matter

This chapter focuses on the ways in which various strands of literature and practice have sought to 'situate' textual and epistemic practices, looking at work on *genre* in applied linguistics, the findings of literacy studies, and related notions of 'digital literacies' in higher education. I argue that, in various moves, researchers and practitioners have done meaningful work to move the conception of textual practices away from the abstract, and towards the particular. I propose that this project has enjoyed partial success via work in new literacy studies, which has drawn attention to the socially-situated and intensively political nature of academic reading and writing. However, literacy studies and applied linguistics have been slower to recognize the material and radically distributed nature of textual practices. However, in recent years a body of work in posthuman literacy studies and posthuman applied linguistics has emerged. I discuss the insights of this work to higher education, and how this shift may open up a more nuanced understanding of how students engage in digital practices, particularly in terms of reading and writing in digitally-mediated spaces, and explore this in more depth with an 'interview' with my laptop.

Chapter 3: Body

In this chapter I will focus particularly on how students are portrayed in policy discourses, and also in the mainstream discourses of 'teaching and learning' in higher education, particularly in relation to the digital. I will argue that these ways of talking about and writing about students tend to make the bodies – the material embodied reality of them as people – disappear from view. I will argue that, instead, archetypes are conjured, which are abstract and disembodied in their nature. I will propose that students collectively are recognized as bodies in a restricted sense, as bodies and voices which are required to perform in ways which reinscribe an ideology of social constructivism. I examine the particular case of the mainstream discourses surrounding 'teaching and learning' in higher education, and argue that that this set of discourses and practices has become dominated by this ideology to such an extent, that interaction and 'participation' have ceased to be regarded as *means* to learning, but have come to stand as a proxy *for learning itself*. I will argue that this is a normative and disciplining discourse, which demands a very particular and restrictive set of interactive performances of students and academic staff, in their embodied practice and online behaviour, drawing on the critical work of Bruce Macfarlane and Gert Biesta. I also look at how student and lecturer subjectivities are generated by texts in the classroom and online, and propose that a posthuman perspective on student-embodied practice offers a more expansive concept of participation. I will develop this analysis to look in particular at how the student is conceptualized in digital education, focusing on an 'interview' with a MOOC. This chapter builds on and develops a paper I first published in the journal Higher Education Policy (Gourlay 2017).

Chapter 4: Presence

This chapter looks at the status of the lecture, taking a historical view, and drawing on the work of Norm Friesen (2017), who traces the gradual shifts in the lecture over the centuries, as a result of changing and continuous media practices and technologies in the university. I focus on what I regard as the distinctive features of a live lecture, as opposed to a broadcast format, such as an online video. Drawing on the work of Erving Goffman, I examine the 'selves' that he proposes the lecturer inhabits, and argue that *ephemerality* and *co-presence* in the live lecture create a situation which is in itself fundamentally interactive, and dialogic. I contrast this with the commonplace criticism in the educational literature that the lecture is inherently 'teacher-centred', renders students 'passive', and is therefore to be considered as 'dead' in the contemporary period. I argue that this is a further instantiation of the phenomenon of Biesta's 'learnification' discussed in the previous chapter, in which student interlocution has come to stand as a proxy for educational 'quality', and the teacher's presence is a problem to be solved, and a body to be dispensed with. I illustrate this point by an 'interview' with the 'flipped classroom', which I propose is a contemporary digitally-mediated return to the notion of lecturer as conduit for a fixed body of knowledge, as in the medieval period.

Chapter 5: Interface

This chapter extends this analysis by focusing on artefacts and devices used for reading and writing in the university, in both analogue and digital settings. I draw further on Friesen's (2017) historical review, looking at the changes but also the continuities over the centuries in terms of the media practices used by teachers and students in universities, following on from his characterization of the book as *interface*. I then turn to look at how digital technology tends to be imagined and discussed in educational policy, research, and popular media discourses, offering a critique of the notion of the digital device as 'tool'. Instead I make a case for viewing the device, and also artefacts of inscription more generally, as nonhuman actors which form part of posthuman *entanglements of epistemic practices*. I contend that this theoretical shift is helpful, in that it moves us away from utopian notions of the 'ideal student', and also away from humanist conceptions of knowledge as *a priori* and latent in the individual – to be 'drawn out', (as with the meaning of the Latin root *educare*) either by traditional pedagogy, or by contemporary social constructivist notions of 'active learning'. I make a case that a posthuman framing of artefacts and devices, which allows digital epistemic practices to be seen not only social, but *sociomaterial*. This moves us away from the commonplace division of practice and context, and reinstates material settings and artefacts as agentive elements of knowledge work, as opposed to inert backdrops or 'tools'. I relate this to the digital, by examining how virtual learning environments are conceptualized in higher education, and again via an 'interview' with a Virtual Learning Environment (VLE), looking at these systems might be regarded as both continuation of historical textual practices, and also posthuman entanglements in themselves.

Chapter 6: Wayfaring

This chapter looks at the various ways in which both analogue and digital texts are restless, non-fixed, mobile, and the how they might be said to 'move'. I consider the notion of 'text trajectories', and the associated body of work which has examined the co-constitutive effects that texts exercise, as they move across media and material and social settings. I then link this strand of research to the work of Tim Ingold, and the relevance of his notion of *wayfaring* to digital higher education. I make the case that digital epistemic practices are fundamentally, and necessarily, restless, emergent and distributed in their nature. I consider this in terms of a critical contrast with mainstream discourses of 'transformation' in higher education, arguing that such changes are subtle, incremental and often situated in the granular, private, unobserved level of private or occluded textual engagement. I conclude by applying this via an 'interview' with the concept of 'hyperwriting' online in the digital university, building on Katherine N. Hayles' (2012) work on 'hyperreading'.

Chapter 7: Quantum

In this chapter I consider the concept of *quantum literacies*, proposed by Vera Buhlmann, Felicity Colman and Iris van der Tuin (2017). Situating their work in feminist new materialist scholarship, they seek to move beyond a conception of literacy in terms of linguistic systems and registers. Their focus is on 'knowledge forms, their production and their meaning' (2017: 47). They also challenge the notion that analogue communication somehow belongs to the medium of 'the real', with digital communication being seen to take place as an immaterial and abstract phenomenon. Central to their concept of *quantum literacy* is what they call *quantum thinking*. They refer to the move in science away from Newtonian physics towards a view of the nature of reality derived from quantum physics. *Quantum thinking* for them is situated and physical. It is concerned with measurement, but also itself generates data which is 'inseparable from the data with which it interacts' (2017: 49). They build on the work of Karen Barad, particular her notion of '... the relationality of object, the apparatus of measurement, and the observer' (Barad 2007: 389, in Buhlmann et al. 2017: 50). Their proposal is that quantum literacy might provide methods to be used to engage with complex social and technological change in the contemporary world. They propose it as a way of bearing witness to changes brought about by digitization in society, without being able to adopt a stance which stands outside of these. Buhlmann et al.'s provocation is challenging, and I attempt in the chapter to unravel it and relate it to digital epistemic practices once again. I conclude by considering the case of OEPs, arguing that they exhibit some elements of quantum literacies, in their distributed, unpredictable and emergent nature.

Chapter 8: Document

In this final chapter, I draw on new materialist work in the field of library and information science, considering recent work in library and information science which has explored the nature of, and differences between, information, documentation, and the nature of the document itself. I focus on an incisive piece by Kosciejew, in which this theme is explored in depth, drawing on range of theoretical sources. Kosciejew concludes that practices such as surveillance, recording, analysis and dissemination are applied to human subjects, this can render the human themselves into the status of a document. Taking the idea of *student as document*, I consider the case of learning analytics in higher education, as a technology of surveillance which – I propose, relates strongly to the series of themes developed in the foregoing chapters. I review critical papers on learning analytics, which critique its practices of surveillance, normativity, lack of transparency, accountability, anti-teaching ethos, links to commercial interests, and reinforcement of the subject position of the student as customer. I draw particularly on Prinsloo's discussion of the algorithmic decision-making and the notion of the *algocracy*, and I conclude that this technology represents the logical end-point of the ideological tendencies I have discussed throughout the book.

Chapter 9: Conclusions, or So What?

In my concluding chapter, I review the various elements of the book, and try to draw together and develop the relationships between the various discussions. I also turn to the question of 'so what?', revisiting the critiques of posthuman theory in general, and posthuman theory in particular, which were raised in chapter 1. I suggest that, rather than avoiding responsibility for human agency around higher education, a posthuman perspective potentially allows for a more focused, and accurate, account for what actually goes on, in the day-to-day of educational processes. I propose in conclusion that posthuman perspectives (defined broadly) offer two things to higher education and digital theorists, researchers and practitioners. The first, I argue, is that it allows for a radical questioning of the fundamental assumptions underlying agency and the unfolding of epistemic practices in higher educational practice, both digital and analogue. My final point is that – at least for me – it allows for a move away from ideological assumptions and stereotypes, towards profoundly ethnographic, observing, noticing stance towards practice. This, I propose, is a potentially valuable approach, which could usefully inform researchers and practitioners who seek to deepen their insights into the complex, emergent world of digital higher education.

More than Human

The focus of this book is on how, in the context of digital technology, our understanding of student engagement, teaching in higher education (in class and online), and also on how our understanding of how students engage with knowledge practices might be enhanced by looking at the university in a different way, drawing on *posthuman* theory. Posthumanism is a complex web of ideas which are not easily defined, are often misunderstood, and may be (mis) identified as an esoteric and highly abstract notions, with little relevance to day-to-day life, and certainly at first glance, to higher education. In this first chapter I will attempt to summarize what I consider to be the most important and useful ideas from posthuman theory, and how they might help us reconceptualize higher education and digital practices.

Posthumanism and the University

The concept of 'posthumanism' is in many respects a puzzling one. This chapter will attempt to define the theoretical 'ground' on which the book is based, and will also attempt to do some clearing work – by setting out how I am using the term, and also what I would seek to exclude, or de-emphasize in my use of it. The apparent oddness of the term posthumanism has arguably contributed to the challenge of making it relevant to educational thought, and bringing it in from what may appear at first glance to be the 'wild fringes' of education theory. The term was first used by Hassan in 1977, the essay based on a keynote speech delivered at a symposium devoted to 'postmodern performance'. In a dense theoretical piece, Hassan proposes posthumanism as a response to what he saw as the rapidly changing nature of the human form and its representations, referring to the development of human space exploration, and also to potential change brought about by artificial intelligence. He also refers to the origins of the universe, and the fact that humans are composed of the atoms created at that time. He goes on to reference contemporary poststructuralist challenges to the notion of the human 'subject' and Cartesian dualism, in addition to referring to future possibilities of human evolution (Hassan 1977). Since that paper, and that rather esoteric focus, the term has evolved and is used in a range of ways.

Bayne (2018) provides an excellent 'navigation aid' for educators seeking to understand the concept, in which she classifies the various strands of thought into three parts: *critical posthumanism, technological posthumanism* and *ecological posthumanism.* I find this helpful, and will follow Bayne's framing here to introduce the idea. Bayne points out that the object of critique within early posthumanism was liberal humanism. She quotes Badmington, who characterizes humanism as holding the following central belief:

> ... that the figure of 'Man' (*sic*) naturally stands at the centre of things; is entirely distinct from animals, machines and other nonhuman entities; is absolutely known and knowable to 'himself'; is the origin of meaning and history; and shares with all other human beings a universal essence.
>
> Badmington 2004: 1345

Bayne offers her own definition:

> To simplify, posthumanism involves us in making an ontological shift from understanding 'the human' as an individuated entity separate from and observant of the world and its (human and nonhuman) inhabitants, to one which is inextricably connected to the world and only conceivable as emergent with and through it.
>
> Bayne 2018

The emphasis here is on the ending of a particular unitary and separate *conception* of the human, as opposed to an ending of the human race itself – this is a crucial distinction. The important idea here is the decentring of the human from our conception of the world, and how it operates. She highlights the dominance of the notion of the autonomous human subject in educational theory, quoting Usher and Edwards:

> The very rationale of the educational process and the role of the educator is founded on the humanist idea of a certain kind of subject who has the inherent potential to become self-motivated and self-directing, a rational subject capable of exercising individual agency. The task of education has therefore been understood as one of 'bringing out', of helping to realise this potential, so that subjects become fully autonomous and capable of exercising their individual and intentional agency.
>
> Usher & Edwards 1994: 24, in Bayne 2018

Bayne first examines what she calls 'critical posthumanism', pointing out the roots of posthumanism in 1960s poststructuralist critiques of the Enlightenment view of 'man' as autonomous and unique, a set of critiques which instead emphasized the discursive construction of human subjectivities, informing movements such as feminism and postcolonial studies. Following these insights, as Bayne puts it, '... it became difficult in critical thought to see the human subject as existing outside history or outside political, discursive and material practice' (Bayne 2018). However, as Bayne argues, this set of insights do not necessarily lead us to a nihilistic perspective which implies an absence or irrelevance of the human, or human agency. She highlights the stance of Braidotti (2013), who proposes a move from 'unitary to nomadic subjectivity' (Braidotti 2013: 49), a subjectivity focused on interconnection between self and others. While some commentators have focused on posthumanism as a reaction to humanism (e.g. Davies 2008), others have claimed that there is nothing new in this state, but simply that it is now being recognized. As Wolfe points out, it was the case:

> ... before in the sense that it names the embeddedness of the human being in not just its biological but also its technological world ... and after in the sense that posthumanism names a historical moment in which the decentring of the human by its imbrication in technical, medical, informatic, and economic networks is increasingly impossible to ignore.
>
> Wolfe 2010: xv, in Bayne 2018

In this book, I also adopt this position, and regard posthumanism as a theoretical framing which provides insights into the nature of human/nonhuman life and practices across historical epochs, as opposed to viewing it as a state of affairs which is new, or unique to our contemporary political and historical moment or predicament. With that in mind, I apply it as a framing throughout, including in consideration of past practices and technologies in the history of the university. Bayne goes on to discuss what she terms 'technological posthumanism', drawing on Hayles (1999, 2006). Her form of posthumanism is focused on:

> ... transforming untrammelled free will into a recognition that agency is always relational and distributed, and correcting an over-emphasis on consciousness to a more accurate view of cognition as embodied throughout human flesh and extended into the social and technological environment.
>
> Hayles 2006: 160–161 in Bayne 2018

As she points out, in a humanist framing, knowledge is seen as 'representing accurately those objects over which we have dominance as autonomous observers' (Bayne 2018). This division of subject and object of knowledge is broken down in a posthuman framing, instead the two elements can be seen as intertwined and co-constitutive. This book focuses particularly on this point, I will argue that this has always been the case throughout the history of the university, but that the advent of digital technology adds further complex dimensions to this set of relationships. Bayne also identifies a third strand, which she characterizes as 'ecological posthumanism'. This work focuses more on human relationships with the natural world, and is associated with writers working in 'new materialism', such as Barad (2007), Coole and Frost (2010) and Dolphijn and van der Tuin (2012). These theorists are influenced by the philosophical writings of Spinoza, Bergsen and Deleuze, focusing on the concept of 'new vitalism' (e.g. Fraser et al. 2005) or 'vital materialism' (Bennett 2010), a perspective which is founded on a 'radical relationality', as Bayne puts it, that '... the world is composed only and always through the enfolding and mutual constitution of matter and meaning' (Bayne 2018). Bayne points out that much of this work has focused on animal studies and 'critical animal pedagogy' (e.g. Dinker & Pedersen 2016) and post-anthropocentric work focused questioning human dominance over the environment. This theme relating to the natural environment is beyond the scope of my project with this book, but undeniably opens up searching new questions and perspectives on the university and its place in the world.

However, there are some objections which may be raised to the notion of posthumanism, and whether it offers anything of value of educational research. The first is that, given the enormous socioeconomic challenges facing the planet in terms of equality and access to basic resources, freedoms and rights, it may seem counter-intuitive to be apparently moving away from the notion of a shared common humanity when discussing education. The project of *humanistic* education is generally regarded to be a benign and 'person-centred' one, focused on inclusion and sensitivity to human needs, emotions and diversity. In contrast, posthumanism, with a name reminiscent of science fiction, literal cyborgs – even robot overlords – is suggestive of a daunting and unknown future, and may seem to represent the opposite of the values of humanistic education.

Additionally, the notion of posthumanism may appear to negate, or elide, the struggles of those who are regarded as 'less human' than others – in a context of extreme power imbalances worldwide, where the 'prototypical' human may be seen as a white, heterosexual, middle-class man. Women, people of colour, LGBTQ people, and the socioeconomically disadvantaged, may be regarded implicitly as 'less human', and therefore not entitled to the full set of rights accorded to those at the pinnacle of privilege. For marginalized and oppressed groups in society, there has been a long and ongoing struggle to be granted full human rights and to be afforded equal status. Viewed from the standpoint of intersectionality, and the contexts of these ongoing liberatory struggles, it may seem unhelpful to apparently move away from the category of human, where the majority of the world's population are still denied that status. For these reasons, for scholars, students and activists working in struggles such as feminism, anti-racism and LGBTQ rights, a move to posthumanism may feel alienating. However, as I hope to clarify, posthumanism offers a way of understanding the world which allows us to see more clearly operations of power, ideology and privilege, by questioning implicit notions of the prototypical 'ideal' human subject placed at the centre of society, or in this case higher education.

One feature of the term 'posthumanism' is that it tends to be associated with notions of a 'robot age', a world dominated by machines and digital technology, in which the human race has been rendered obsolete, or has in some sense been replaced – or even defeated – by dominant technologies. This book is concerned with the relationship between digital technologies, the university and what I broadly term *epistemic practices*. However, my central thesis is not that the university – or indeed society as a whole – is being 'taken over' or supplanted by digital technology, or that it should be. Instead, my work is rooted in a desire to examine the existing and emergent relationships between the digital, the material, the textual and the human in the university. I seek to do this in such a way as to refocus attention on the embodied nature of human subjects, on the various forms and actions of texts and devices which make up the university, and the materiality of *how* epistemic practices – digital and analogue – emerge. In doing this, I situate my work under a fairly loose canopy of posthumanism, defined broadly to include work which might also be categorized as part of new materialism. The emphasis in this work is not on a replacement of the human, but more of a questioning of the central role that has been granted to the human in educational thought, seeking to focus instead on how the human and nonhuman entities entangle, to create knowledge in the university. The bedrock of posthumanism is a questioning of supposed taken-for-granted binaries, such as the division between nature and culture, human and animal, subject and object, or between human and nonhuman. My interest in this book is on the digital, but similarly I do not regard this as existing in a separate and clear binary with the analogue, or nondigital, therefore I also focus on how these technologies relate to each other and entwine in the day-to-day life of the university.

In some respects, the 'post' element of the term is unhelpful, as it implies 'after' in a chronological sense, leading to notions of future cyborgs, technological enhancements, implants or prostheses to be added to the body, or attempts to increase human longevity via technology – notions which, I argue, need to be clearly delineated as belonging to a distinct, and very different theoretical stance, *transhumanism*. Transhumanism is a school of thought which actively promotes the notion of enhancement, or even transformation, of the human body via technology. This idea has historical roots in philosophy, and is strongly associated with ideas from science fiction. However, due to the similarity of the terms *posthumanism* and *transhumanism*, they are often regarded as being related. I would like to argue that they are in fact diametrically opposed to each other in a range of ways. Transhumanism is focused on the notion of the human body as problematic, imperfect, and in need of remediation, extension or replacement via technology. It is closely associated with utopian notions of potential extensive human abilities, and imagined superpowers in the future, and hinges on the fantasy of transcending the biological body, which is regarded as implicitly weak and faulty. The limits of the biological human body, the existence of human mortality, and the process of aging are all regarded as problems to be solved via technology. As Ferrando (2013) points out in her comparison of posthumanism and transhumanism:

> They share a common perception of the human as a non-fixed and mutable condition, but they generally do not share the same roots and perspectives. Moreover, within the transhumanist debate, which causes further confusion to the understanding of the posthuman: for some transhumanists, human beings may eventually transform themselves so radically as to become posthuman, a condition expected to follow the current transhuman era. Such a take on the posthuman should not be confused with the post-anthropocentric and post-dualistic approach of (philosophical, cultural, and critical) posthumanism.
>
> Ferrando 2013: 27

As she clarifies, transhumanism problematizes our understanding of the human in terms of '... the possibilities inscribed within its possible biological and technical evolutions.' (2013: 27). In this regard, transhumanism is in fact an offshoot of humanism, and has even been referred to as 'ultrahumanism' (Onishi 2011). Both ideologies are dominated by the centrality of an idealized figure of the human. In the case of humanism, it is the privileged white heterosexual and socioeconomically powerful white man. In transhumanism, I would argue, this essentially patriarchal and racist logic of power within humanity is radically extended, by a move to a fantasy of 'escape' from the confines of the biological body. As Ferrando argues:

Furthermore, the transhumanist perseverance in recognizing science and technology as the main assets of reformulation of the human runs the risk of techno-reductionism: technology becomes a hierarchical project, based on rational thought, driven towards progression. Considering that a large number of the world's population is still occupied with mere survival, if the reflection on desirable futures was reduced to an overestimation of the technological kinship of the human revisited in its specific technical outcomes, such a preference would confine it to a classist and technocentric movement.

Ferrando 2013: 28

In this respect, it is a profoundly ideological notion, and expression of a set of desires, as opposed to a means of understanding the world as it unfolds now, and has unfolded in the past. In contrast, posthumanism should be viewed not as referring to a putative future era 'after humans', despite the term, but instead should be seen as an alternative means of understanding and responding to life and society, which does not place the human at the front and centre of the theoretical model. Here, *post* may be read as *beyond*, or *more than*. The emphasis then is on a move beyond the notion underpinning our contemporary beliefs, that the human is, or should be, a sole autonomous agent, acting on the planet, animals, objects and technology. Central to the idea of posthumanism is this change in perspective – a subtle but also radical shift in our sensibility – but not a change to biological humanity itself.

Posthumanism also has a very different understanding of technology. As Ferrando puts it, 'Technology is neither "the other" to be feared and to rebel against (in a sort of neo-Luddite attitude), not does it sustain the almost divine characteristics which some transhumanists attribute to it (for instance, by addressing technology as an external source which might guarantee humanity a place in post-biological futures).' (Ferrando 2013: 28). Posthumanist consideration of technology has its roots in the feminist scholarship of Donna Haraway (1991), in particular her challenge to the notion that there are strong boundaries between human and nonhuman animals, biological organisms and machines, and crucially here, technology and the self. Ferrando links this to Heidegger's essay 'The question concerning technology', in which he states 'Technology is therefore no mere means. Technology is a way of revealing.' (Heidegger 1953: 12, in Ferrando 2013: 28). She also links posthumanism to Foucault's (1988) notion of the 'technologies of the self', which also serves to break down division between the self and others. Ferrando reviews the contribution of work in feminist new materialism, such as that of Karen Barad (2003), Coole and Frost (2010) and Dolphijn and van der Tuin (2012), stating that:

New materialisms perceive matter as an ongoing process of materialization, elegantly reconciling science and critical theories: quantum physics with a post-structuralist and postmodern sensitivity. Matter is not viewed as in any way as something static, fixed, or passive, waiting to be molded by some external force; rather, it is emphasized as a 'process of materialisation'.

Ferrando 2013: 31

A core idea in posthumanism and new materialism is the notion of agency being distributed across a range of actors, both human and nonhuman. Artefacts and material things which would normally be seen as 'tools', inert objects, or simply elements of material or natural context, are instead seen as lively, active elements of how life and social practice unfolds. This for me, is the fundamental change in viewpoint which I regard as valuable to educational theory and practice, which I argue is dominated by humanism, and increasingly influenced by elements of transhumanist thinking. Throughout the book, I analyse educational practices in the university, both face-to-face and online, in terms of this sensibility, and make a case that a posthumanism provides insights into aspects of higher education practices in the 'digital age', which are hidden, or distorted, by a dominant humanist framing.

However, it must be acknowledged that posthuman approaches to education in particular are not without their critics. Friesen gives a response to Bayne's overview in the same journal issue, raising several questions about the utility of this approach (Friesen 2018). Friesen's main objection centres exactly on the point surrounding agency – in particular, what he sees as a disavowal of human agency implied by the tenets of posthumanism, which by positing human agency as entangled with nonhuman actors, questions for him the humanist notion of human autonomy. As he puts it:

Education, from the Latin *educare* – to 'bring out, lead forth' – implies someone acting on another, typically an older person drawing out or in some sense leading a younger. To say that such action requires a significant and responsible exercise of agency, decision, intention and will is to state the obvious. What might be less obvious, though, is that such agency and intention is also expressed in the widest range of educational actions, plans and designs – from everyday acts of communication and instruction to the design of the school, classroom and lesson plan. Practically speaking, education, its engagements, artefacts and discourses are all unavoidably *purposive* and *normative*.

Friesen 2018

For Friesen, a posthuman framing renders invisible the human intentionality behind education. He also argues that a blurring of human agency lessens our ability to take responsibility for our actions as social and political actors, and he raises the point that in education, posthumanism is essentially an oppositional stance. These are very legitimate points – posthumanism may indeed appear attractive due to its apparently radical overturning of 'commonsense' binaries, and assumptions about the nature of the human and our relationships with the nonhuman and the world. A wholesale rejection of mainstream theory can be a heady and seductive academic project, and arguably, it is always easier to question established 'truths' and tired old binaries, than it is to propose alternatives. It could be accused of being merely fashionable, wordy, and short on detail in terms of what it might offer in practical terms. Sooner or later, the question arises – 'so what?' My motivation in writing this book is – in part – to try to address this question, which I feel is incumbent on educational theorists in the field to attempt to tackle. What do we really mean when we talk about agency being entangled between the human and the nonhuman? Does this stance serve to break down restrictive views of 'the human', or does it serve to erode our sense of responsibility, as Friesen suggests? Are we risking a collapse into banality and statements of the glaringly obvious, by focusing on the embodied and the material? What, if anything, does posthumanism offer analyses of digital higher education? These are some of the questions I hope to address. By discussing the theoretical literature in terms of various educational practices, I will argue that, despite these critique, posthumanism offers broad sets of insights which are of potential value. I will return to address these objections directly in the conclusions.

I situate this project under Bayne's technological posthumanism, and argue that this stance allows for better theoretical, descriptive, granular and ethnographic purchase on the nature of practices and meaning-making via speech, writing and reading in the university. I take the view that these practices have always been posthuman, in the sense of *beyond*, or *more than*. This is my main use of posthumanism as a scholar, and this thread forms the main line through the book. I argue that a posthumanist framing – rather than leading us into a rarefied world of high theory and fantasy – can in fact have the effect of bringing us right 'back down to earth', by anchoring our attention as researchers, theorists and practitioners in the fine-grained, detailed 'nitty-gritty' of everyday higher education *as it unfolds,* in a mesh of bodies, nonhuman actors, and technologies. In this regard, I propose posthumanism as a profoundly practical, observational, ethnographic stance, which is concerned with noticing, and recognizing the complexity and detail of *how* life, or in this case digital higher education, actually operates in the complexity of the day-to-day. This stance may be critiqued as superfluous or banal, but my contention is that many of the errors and weaknesses of contemporary higher education policy, discourse and research, stem from a lack of close attention to the 'how', in particular to the 'how' of epistemic practices as specific, emergent, material entanglements which cannot be reduced to ideological fantasies, or apparently obvious archetypes – a tendency which can be observed in educational discourse when examining the nature of the digital in particular. I also argue that the 'decentring' (not removal) of the human, both ontologically and epistemologically, has potentially beneficial effects for higher education research and practice, and need not lead to a denial of human agency or ethical responsibility. I contend that humanism (and social constructivism) underpin strongly ideologically-freighted conceptions of the human subject in higher education, as students, teachers, scholars, writers, readers and graduates. I propose that these apparently benign archetypes are too easily and frequently put to work, in the service of ideologies which in fact reproduce privilege, or govern what are deemed to be 'acceptable' academic subjectivities. The 'human' can never be a neutral conception, and when placed strongly at the centre of the model, an implicit hierarchy of who counts as 'most human' is implicitly, or explicitly, invoked, as discussed above, maintaining existing power structures in terms of sex, ethnicity, sexuality and socioeconomic status. I propose that to maintain a critical tension around this point is complex, but ultimately generative. Finally, although it lies outside the scope of my work, I support the view that posthumanism throws down a radical set of challenges in terms of what should be the focus of education and human endeavour in the contemporary period. Here, I regard the claims of writers in Bayne's category of ecological posthumanism to be highly relevant – a decentring of the human in terms of our view of animals, and of the natural world is likely to lead to an increased sense of human responsibility and interconnectedness towards biodiversity and the environment, at a time when these are under extreme threat.

These perspectives are particularly generative when applied to datafied societies and 'algorithmic selfhoods' (Pasquale 2015), as Bayne points out. However, my project is to apply them to digital practices, also in combination with 'traditional' practices and devices for meaning-making, in accordance with my stance that in a sense 'we have always been posthuman'. I also look at theorists writing on *new materialism*, and explore how these ideas might have relevance to knowledge practices, both in the past, and in the contemporary period. In this regard, this work is highly interdisciplinary. It is situated in the field of higher education studies, but draws on science and technology studies, social anthropology, cultural theory, literacy studies, media studies, applied linguistics and library and information science. I combine these disciplinary perspectives in the chapters that follow, attempting to interweave and 'refract' those ideas through the notion of posthumanism more broadly. In doing so, I resist the adoption of a doctrinaire stance towards any particular 'school of thought', or a monolithic orientation towards any particular theorist. In contrast, I seek to explore the potentials, but also the limitations, of a range of these interconnected theoretical perspectives for higher education, attempting a more eclectic bricolage. This, of course, risks loss of theoretical coherence, and may offend the purist. However, I feel the potential gains of a 'messy', speculative approach to theory outweigh the lure of a superficially 'neat' analysis. The rest of this chapter will narrow its focus to look at theoretical work which I regard to be of particular relevance to the aims of the book.

Returning to agency, Pickering (2001) looks at the concept in relation to practice and posthumanism. He is particularly concerned with analyses of scientific practice 'at the microlevel' (2001: 163), and how they might relate to more macrosocial issues. He refers to a 'mutual tuning of social and material agency' (2001: 163) as means of understanding agency, and argues for a posthumanist social theory, '... that recognises from the start that the contours of the material and human agency reciprocally constitute one another' (2001: 164). For Pickering, practice is always temporally emergent, with nothing given in advance:

> A theory of practice, then, would focus our attention on specificity, on particular interdefinitions of machinic and social fields. This is not, of course, how traditional theory functions. Traditionally, as I have said, the invitation is to extract an invariant skeleton from the flux of appearances. Perhaps we should say that a theory that recognises temporal emergence is an antitheory in the traditional sense.
>
> Pickering 2001: 164

He goes on to ask '... what use is a posthuman antitheory that continually returns us to specifics?' (2001: 165). He argues that such a stance directs us to conduct a history of agency in a way which centres on '... visible sites of encounter of human and nonhuman agency' (2001: 165), such as the factory, the battlefield, or the home. He gives the example of science '... within the *plane of practice*: continually emerging from and returning to enduring sites of encounter of material and human agency' (2001: 165). He contends that a humanist social theory cannot properly take account of these developments. 'All that one can do is register the visible and specific intertwinings of the human and the nonhuman. But this is enough; what more could one want or need?' (2001: 165). He also provides an example from Schivelbusch's (1986) study of the nineteenth-century railway as a site for the development of an 'industrialised consciousness' (167). Schivelbusch focuses on how rail travel allows for what he calls 'panoramic seeing', which was quite different from the form of seeing made possible while walking, or travelling by horse-drawn cart. He proposes that the experience was constitutive of the subject of a panoramic voyeur – this he characterizes as an *emergent phenomenon*. Pickering commends Schivelbusch's work as '... opening up to analysis the relations between technology, bodily states, and inner human experience: a terrain which ... has been ignored by the science and technology studies mainstream, on one side, and also by humanist social sciences on the other.' (Pickering 2001: 169). He goes on to consider the relationship between the human and the digital, as '... part of a project with a long history that simultaneously defines the human and nonhuman in relation to one another.' (2001: 169). He argues that in video games, for example, '... the interface achieves its apotheosis as pure thing-in-itself: all that matters is destroying the space invaders as they appear on the screen' (2001: 170). He concludes by highlighting the interconnection between cybernetics and posthumanism, such as the notion that the unit of analysis is not an organism, but organism *plus* environment in mutual co-evolution, drawing on Maturana and Varela (1992). This framing of agency is highly relevant to the project of this book, and represents an understanding of human-nonhuman agency which I will return to throughout the chapters.

In another relevant work focused specifically on knowledge, Knorr-Cetina (2001) discusses the concept of *objectual practice*, pointing out the prevalence of the notion that practices are governed by schemata, and are repetitive. She raises the question of how we can characterize practice in settings where the knowledge base is not static, but is constantly developing, giving the example of research work. She poses the question:

> Research work seems to be particular in that the definition of things, the consciousness of problems, etc., is deliberately looped through objects and the reaction granted by them. This creates a disassociation between self and work object and inserts moments of interruption and reflection into the performance of research, during which efforts at reading the reactions of objects and taking their perspective play a decisive role. How can we conceive of practice in a way that accommodates this dissociation?
>
> Knorr-Cetina 2001: 175

She looks at knowledge-centred, *epistemic practices* 'in a relations rather than performative idiom' (2001: 176) focusing on the relationship between subject and object. She characterizes *epistemic objects* as inherently incomplete, posing further questions to science. She points out the tendency in social theory to treat contexts as '... alien elements in social systems' (2001: 177). She argues that the move to a 'knowledge society' brings with it not only experts and technology, crucially it involves knowledge processes, or epistemic practice, and proposes the notion of *relational undergirding* to understand the functioning of epistemic practice, drawing on Heidegger's (1962) concept of 'ready-to-hand' to describe the relationship between driver and car '... the car becomes an unproblematic means to an end rather than an independent thing to which I stand in relation. It becomes an instrument that has been absorbed into the practice of driving – I, too, become transparent.' (Knorr-Cetina 2001: 178). She suggests that this provides an apt description of habitual practice, in a performative idiom, but that it is not adequate as a description of knowledge-centred work, or epistemic practice. Using the example of a researcher who is working on an unfamiliar protein – the protein is no longer invisible, but is enhanced. The researcher must use *relational resources* to overcome subject-object separation. Knorr-Cetina likens this to Heidegger's (1962) 'envisaging', 'deliberate coping' and 'theoretical reflection' on entities. She goes on to tackle the question of how to characterize epistemic objects, referring to the historian of biology Rheinberger (1997), who uses the construct of 'epistemic things', which Knorr-Cetina describes as:

> ... any scientific objects of investigation that are at the centre of a research process, and in the process of being materially defined. Objects of knowledge are characteristically open, question-generating and complex. They are processes and projections rather than definitive things. Observation and inquiry reveals them by increasing rather than reducing their complexity.
>
> Knorr-Cetina 2001: 181

She builds on Rheinberger, by characterizing epistemic objects '... in terms of a lack in completeness of being that takes away much of their wholeness, solidity, and the thing-like character they have in our everyday conception.' (Knorr-Cetina 2001: 181). She argues that the everyday view of objects, or tools, is that they are ready-to-hand, while epistemic objects '... have the capacity to unfold indefinitely. They are more like open drawers filled with folders extending indefinitely into the depth of a dark closet.' (2001: 181). She contends that due to their shifting nature, epistemic objects are '... never quite themselves', and what is encountered are in fact '... representations or stand-in for a more basic lack of object' (2001: 181).

The *lack in completeness of being* is crucial: objects of knowledge in many fields have material instantiations, but they must simultaneously be conceived of as unfolding structures of absences: as things that continually 'explode' and 'mutate' into something else, and that are as much defined by what they are not (but will, at some point, have become) than by what they are.

Knorr-Cetina 2001: 182

It is this *unfolding ontology*, she argues, that engages experts in creative practice. Another feature of epistemic objects is that they can exist in multiple forms at the same time – for example, a detector in a physics experiment may take the form of simulations and calculations, drawings, photographs, written and verbal reports, and so on. These are partial instantiations of 'the detector', *partial objects* standing in internal relation to the whole. Crucially, she argues that these should not be regarded as a 'halo' of representation – instead the real thing, in this case the detector, has an ontology which is unfolded by the partial objects. The boundaries of an object are always blurred and unfinished, it is itself *partial*. It is not however, a referent, or replacement for a 'real' object. Epistemic objects are both meaning-producing, and practice-generating:

Thus in creative and constructive practice, (partial) epistemic objects have to be seen as transient, internally complex, signifying entities that allow for and structure the continuation of the sequence through the signs they give off of their lacks and needs. Their internal articulation is important for the continuation of epistemic practice; not just their differ(a)nce to other objects, as in a Saussurean linguistic universe.

Knorr-Cetina 2001: 183–184

She sees naming of objects here not as a signifier of stability, but as a way to 'punctuate the flux' (2001: 183–184). She then makes a case for knowledge practices as an expression of desire, as opposed to cognitive, as a relational process of 'wanting'. Knorr-Cetina's conceptual work is also pertinent to the analyses I will make throughout this book, where I will draw on the notion of emergent *epistemic practices* and *epistemic objects*, in the case of the digital university.

Meaning-making

To a large extent, higher education is concerned with meaning-making. Knowledge in the university is conveyed and understood via speech, writing and reading, in additional to other forms of communication, using multimodal and embodied semiotic practices such the use of diagrams, demonstrations and experimentation. In this regard, meaning-making and higher education knowledge practices are strongly intertwined. However, until relatively recently, the relevance of a posthumanist sensibility to our understanding of language use, communication and semiotics was not particularly well-developed, with the discipline of applied linguistics only recently beginning to explore these perspectives. As Pennycook (2018), puts it:

> From proclamations about the death of Man to investigations into enhanced forms of being, from the advent for the Anthropocene to new forms of materialism and distributed cognition, posthumanism raises significant questions for applied linguistics in terms of our understandings of language, humans, objects and agency.

Pennycook 2018: 6

However, as he points out:

> Applied linguistics has taken on board, and indeed has been a major promoter of, humanist accounts of language, literacy and learning. To the extent that applied linguistics has for a long time supported a view of humans as self-governing individuals and languages as separable objects it has been an important player in the promotion of a humanist vision.

Pennycook 2018: 8

However, Pennycook traces how the field has begun to engage with these ideas, such as via the work of Scollon and Scollon, whose concept of the *nexus analysis* as a 'semiotic ecosystem' (2004: 89), focusing on the role of objects, in particular how '... historical trajectories people, places, discourse, ideas, and objects come together' (2004: 159). Pennycook proposes the construct of *relocalisation* (Pennycook 2010), which he sees as '... not only a process of remaking meaning in different contexts, of the reinscription of different meanings onto different surfaces, but also of a redistribution of meaning in a physical space, a reorientation of meaning in relation to the body and the physical surroundings.' (Pennycook 2018: 40). He also proposes the concepts of *navigation* and *material anchors* to illustrate the role of artefacts in *distributed agency* (Bennett 2010), in contrast to a humanistic view which emphasizes individual and bounded cognition. He sets out the need to move away from language as a representational system, instead proposing a move towards *distributed language,* and asserting that sociolinguistic repertoires '... need to be understood in terms of spatial distribution, social practices and material embodiment rather than the individual competence of the sociolinguistic actor who has held centre stage over the last few decades.' (Pennycook 2018: 47). He critiques established theories of linguistic and communicative repertoires as being essentially humanistic in their underpinnings, arguing that:

> Once we start to think in terms of networks of texts, artefacts, practices and technologies (Gourlay et al. 2013), the distinction between being online and offline, between real and virtual, and between paper text and screen text become much less important than an understanding of the relations between linguistic and cultural assemblages.
>
> Pennycook 2018: 48

Pennycook also incorporates Deleuze and Guattari's notion of the *assemblage*, specifically a '... collective assemblage of enunciation, of acts and statements of incorporeal transformations attributed to bodies' (Deleuze & Guattari 1987: 88), proposing the notion of the *semiotic assemblage* (Pennycook 2017, Pennycook & Otsuji 2017). As argued elsewhere in this book, Pennycook regards online space as follows, with reference to Gourlay and Oliver (2013):

> The notion of the repertoire in such contexts can consequently be understood as an emergent and interactant affordance of the online space rather than an individual or communal capacity. From this point of view, digital literacies can be understood as social practices that are produced collaboratively through the manipulation of human and nonhuman.
>
> Pennycook 2018: 49

Pennycook gives a series of examples taken from work in linguistic ethnography in markets and restaurant kitchens, (e.g. Pennycook & Otsuji 2014a, 2014b), concluding that these complex linguistic practices are embedded in spatial repertoires. He goes on to discuss *distributed language* in more detail, a concept which raises questions about the mainstream notion in orthodox linguistics of language as essentially an internalized, cognitive entity. Instead, he proposes it as '... embodied, embedded and distributed across people, places and time.' (Pennycook 2018: 51). He proposes language as part of a wider set of semiotic resources, suggesting a move away from the idea of linguistic options being predetermined, and towards the concept of 'the radical indeterminacy of the sign' (2018: 51), with reference to Harris (1996), in which communication is theorized as consisting of open-ended opportunities. He links this notion to Canagarajah's *translingual practices* (2013) and argues that the mind should be seen as not only integrated with, but also itself part of the exterior world. As he puts it, '... language cannot be reduced to a notion of system, is bound up with real-time activity, and plays a role in socially moulded cognitive and linguistic niches, rather than individual cognition.' (Pennycook 2018: 52). He exclusively refers to this as follows:

The shift away from a Cartesian view of a mind engaged in symbolic processing involves an understanding that humans are metabolic before they are symbolic. From this point of view language and cognition are on the one hand embodied, embedded and enacted (far more than representational activity in the mind) and on the other hand extended, distributed and situated (involving the world outside the head).... While language can still be understood as a human capacity ... its operation and distribution are not limited to a process occurring in and between humans.

Pennycook 2018: 52

In conclusion, he argues that linguistics has placed too much emphasis on the notion of the 'cognitive sandwich' (Hurley 1998), with cognition being the filling between input and output in the world. He argues that this is an overly restrictive view of language. Crucially, he makes the point that:

This is not just to include nonverbal communication in the model, or to acknowledge that context plays a role in language use, but rather to shift the locus of where things happen and to suggest that language use is not an internally motivated process choice between language items – not the white-bread output resulting from the cognitive processing of sandwich filling but a far more distributed process, involving places, things, senses, bodies.

Pennycook 2018: 53

He refers to humans using 'tools' such as facial expressions, gesture and bodily orientation and material objects, these are posited as part of distributed language. He rejects the notion of material surrounds as 'context', but instead part of the interactive whole. *Practices* are defined as '... those repeated social and material acts that have gained sufficient stability over time to reproduce themselves' (2018: 53), plus what Thrift calls '... the vast spillage of *things*' which form '... part of hybrid assemblages: concretions, settings and flows' (2007: 9). He also refers to Jane Bennett's concept of *thing-power*, and ways in which things form *assemblages*.

Pennycook also draws on Deleuze and Guattari's concept of the assemblage, which they define as a '... collective assemblage of enunciation, of acts and statements of incorporeal transformations attributed to bodies' (1987: 88, in Pennycook 2018: 53/54). He points out how their work focuses on challenging an overemphasis on stability, and languages as systems. He also refers to Fenwick and Edwards' focus on '... the effects of relational interactions and assemblages, in various kinds of more-than-human networks entangled with one another, that may be messy and incoherent, spread across time and space.' (2011: 712). He proposes that the notion of *semiotic assemblages* (Pennycook 2017; Pennycook and Otsuji 2017) allows for a more expansive conception than the traditional narrow, humanist, cognitive view of language. In conclusion, he states:

> Looking at language use in relation to distributed language and semiotic assemblages gives us a way to think in much more inclusive terms than individualistic accounts of linguistic or communicative competence or notions such as language in context. The focus, rather, moves away from the humanist concern with individuals and systems in their heads and looks at the greater totality of interacting objects, places and alternative forms of semiosis.
>
> Pennycook 2018: 54–55

This move is a significant departure from the mainstream view in applied linguistics, that language is essentially cognitive and bounded, as discussed above. In this regard, this work and those related to it mark an important shift towards a recognition of the nonhuman, the embodied, and the material, as integral elements of semiotic assemblages, challenging taken-for-granted notions of 'context' and 'tool'. This marks an expansion of these ideas into how language and semiotics are conceptualized, providing further support for the central ideas of this book concerning the posthuman nature of digital knowledge practices. In literacy studies, there has also been an increased interest in posthumanism, with recent works focusing on a range of research projects and pedagogic interventions (e.g. Kuby et al. 2019), many focusing on early years or school-level education. There has been little work, however, linking academic or digital literacies at higher education level with posthuman theory. The next section will return to focus to this project, deploying an approach to researching digital practices from a posthuman set of framings. This methodology is described in detail, as it is used throughout this book, to analyse a series of practices commonly used in and around the digital university.

Interviewing Objects

Adams and Thompson (2016) provide an engaging overview and synthesis of posthumanism and related theory, and how these perspectives might shed light on our understanding of the nature of the digital. They point out the particular difficulty of operationalizing posthuman theory into a research agenda, given that '. . . little guidance has been offered so far on how researchers might translate the insights of posthumanism into tangible, theoretically sound research practices.' (Adams & Thompson 2016: 3). Drawing on actor-network theory and phenomenology, they propose an approach in which objects are 'interviewed' as part of 'researching a posthuman world'. Insightfully, they go back to the etymological roots of the word 'interview', which is derived from the old French verb '*s'entrevoir*', and is composed of two parts, '*entre*' meaning between or mutual, and '*voir*', meaning to see. As they put it, 'To inter-view an object or thing is therefore to catch insightful glimpses of it in action, as it performs and mediates the gestures and understandings of its human employer, and as it associates with others' (Adams & Thompson 2016: 17–18). They relate this concept of the mutual gaze with Barad's (2003) *intra-action*, through which '. . . the boundaries and properties of the "components" of phenomena become determinate and that particular embodied concepts become meaningful' (Barad 2003: 815). In Adams and Thompson's words, '. . . an object (indeed any human and nonhuman) becomes what it is through the mesh of relations in which it is entangled' (2016: 19). They propose eight heuristics which can be applied in order to 'interview' a digital object, elaborating on each in terms of the relevant theoretical literature. In their book, they focus these on iPod Touch handheld devices, and also on the qualitative data analysis software package NVivo. They divide the eight heuristics into two groups. The first group if focused on 'attending to objects, attuning to things' (2016: 23).

1. Gathering Anecdotes

This heuristic is accompanied by the suggested 'interview' question 'Describe how the object or thing appeared, or was given in professional practice or everyday life. What happened?' (Adams & Thompson 2016: 24). Anecdotes are characterized as 'little stories', which '. . . reassemble via textual description the unfoldings of everyday events' (2016: 25). They argue that anecdotes show humans and things as they are, and as they are becoming, in order to '. . . reassemble the eventing lifeworld' (2016: 26). They distinguish between first-person experiential anecdotes, and third person observational accounts, both used in phenomenology (which favours the former), and actor-network theory (which makes more use of the latter in the form of observations and reports). In constructing posthuman anecdotes, they suggest that multiple sources can be used, including interviews, field observations, online sources, journals, documents and visual artefacts. Their criterion for inclusion is '. . . does this source reveal something about how a given technology is taken up, used, integrated, mobilized in professional practice or everyday life?' (2016: 27). They also suggest that this approach can be used to investigate one's own relationships with technology, using two potential approaches. One approach is to recall a memorable event involving technology, and to write a detailed account of it. The other approach suggested is to self-observe, intermittently recording one's own observations – I use both of these approaches in this book. They refer to the approach to sociomaterial enquiry taken by Mulcahy (2012, 2013), whose relational materialist accounts are scaffolded using humans as starting points, in which the human individual is not regarded as autonomous, but is instead a '... network effect comprising a myriad of social and material relations' (2012: 29, Mulcahy 2013: 1287). Adams and Thompson emphasize the importance of attending to our '... prereflective conversations with (digital) things' (2012: 30). They point out that anecdotes are themselves performative assemblages which act on the world, in Knorr-Cetina's (2001) terms, they are *epistemic objects*, or *objects of knowledge*, which:

> ... have the capacity to unfold indefinitely ... since epistemic objects are always in the process of being materially defined, they continually acquire new properties and chance the ones they have. But this also means that objects of knowledge can never be fully attained, that they are, if you wish, never quite themselves.
>
> Knorr-Cetina 2001: 181, in Adams and Thompson 2016: 31

2. Following the Actors

This next heuristic comes from actor-network theory, and focuses on tracing the human and nonhuman actors in a sociomaterial assemblage, as a way of '... mapping the relations of practice' (Law & Singleton 2013: 491), at a micro level. They refer to Thompson's (2012a) study in which she 'interviewed' the delete button on a computer keyboard, and in doing so uncovered a range of practices relating to working online, which '... acted as a line of defence against information overload, arbitrated relevance, served to presence and absence other actors, safeguarded against intrusion, and both opened and enclosed spaces' (Adams & Thompson 2016: 37). They set out that 'following the actors' involves two activities, first identifying actors of interest, then mapping micro-practices which seem worthy of further analysis. The goal is to render visible what is not normally seen, in terms of objects and also negotiations taking place in order to create and maintain an assemblage. Thompson (2018) examines mobility and work practices in relation to mobile technologies, and in doing so uncovered how the mobile device is itself entangled with a range of other actors, such as '... data plans, bits of computer code, digital screens, YouTube videos, external hard drives, e-books, roaming charges, mobile hotspots, batteries, keyboards, Bluetooth, and server farms.' (Thompson 2018: 1035). The object is seen as an entry point in this approach, in order to explore the assemblage and practices of which it forms a part. As they put it. 'Attending to the different gatherings around an object and its varying material performances propels the researcher and practitioner to think beyond separate entities toward something far more intertwined and practice oriented.' (Adams & Thompson 2016: 38).

3. Listening for the Invitational Quality of Things

This third heuristic places emphasis on the agency of objects, and the ways in which objects act upon us. Thompson and Adams provide an everyday example:

> Arriving at my office, the closed door invites me to open it, the chair behind my desk beckons me to sit in it, the dark screen on my desktop tells me I must power on my computer, my e-mail tugs at me to check it, the smartphone vibrating in my back pocket insists that I answer it, etc.
>
> Adams & Thompson 2016: 41

They describe how things speak to us in 'tacit tongues more primordial than the familiar language of human discourse' (2016: 41). They refer to Adams' (2010) study of PowerPoint, in which '... the teacher find herself simultaneously enmeshed or *caught* up in the particular design imperatives, decisions, and suggestions embedded in this software.' (Adams & Thompson 2016: 44). They also cite the media theorist Marshall McLuhan, who regarded technology as having an 'utterance', and point out the etymology of the word 'utter', which comes from the Old English *uttra*, meaning 'outer'.

4. Studying Breakdowns, Accidents and Anomalies

The fourth heuristic focuses specifically on breakdowns, where things go wrong with objects. They point out that when a technology functions as expected, it is taken for granted and its workings are not regarded as salient. However, when there is a breakdown, or when an object is missing, its material presence is noticed and becomes visible, '... affording the alert observer a unique aperture into our ongoing, co-relational entanglements and tacit conversations with our material surround.' (Adams & Thompson 2016: 50). This is an approach used frequently in actor-network theory, media ecology and phenomenology. Thompson's (2018) study of mobility and work practices also uncovered examples of breakdowns, which she used as an 'entry point' for sociomaterial analysis, such as broken wireless cards, unaffordable data plans, or a lack of Wi-Fi rendering mobile devices immobile, and enmeshed in their immediate sociomaterial setting. They proceed to describe four more heuristics, which they characterize as '. . . lifting the entangled digital thing of interest into relief, and then reflectively analysing its medial relations and material contributions.' (Adams & Thompson 2016: 57).

5. Discerning the Spectrum of Human-technology-world Relations

The first of these enquires into the nature of the human-technology relationship at hand, referring to Ihde (1990), whose work in the postphenomenology of technics identifies three types of human-technology relations: *embodiment*, *hermeneutic* and *alterity*. The embodiment relation is one in which the technological artefact is an extension of the corporeal self, examples of this include cars, smartphones and pens. We use these technological artefacts to extend our senses and the capabilities of our bodies in an 'intimate assemblage' (Adams & Thompson 2016: 59). *Hermeneutic* relations for Ihde pertain when the technology must be 'read', the examples given are a thermometer, a map, PowerPoint and a book. The technology is seen as forming a linkage with the world, which appears 'translated'. This also involves intimate embodied relations with the technology. *Alterity* relations apply when the artefact is perceived to be 'other', as Adams and Thompson put it, 'Such relations occur when a technology seems to have a mind of its own, does not obey our desire, or acts in an unexpected manner.' (2016: 62). The example of a 'user attachment' to a smartphone is given (Thorsteinsson & Page 2014), but this category also includes relations with artefacts characterized by awkwardness or difficulty, where the technology is not transparent, but is instead encountered as 'other'. The final category proposed is 'background relations', which apply to those technologies which are taken for granted and work outside of our awareness in infrastructures such as heating, communications systems and big data analytics. These relations may also be described as 'interpassive', in which our work is outsourced to a device, the example of the Tibetan prayer wheel is given (Zizek 1998). Objects are seen as having 'actorship' (van Oenen 2006). Adams and Thompson relate this to education:

In today's classrooms, for example, teacher's disciplinary knowledge, once presented and represented at the hand of chalk and blackboard, pens and notebooks, books and desks, is increasingly being distributed across broad and deep digital networks reaching well beyond the local enclave in the neighbourhood school. In this respect, the interactive whiteboard (IWB) could also be described as an interpassive whiteboard, inasmuch as the board performs tasks on the teacher's behalf, such as showing a YouTube lesson on wheels and levers or running a simulation of population growth.

Adams & Thompson 2016: 64

6. Applying the Laws of Media

The next heuristic draws on work in media ecology, and notion of the medium. As they put it:

Every medium of lived technology is recognised as ecological. It dilates and contracts, infects and infuses human perception, action, and understanding, with potentially far-reaching implications and reverberations in our personal, social, cultural, and political lives.

Adams & Thompson 2016: 66

They refer to the 'four laws of media' proposed by McLuhan and McLuhan (1988): enhancement, obsolescence, retrieval and reversal, which they presented as questions:

- What does [a technology] enhance or intensify?
- What does it render obsolete or displace?
- What does it retrieve that was previously obsolesced?
- What does it produce or become when pressed to an extreme?

McLuhan & McLuhan 1998: 7, in Adams & Thompson 2016: 66

Enhancement focuses on extension or improvement of bodily functions and/or cognitive capabilities, GPS technology is suggested as an example. In contrast, *obsolescence* closes down or reduces an aspect of experience, such as virtual reality technologies. As Adams and Thompson point out, these two are in tension, in that '... we are simultaneously augmented and diminished by the technical' (2016: 69). An example from the classroom is the calculator, a technology which simultaneously augments what students can do, while weakening their mental arithmetic capacities. *Retrieval* involves the renewal of something which was obsolete, the example given is of GPS replacing the act of exploring the world using a compass (as opposed to a map). Finally, *reversal* relates to breakdowns. They offer the example from Adams (2006), in which she explored how NASA had found the ubiquitous use of PowerPoint to be implicated in the *Columbia* space shuttle tragedy. The PowerPoint slide deck used during the project had apparently broken complex information across multiple slides, with the most important point apparently 'buried' low down in a group of nested bullet points, which as a result was insufficiently emphasized. Again, the example of GPS is used, with reference to GPS misleading drivers.

7. Unravelling Translations

The next heuristic draws on the actor-network theory concept of *translation*, in order to explore how an assemblage of actors has come into being. It also enables us to ask questions about the politics of an assemblage, and how some actors are made more powerful. Callon (1986: 196) proposed a 'sociology of translation', in order to explore how actors are defined, and also how some may be allowed to speak for others. They draw once again on the study of mobile technologies, turning their attention to how the market for mobile devices influence day-to-day life, utilizing a powerful discourse of continuous connectivity, and indispensability. Using the *translation* heuristic, they look at the way in which these devices align with other actors such as apps. These alignments cause changes to how human actors engage, for example by travelling light, instead of carrying larger devices. The mobile device acts as a 'unit of force' (Callon 1986: 216), which draws together actors. They also explore the work of Rohl (2015), who analysed geometrical prisms and model airplanes used in geometry classes. Rohl argues that these objects are actively transformed by various actors into educational objects, via a series of transformations from the factory to the classroom. Rohl described this process as *transsituative*, '... a nexus of practices conducted at various sites but connected to each other via mediating material objects.' (Rohl 2015: 143, in Adams & Thompson 2016: 79).

8. Tracing Responses and Passages

The final heuristic identified by Adams and Thompson draws on the work of Tim Ingold, to ask questions about how human actors join with the things around them, in Ingold's (2012b) terms, how they *co-respond* to what is happening around them. They also pose the question, drawing on Ingold (2012a), of how passages are made '... as entities thread their way through the ways of others' (Adams & Thompson 2016: 82), drawing on Ingold's concept of *meshworking* – which he defines in contrast with a network: '... the lines of the meshwork ... are the trails along which life is lived. And it is in the entanglement of lines, not in the connecting of points, that the mesh is constituted' (Ingold 2005: 47). Anusas and Ingold (2013) argue that the network is an inadequate construct, as it conjures the notion of an assembly of discrete objects, instead they argue for an '... entangled mesh of materials in energetic movements, out of which the forms of things are continually emerging' (2013: 66). Another concept used here is Ingold's (2012a) notion of *improvising passages*, where each new passage forms another line in the meshwork. *Knots* are formed, in which more permanent practices may coalesce, but these are still contingent. Drawing again on Thompson (2018), they illustrate this with reference to how mobile devices and humans co-respond to create not only practices, but the objects themselves – the mobile phone *becomes* a mobile device through activities, which are emergent, contingent and unstable. This framing, as they point out, forces us to think differently about objects as static entities, instead seeing them as being in a constant process of movement and becoming. The emphasis here is on flows, movement and the intersection of people and things.

These heuristics combine empirical and theoretical forms of enquiry drawn from a range of perspectives in the literature. It might be argued that there is a degree of overlap between them, and perhaps even some redundancy. However, they also offer subtly different ways in which to probe, question and interrogate digital objects, which serve to 'operationalize' concepts which hitherto have perhaps remained at a fairly abstract level – disruptive concepts yes – but also prone to raise the question among researcher or practitioners of 'so what?'. It is undoubtedly easier to critique mainstream orthodoxies and theoretical positions in social science and education, than it is to find generative alternatives, and these heuristics seem to offer a 'way in' to an examination of practices which may render posthumanist thinking more practical, and applicable. Thompson and Adams use their heuristics to 'interview' the text-tagging software package NVivo, the iPod Touch device, and the VLE Blackboard. This book will also take this approach, elaborating on and drawing on these heuristics throughout, as in over several chapters I consider (or 'interview' in Adams and Thompson's terms) a *digital epistemic object* (combining Adam and Thompson's framing with that of Knorr-Cetina) in relation to a foregoing theoretical argument or critique. In my investigation, I find *digital epistemic practices* is also a useful term, as the focus of my analysis are in some cases broader and less clearly delineated than that of an object. Over the course of seven chapters, I will 'interview' my laptop, a MOOC, a flipped classroom, a VLE, 'hyperreading', and will also consider more broadly OEPs, and leaning analytics, all as instantiations of *digital epistemic practices* in the contemporary digital university.

2

Matter

My intention is to consider how meaning-making takes place in and around contemporary universities, in the context of digital technologies and mediation. In relation to this, the title of this book was difficult to formulate, and went through several iterations. I still find it problematic – particularly the formulation 'the digital university'. This construct throws up a couple of problems. First, it is singular, therefore implying a unified and monolithic institution or concept, as opposed to the reality of a highly diverse international sector where digital technologies may be omnipresent in one setting, and entirely absent, or very scarce in another. Also, the adjective 'digital' reproduces one of the effects I aim to critique in this book, the binary notion that a 'pure' digital realm exists, separate from the analogue, the material and the embodied. I use and tolerate the phrase as a kind of shorthand for 'universities in the time of digital technology', but the focus of this and subsequent chapters is frequently not on the digital itself as a separate field of enquiry, such as might be expected in a book on 'elearning' of 'technology enhanced learning', but more holistically on what I regard as expansive human/nonhuman assemblages of practices in higher education, which include or involve entanglement with the digital.

Contemporary academic engagement, textual practices and the related notion of 'digital literacies' are theorized and imagined in a range of complex and contradictory ways in higher education research, policy and practice, leading to a situation where the day-to-day practices of reading and writing in digital contexts may be lost from view. Instead, there has been a tendency in mainstream policy development in particular to collapse into a generic 'skills and competencies' model, which underscores the notion of the neoliberal individual student, imagined as context-free, as both repository and sole agential source of digital practices. Alongside this, there is a somewhat contradictory 'brave new world' discourse in higher education associated with the digital in particular, which also operates on a fairly abstract level, imagining the 'digitally literate' student or graduate as able to 'harness' what are portrayed as awe-inspiring potentials of the digital for learning and future employment. Although both of these framings may reflect some aspects of digital epistemic practice, the nature of embodied and emergent day-to-day engagement is arguably 'tidied up' by both, resulting in a strongly humanist model which regards devices and artefacts of inscription as 'tools' at the command of the idealized 'user', who is stripped of markers of identity such as gender, race and social class. It also elides the specifics of social setting, temporality and spatiality, all of which are rendered as neutral backcloths to engagement.

In this chapter, I aim to explore these tensions, and draw out the effects that flow from these overly-abstract and ideologically-freighted humanist assumptions about the nature of texts, devices, the writer, and epistemic practices in the digital setting. I will trace what I characterize as a series of moves in the literature, from a rejection of humanist abstraction, towards a posthuman framing. In doing so, I will review the contributions and ongoing potentials of new literacy studies, actor-network theory, and theoretical challenges surrounding the notion of spatiality and temporality as 'contexts' to practices. The first important point is that, following work in new literacy studies, textual practices are central to, and constitutive of, educational practices, student engagement, teaching face-to-face and online, and in the uses of artefacts and digital devices. However, despite the central position of texts, they are frequently rendered somewhat opaque, and have been 'naturalized' almost to the point of invisibility, and as a result are elided and paid scant attention throughout educational research, theory and policy discourses. The practices of higher education, and the subjectivities conjured by it tend to be discussed in relatively abstract, even ideological terms. The 'nitty-gritty', fine-grained 'doings' of what actually goes on in the day-to-day of higher education face-to-face and online, have received less attention, and even where ethnographic studies have been carried out, arguably these textual practices have not been foregrounded to a huge extent. An exception can be found in the generative strand of work coming out of new literacy studies (e.g. Barton 2007), in particular work on academic literacies (e.g. Lea & Street 1998), which identified the co-constitutive relationship between academic writing, knowledge and subjectivities. Researchers working in this field have subsequently turned their attention and ethnographic gaze towards the digital (e.g. Goodfellow 2011, Bhatt 2017).

Textual, Digital, Embodied, Material

One of the key contributions of work on academic literacies has been that it has foregrounded the central importance of reading, writing and texts in higher education, both in face-to-face contexts and online. This may seem obvious, but the literature on 'teaching and learning' in universities, I would argue, tends to render textual practices invisible. Instead, the focus frequently remains on somewhat abstract concepts such as 'student engagement', 'active learning', or 'connectivism', as opposed to recognizing that almost all activity in the university is intertwined with texts. Take for example, the prototypical form of university teaching through the ages, the lecture. It may appear to be primarily a spoken event, and it is this spoken, ephemeral nature which is intrinsic to what makes it distinctive, and if done well, compelling as a form of teaching and engagement. However, a closer examination of what underlies a lecture, and how it comes about, reveals its fundamentally textually-entangled nature, from inception, to performance, and beyond. A consideration of the various steps taken 'off stage' reveals this. Firstly, when a new module or course is proposed, it will be initiated and led by an academic specialist, or group. The specialist has gained knowledge through years of reading and writing on the specific field of expertise, even if the subject is practical or vocational. A written proposal for a new course must be submitted, then read and scrutinized by a panel concerned with quality assurance. They are likely to respond with written comments. If the proposed course is approved, the lecturer is likely to spend several months developing and preparing the lectures, seminars, practical activities and assessments which make up the course. This preparation will take place via engagement with a range of texts – books, articles, visual and multimodal artefacts, and so on. Email is now the primary means of communication in the contemporary university in contexts where digital mediation is widespread, and dozens, if not hundreds of emails may be written surrounding a new course. Students will obtain information about their course through written information and are likely to enrol online, via a form of some kind. A handbook may be distributed, again most likely to be online, and a reading list prepared, directing students to a range of texts they should read in advance or during the course. PowerPoint slides are frequently used and may even be mandatory, these are both textual and multimodal. During the lecture, these may be shown alongside the speech of the lecturer, who may also be referring to written notes. Students may take notes while listening. After the lecture is over, they may review these textual materials on the VLE. Overall, the lecture may be seen as a verbal event, but one which is nested in a complex set of digital textual practices, which I would argue are broadly 'taken for granted' and not focused on in mainstream educational literature and policy. This is one example of an educational set of practices which is suffused with meaning-making and textual practices, a similar analysis could be brought to bear on other practices in the university.

A further aspect of higher education which is often missed, is the extent to which the 'face-to-face', physical campus is permeated with digital technology and mediation. Reviewing the various steps underlying the lecture described above, it is worth noting that almost all of them are, partly or wholly, mediated by textual practices in digitally-resourced settings – the online prospectus, online forms, PowerPoint, students' personal digital devices, the VLE, the online library catalogue, PDFs, and so on. The same could be said for any form of engagement which we do not normally think of as 'online learning' – for example, independent study and academic writing are increasingly conducted through engagement with digital devices and texts. Crucially, this is not to say that these practices are disembodied or somehow outside of the material world – I will return to this point later in this chapter – but they are *entwined* with the digital. In this regard, the persistent binary in educational thought and discourse between 'face-to-face' and 'online' higher education starts to appear meaningless. A familiar trope related to digital education is the notion that digital technologies lead to a breaking away from the confines of the material world, and that through their use, the student is converted into some sort of freefloating agent, untrammelled by physical or bodily limitations. It is undeniable that digital technology allows for the instantaneous circulation of messages, texts and images around the world, removing or reducing the need for some of the physical systems relied upon on the past, such as mail delivery, posters, written memos, exclusive reliance on analogue books and papers, and so on. This can give the impression of a wholesale disjuncture from the physical world, almost resembling a form of 'magic'. However, all computer systems are in fact material, are composed of hardware, and rely on electricity, as we are reminded whenever the server breaks down at work, a laptop is dropped on the floor, or a phone battery goes flat. Kirchenbaum describes electronic textuality as:

> ... locatable, even though we are not used to thinking of it in physical terms. Bits can be measured in microns when recorded on a magnetic hard disk ... When a CD-ROM is burned, a laser superheats a layer of dye to create pits and lands, tiny depressions on the grooved surface of the platter. The length of these depressions is measured in microns, their width and depth in nanometers.
>
> Kirchenbaum 2012: 3

He cites Thibodeau (2002), who proposes a three-part model of digital objects: as *physical objects* such as those described above; *logical objects* such as data as it is recognized by particular software; and *conceptual objects*, defined by Thibodeau as '... objects we deal with in the real world' (Thibodeau 2002, in Kirchenbaum 2012: 3) such as a digital photo. Thibodeau defines a digital object as something whose ontology necessitates all three aspects. Kirchenbaum goes on to quote posthuman theorist Katherine Hayles, discussing the materiality of multimedia literary works, which she calls *technotexts*:

> The physical attributes constituting any artifact are potentially infinite; in a digital computer, for example, they include the polymers used to fabricate the case, the rare earth elements used to make the phosphors in the CRT screen, the palladium used for the power cord prongs, and so forth. From this infinite array, a technotext will select a few to foreground and work into its thematic concerns. Materiality thus emerges from interactions between physical properties and a work's artistic strategies. For this reason, materiality cannot be specified in advance, as if it pre-existed the specificity of the work. An emergent property, materiality depends on how the work mobilizes its resources as a physical artifact a well as the user's interaction with the work and the interpretive strategies she develops – strategies that include physical manipulations as well as conceptual frameworks. In the broadest sense, materiality emerges from the dynamic interplay between the richness of a physically robust world and human intelligence as it crafts this physicality to create meaning.
>
> Hayles 2002: 32–33

Kirchenbaum demonstrates in his book that electronic texts are artefacts, '... subject to material and historical forms of understanding' (Kirchenbaum 2012: 17). His aim is to challenge the widespread perception that digital texts are ephemeral, inherently unstable, or identical copies of each other. His examples are drawn from literary works, but the analysis applies equally well to digital texts in higher education, where digital texts are routinely assumed to be nonmaterial, and therefore fundamentally different to print texts in their nature. He refers to specific technologies, such as the hard drive, as *actants*, a term central to actor-network theory (Latour 1987), which Kirchenbaum states '... seems indispensable to developing robust theories of computational processes, where the human agent – the user – is only one participant in a long chain of interdependent interactions.' (Kirchenbaum 2012: 17). Likewise, all digital texts and images are partly *handmade* – not in the same sense as an artefact crafted by hand, but at the root of all digital texts human hands have typed a text or command, human bodies have hunched over keyboards, and human eyes have looked at a screen. Again, this is not to deny the powerful agentive and generative force of technologies and nonhuman actors, but this is a human-nonhuman set of entanglements, not exclusively one or the other. The tendency in discourses surrounding the digital in society in general, and also in higher education, has been to collapse into one or other side, while seeking to account for the role of the digital. Therefore, digital devices may be described as 'tools' for human use, which denies their agency, or conversely digital technologies may be portrayed as an awesome force to be 'harnessed'. The more extreme version represents digital technologies as an adversary to be feared, in a view of technology as all-powerful, and humans as helpless pawns. However, a closer look at day-to-day practices serves to break down these strong utopian/dystopian interpretations, in order to gain a better understanding of how this complex entwining actually takes place.

Situating of Textual Practices

There is a tendency in contemporary higher education to regard academic reading and writing practices as somewhat problematic, and in need of remediation, with issues like plagiarism often focused on as a crisis which needs to be accounted for via blame (e.g. Gourlay & Deane 2009). In this section I will examine how writing and meaning-making is theorized in the university, by examining the various ways in which it is framed in practices. My analysis refers primarily to the UK higher education system, and builds on my consideration of this point in Gourlay (2019), it is hoped that this analysis will have relevance in other contexts. In the UK, and in other countries, universities normally offer some form of 'study skills' support for students. This normally includes a focus on academic reading and writing, and often takes the form of extracurricular provision which may be accessed voluntarily by individuals, although there may also be guidance offered online, or as part of academic programmes. However, as this provision is offered outside of the curriculum, there is a tendency for it to be generic, as opposed to being specifically focused on the conventions or expectations of a particular discipline. Arguably, the assumption is that the students accessing this type of support will have English as a first language, as there is generally a separate strand of support for students for whom English is an additional language. This type of support has grown in scale and scope partly in response to the increased proportion of young people going to university in the UK, from a wider range of social backgrounds, including what are known as students from 'non-traditional' backgrounds, meaning socioeconomic circumstances where parents and other relatives or associates did not attend university. These students are seen as in need of extra support, due to less academic school preparation, and a lack of support or understanding of academic study in their family or social background. In terms of the framings used in this book, in the case of these students, the 'problem' is positioned as residing in a mismatch between the literacy practices of the students' home lives and school backgrounds, and those required by the university.

In the case of 'international' students, there is normally provision of support for writing in a separate unit, often a Language Centre staffed by specialists in Teaching English as a Foreign Language. In the case of this form of provision, attendance is generally also voluntary, but more commonly offered in the form of structured classes focused more on language, specifically English for Academic Purposes, or EAP. This branch of teaching has been strongly influenced by the concept of *genre* in texts (e.g. Swales 1990), a construct which recognizes the disciplinary and context-specific conventions that govern textual conventions. However, by necessity, EAP also tends towards the generic, due to the logistical difficulties of providing classes for students from a range of subject areas. An analysis of international students and EAP provision would suggest that the 'problem' or deficit being addressed is somewhat different from that of the students accessing 'study skills' support. In the case of international students, their practices are seen to be mismatched in terms of the presence of another language, and the lack of proficiency in English. Additionally, international students may also be perceived to lack familiarly with writing conventions required, not due to socioeconomic status, but because of the presence of a further element, the academic conventions of their own cultural background.

Another way in which meaning-making is portrayed, although more indirectly, is though the concept of 'digital literacy'. This concept has its roots in 'technology enhanced learning', and has evolved from a concern to ensure that students are confident and capable of using digital technologies as a core medium in their studies. These capabilities tended in the past to be framed via 'skills and competencies' models, which did not emphasize social situatedness, identities and so on, but recent work in the area has adopted the term 'literacies' to broaden the focus. However, it is worth noting that this usage does not map easily onto the sense of the word used in new literacy studies, but is more associated with a sense of 'know-how', as in popular coinages such as 'media literacy'. In sociomaterial terms, the range of issues to be addressed here is complex, ranging from procedural familiarity, through to a more critical and nuanced understanding of how subjectivities might be expressed via social media platforms, for example. The emphasis here is on meaning-making as primarily situated in human individual cognition. Knowledge practice are also seen as generic and transferable, as opposed to residing in a particular sociomaterial setting.

In an insightful piece, Leander and Boldt (2012) address the limitations of a key foundational text in new literacy studies, the New London Group's (1996) 'A Pedagogy of Multiliteracies: Designing Social Futures'. This text has been highly influential in moving the field away from a notion of 'literacy' as a singular conception, towards a plural framing of 'literacies', thought a recognition of the range of ways of meaning-making, taking in the visual, auditory, behavioural and gestural (New London Group 1996: 64). The paper was inspired to a large extent by the increasingly digitized, connected and multimodal nature of texts engaged in, particularly by young people in that period. Although groundbreaking at the time, Leander and Boldt reflect on the limitations of the paper from a more contemporary standpoint. The first aspect of their critique focuses on the emphasis in the New London Group on rational design, which they argue artificially 'tidies up' practices and in doing so elides the indeterminate and emergent nature of engagement, this point echoes that made by Knorr-Cetina in her concept of the *epistemic object*. Their argument is that the New London Group, drawing on systemic functional linguistics (Halliday 1978), collapses all forms of meaning-making into forms of texts, which are assumed to be under the rational control of teachers and students. Essentially, they argue, the logic of grammatical texts is expanded in the analysis to take in all forms of meaning-making, including the body-as-text, in 'spatial', 'gestural' and 'behavioural' modalities. As Leander and Boldt put it, in this conception 'The human body was treated as a sign system and sign-generating system that expands our ways of writing and reading the world.' (Leander & Boldt 2012: 24). The central concept is one of 'design grammars', the difference between bodies and signs is not recognized, but instead they are assumed to be the same. They point out that this document has been taken up in the research and pedagogic literature and has attained the status of 'fact', and established as a 'framework'.

They go on to draw on Deleuze and Guattari's (1987) critique of representationalism, arguing that representational readings of meaning-making render actors and practices as a set of signs '... to be coordinated via expanded "grammars"' (Leander & Boldt 2012: 25) to convey meaning. They make a case instead, using Deleuze and Guattari's terminology, for *nonrepresentational emergence*, which they associate with the *rhizome* – the root system of bulb plants which spreads out unpredictably and in an emergent manner. Deleuze and Guattari argue for a rhizomatic understanding of life as emergent, without fixed barriers or boundaries. They also draw on Deleuze and Guattari's notion of the *assemblage*, which Leander and Bolt define as:

> ... the collection of things that happen to be present in any given context. These things have no necessary relation to one another, and they lack organization, yet their happenstance coming together in the assemblage produces any number of possible effects on the elements in the assemblage.
>
> Leander & Boldt 2012: 25

They provide an example of Lee, a twelve-year-old boy, and his activities surrounding Japanese Manga comics, which involve the assemblage of hand gestures, dialogue, cards, a website, television programmes and drawings. Crucially, they point out that from the perspective of Deleuze and Guattari, '... texts are not "about" the world; rather, they are participants in the world. Texts are artifacts of literacy practice, but do not describe practice itself.' (Leander and Boldt 2012: 25).

> This nonrepresentational approach describes literacy activity as not projected toward some textual end point, but as living its life in the ongoing present, forming relations and connections across signs, objects and bodies in often unexpected ways. Such activity is saturated with affect and emotion; it creates and is fed by an ongoing series of affective intensities that are different from the rational control of meanings and forms.
>
> Leander & Boldt 2012: 25

The emphasis is on moment-by-moment *unfolding*, in Deleuze and Guattari's terms. In their discussion of Lee's activities, they emphasize the body, which is seen as an assemblage – beginning with Lee-as-body rather than Lee-as-text.

> Because the body is in constant movement in an environment that is itself always in motion, the potential for variation is almost infinite. The body is always indeterminate, in an immediate, unfolding relation to its own potential to vary.
>
> Leander & Boldt 2012: 29

Massumi (2002) also emphasizes that change is constant as assemblages shift and emerge. Leander and Boldt contrast this conception with the New London Group paper, which is based on Fairclough's (1992, 1995) theory of *discursive hegemony*, drawing on Gramsci (1971). In this view, language is seen as '... the key site for the reworking of social conventions' (Leander & Boldt 2012: 30). Massumi (2002), who rejects the notion that the body can be reduced to discursive subject positions, on the basis of scripts governing '... every possible signifying and countersignifying move as a selection from a repertoire of possible permutations on a limited set of predetermined terms.' (Massumi 2002: 3, in Leander & Boldt 2012: 31). They make the case, with Massumi, that 'text-centric' ways of understanding how subjectivities are produced elide movement and materiality. A further effect of 'text-centrism' in their view is that literacy practices are inferred back from the standpoint of the texts themselves, while a nonrepresentational reading focuses on the temporal unfolding and emergence of practice.

> From an emergence perspective, texts are artifacts of literacy practice but do not describe practice itself. Texts are participants in the world, one piece of our ever-changing assemblage, along with material objects, bodies, and sensations. A nonrepresentational approach describes literacy activity as not determined by past design projected toward some future redesign, but as living its life in the ongoing present forming relations and connections across signs, objects and bodies in often unexpected ways. Such activity is created and fed by an ongoing flow of affective intensities that are different from the rational control of meanings and forms.
>
> Leander & Boldt 2012: 34

They also draw on Massey, who urges us to see social space as temporal process, as '... simultaneity of stories-so-far' (2005: 24, in Leander & Boldt 2012: 40). In the New London Group paper, texts, identities and so on are cast as resources, which are seen as static and awaiting use. As they put it, 'Literacy is unbounded. Unless as researchers we begin travelling in the unbounded circles that literacy travels in, we will miss literacy's ability to participate in unruly ways because we only see its proprieties.' (2012: 41).

In a related paper, Lenters (2014) also reviews a seminal text in literacy studies, with her reconsideration of Shirley Brice Heath's (1983) 'Ways with Words', a groundbreaking longitudinal ethnographic study of three communities in rural Carolina, USA in the 1960s and 1970s. Heath established the concept of the *literacy event* as a means by which to understand home and school literacy practices. Lenters suggests, however, that this construct may not be adequate for gaining insights into contemporary urban and diverse school environments, and seeks to bring a sensibility towards materiality to the notion of the literacy event, thinking of it as '*literacy-in-action*' (Lenters 2014: 48). Heath bases the literacy event on Hymes' (1977) construct of the *speech event*, and defines it as '... any occasion in which a piece of writing is integral to the nature of participants' interactions and their interpretive processes' (Heath 1982a: 350). She points out that literacy practices themselves (Street 1993) are inferred in this model, as not all of aspects of these can be directly observed. Drawing on Baynham's (2004) historical review of the field of literacy studies, she points out that the concept of *literacy event* had become naturalized to the point where it had been taken as 'fact', and had tended not to be critiqued or problematized. Lenters moves on to discuss what she calls 'third generation' literacy studies, (she cites Barton & Hamilton 2005, Baynham & Prinsloo 2009, Collins & Blot 2003, Kell 2006, Reder & Davila 2005) which have raised questions about the nature of agency and context, the human-centred stance, and the adequacy of the literacy event as a unit of analysis. She raises the question of how an event or practice may be seen as straightforwardly situated or local, given the interconnected nature of contemporary digital media. She also raises the point about whether agency can be clearly attributed to individuals. She cites recent work in literacy studies which has sought to incorporate materiality into the analysis, such as work using object ethnography (Carrington 2012), multimodality (Pahl & Rowsell 2006, 2010), activity theory (Kell 2006), and actor-network theory (Hamilton 2001, Leander & Lovorn 2006, Michaels & Somer 2000, Nichols 2006). She highlights the work of Brandt and Clinton (2002) as groundbreaking in their approach to materiality and transcontextual literacy practices, and refers to the work of Latour (2005) and the concept of objects as *actants* which exert agency. Brandt and Clinton (2002) also recognize that texts are often constructed outside of the literacy event, and therefore should not be seen as contextual features to be acted upon, but as *actants*. Lenters points out the possibilities inherent in viewing texts and also digital technologies in this way. Brandt and Clinton propose *literacy-in-action* as a unit of analysis, allowing for a tracing of objects such as print artefacts, paper and digital devices. Lenters goes on to re-analyse vignettes from Heath's (1983) data, using a literacy-in-action approach, which allowed for a more nuanced analysis which takes into account the agentive effect of texts as agentive objects, in one case the effect on students of viewing transcriptions of their speech on a video, in another it brought into view the 'bureaucratic maze' faced by African American parents who were required to obtain certification to place their children in daycare.

Micciche (2014) also offers an incisive critique of the limitations of the 'social turn', also making the point that an overemphasis on texts, with a neglect of matter. She quotes Karen Barad, who states 'Language matters. Discourse matters. Culture matters. There is an important sense in which the only thing that does not seem to matter anymore is matter.' (Barad 2003: 120). She draws on new materialism, setting out how it allows her to '... recognize writing as radically distributed across time and space, as well as always entwined with a range of others.' (Micciche 2014: 489). Echoing other critiques, Micciche refers to Coole and Frost (2010) who also reject textual analysis, structural Marxism and 'radical constructivism' as '... incapable of describing complex material realities and resulting radical agencies.' (Micciche 2014: 489). She also refers to Deleuze and Guattari's *assemblage* and Latour's *actants*, as ways in which we can see matter as active, decentring the human. She highlights the importance of a focus on bodies and corporeality for feminism, and in accounts of writing, points out what she regards as a tendency among male academics in the field to elide bodies, in order to render writing as a 'ghostly' effect of tools and technologies. She points out the need for a focus on materiality in the contemporary context, in which platforms and forms of writing have been transformed.

The notion of the vitality and active nature of objects is also emphasized in *new materialist* perspectives. This term emerged in the 1990s as part of a rejection of human/nonhuman dualisms in cultural theory, and as such it shares a lot of ground with posthumanism. Bennett's work emphasizes the distributed nature of agency across human and nonhuman actors, what she calls 'thing power', which she defines as follows:

> Thing-power gestures toward the strange ability of ordinary, man-made items to exceed their status as objects and to manifest traces of independence or aliveness, constituting the outside of our experience.
>
> Bennett 2010: 14

This is also clear in elaboration of the conception of 'vitality':

> By 'vitality' I mean the capacity of things – edibles, commodities, storms, metals – not only to impede or block the will and design of humans but also to act as quasi agents or forces with trajectories, propensities and tendencies of their own.
>
> Bennett 2010: viii

Bennet rejects the notion of constructivism:

> This impulse toward cultural, linguistic, or historical constructivism, which interprets any expression of thing-power as an effect of culture and the play of human powers, politicises moralistic and oppressive appeals to 'nature'. And that is a good thing. But the constructivist response to the world also tends to obscure from view whatever thing-power there may be. Thus there is something to be

said for moments of methodological naiveté, for the postponement of a genealogical critique of objects. This delay may render manifest a subsistent world of nonhuman vitality. To 'render manifest' is both to receive and to participate in the shape given to that which is received. What is manifest arrives through humans but not entirely because of them.

Bennett 2010: 17

In this regard, texts in digital epistemic practices might also be described as 'vibrant texts', which exhibit the features Bennett describe above. I will conclude this chapter by looking at an example of digital epistemic practice, laptop use, drawing on Adams and Thompson's heuristics.

An Interview with my Laptop

Adams and Thompson's (2016) second heuristic invites us to 'follow the actors', drawing on actor-network theory. They propose the following interview questions:

- Consider the main practices you are interested in examining. What micro-practices can you discern? Look closely at how materialities and material actors are implicated in the way these micro-practices are performed.
- Who-what is acting? What are they doing? Are some actors more or less powerful than others? Who-what is excluded?
- How have particular assemblages of actors come to be configured this way? How have these people, objects, ideas, discourses, and events gathered? What is related to what and how?
- What sort of work does this assemblage do or try to do?
- Choose an object of interest. What is the sociality around the object? The materiality?

Adams & Thompson 2106: 33

In their first heuristic, 'Gathering Anecdotes', they also encourage a process of detailed self-reflection and noticing of practices. Drawing on the questions above, the rest of the chapter will endeavour to deepen the analysis of practices in higher education discussed above, by conducting an 'interview' with my laptop. This object was chosen as a research 'participant' in order to bring a focus to a specific set of academic writing practices at a micro level.

I wrote this book during a one-year sabbatical afforded by my institution, UCL Institute of Education, after a period of four years as a Head of Department.

I had the fortunate opportunity to relocate to Italy for a year, with the agreement that I would continue in my leadership of the UCL Institute of Education Academic Writing Centre, at a distance and also via regular visits. I was also supervising several doctoral students at this time, based in various countries. I took up a part-time professorial appointment at the European University Institute (EUI), contributing to a course on teaching and learning for doctoral students. An office space was provided, but I seldom used it. Instead, all of these roles and their associate practices were conducted with my laptop, and a range of other nonhuman actors. There is nothing exceptional about the account which follows – in fact, it is mundane to the point of apparent banality. But it is precisely for this reason that I have chosen to focus on it, its everyday nature seems to be obvious, to the point of invisibility.

The house in Italy was in a village just outside Florence, in a semi-rural location. I worked in a small bedroom which I designated as my office. An important object was the power supply, and the Italian adaptor plug. A further vital element of this assemblage was the Wi-Fi router. These, formed the shifting assemblage which together wrote this book, emailed and Skyped my students, planned the EUI course, stayed in touch with my team in London, booked tickets and arranged visits back. In this chapter I will focus on the micro-practices which were involved in writing the book.

From the beginning, I decided to write the book on a single Word document, as opposed to multiple documents for chapters or notes from the literature. I also decided to set myself a target of a number of words each day (usually 1,000 or 2,000). Therefore, from an early stage, a vital element of the assemblage and practice was the 'Word Count' feature in Microsoft Word. This feature (in the Tools menu) became an entity with which I was in constant dialogue. I would repeatedly check it towards the end of the morning (my normal writing period), hoping to see a round number with three zeros. The sight of such a number (e.g. 53,000), gave me great satisfaction and a sense of achievement. At that point, once the Word Count feature had 'spoken', I could stop writing for the day. From that moment, I was free to have lunch, or do whatever other work I needed to do. I came to see the Word Count as my helper and encourager, but also a confidante and confessor – the only other entity who 'knew' when I had not had a particularly productive day. I also downloaded Freedom, an app which blocks websites, in order to help to retain focus. I would set Freedom for three hours at a time, in order to stop myself from checking email or looking at social media. Once the Word Count feature had given me permission to stop writing, I would send the draft manuscript to myself as an email attachment, with the latest word count as the subject line. I trusted my email in a way that I never came to trust the new, large-capacity external hard drive I had brought to Italy, as its predecessor had become corrupted, leading to the loss of files. The daily emails were stored in a folder, at the time of finishing this book, they numbered over ninety emails. Each email represented a writing session, and also progress. It was also a record of a particular day in that room, perhaps hot in the summer with birds calling in the garden, or cold in the winter with the wind howling in the cypress trees around the house. Every day was full of sounds, such as bells in the village, the occasional car, my neighbour watching Italian TV, the other neighbour's cat, and so on. Each day was different for me as an embodied writer, hunched over the laptop, typing, turning the pages of books, getting up occasionally to fetch a glass of water. Looking at the emails in the folder, I could see an ascending number, which gave me a sense of hope and confidence, at the many times when I felt I could not finish the book, felt overwhelmed by the literature, could not marshal my ideas, or felt generally stuck. Pencils and Post-it notes were vital components of the assemblage when I came to read research and theory literature in the form of physical books (as opposed to digital texts). I bought a pack of pencils, and a stack of Post-it notes. As I read, the laptop stayed in front of me and the book was held or placed on one side. I wrote summary notes on Post-its, which I arranged to stick up out of the top of the book. I also underlined important passages and drew circles on the text in the books. I would stop to write into the draft on the laptop during this process, if I found an element which I felt was sufficiently important. I placed a single Post-it note at the beginning of the references section of the book, sticking out of the side, in order to let me see how much more I had to read. The yellow thicket of Post-its acted as a host of small helpers, in a similar way to the Word Count feature, in that it showed me visually, and in a tactile manner, how far I had progressed.

In terms of the questions in the heuristic posed above, I myself formed part of this assemblage, working closely with a number of material actors in this emergent practice. The elements identified above were the most powerful actors, alongside the infrastructural elements such as the electricity in the house, the Wi-Fi (slow), the adaptor plug (very often missing when needed) and the power supply. I was literally entangled with the latter cable, which spent a lot of the year draped across the room from an inconveniently-positioned power socket halfway up the wall. The cable was irritating, often fell down the back of the desk, and received harsh words from me on many occasions as a result. It got worryingly hot if plugged in for more than an hour, I assumed it must be due to the electrics in the old house. However, I also viewed this grubby, tangled white cable as my ally, powering up the laptop when it was flat, and accompanying me on my travels – an unruly and messy snake, which would spring out of the top of my bag, seemed to tie itself in knots every night by itself, but also was a form of friend – my vital line or thread which allowed me to connect with the world.

After the daily target had been reached, both me and the laptop were off duty from writing. I could then use it for email, Skype or literature searching. Another important actor was the UCL library portal, which allowed me to access online journals. In the evening, I normally moved to the kitchen or the outdoor terrace and browsed the laptop for pleasure or interest. The laptop used in the kitchen, or while sitting outside, at that point seemed a different device, associated with relaxation. The laptop also accompanied me while teaching, and in this context, it was different again – it provided me with a private portal I could use to communicate with UCL Institute of Education students and colleagues on break times, or at lunch. In that sense, it allowed me to be 'present' at two universities at once, something I found oddly comforting in this new environment. I found the screen facing me while in the classroom at the EUI to be soothing, familiar, and in some sense a positive presence, (despite the frequent emails). On one occasion towards the end of my stay in Italy, I left the laptop in a bag at a bus stop – a wave of panic washed over me when I realized, I got off the bus and ran up the steep hill in intense heat to retrieve it. While panting up the hill, I told myself it would be OK even if missing – after all I had everything backed up, and although expensive, it could be replaced. However, the sense of loss was deeper than that, and my joy and relief on finding the bag waiting by the bus stop in the sleepy village square was profound. My collaborator, confidante and ally was safely back with me again.

Returning to Adams and Thompson's interview questions:

- Consider the main practices you are interested in examining. What micro-practices can you discern? Look closely at how materialities and material actors are implicated in the way these micro-practices are performed.
- Who-what is acting? What are they doing? Are some actors more or less powerful than others? Who-what is excluded?
- How have particular assemblages of actors come to be configured this way? How have these people, objects, ideas, discourses, and events gathered? What is related to what and how?
- What sort of work does this assemblage do or try to do?
- Choose an object of interest. What is the sociality around the object? The materiality?

My account above reveals the central role of materialities and material actors in this practice, one which is often conventionally presented as 'virtual' and somehow nonmaterial. The minutiae of the material micro-practices had huge salience to the whole assemblage and my experience of it. In terms of actors, I would suggest they were multiple and shifting in terms of their presence and influence on the flow of practice. Exclusions had to be engineered by me, using a combination of will-power, temporal routine, and the blocking app Freedom. The assemblages and gatherings that took place around the laptop were enormously fluid, as I suggest the account above reveals. In addition to the constantly shifting digital/material assemblages which were in constant flux, the laptop also moved around in embodied, social settings. It was mostly my solitary companion, but at times in terms of sociality, it took part in group activities, and also served as a gathering point for planning trips, looking up cultural events, social media and so on. The assemblage as a whole tried to primarily produce a book-length text. As I type this, a couple of days before the deadline agreed with the publisher, I can now say it succeeded, and I feel a sense of gratitude towards my diminutive, but also endlessly expansive, 'second author'.

3

Body

This chapter develops the analysis by turning my attention to the students themselves. In many ways, this may seem an odd focus, in a book which sets out to question humanist assumptions and ideologies surrounding meaning-making, appearing to 'place humans at the centre', in a way that I have argued is not productive or accurate. However, this is not my intention. Instead, what I argue here is that within the humanist framing, the human is simultaneously foregrounded, but also paradoxically made *invisible* and *disembodied*. My contention is that mainstream educational discourses of the student and the graduate, particularly in terms of how the digital is constructed, are in fact highly abstracted, ideological and reductive. This, I suggest, leads to two main effects. The first is a reinforcement of a particular type of neoliberal subject, who is expected to display certain values prized by contemporary society – the student should be 'active', individualistic, competitive, adaptive, 'self-regulated' and performative, imagined via a highly utopian lens of the 'transformative' potential of the digital. Secondly, I argue that this conjured digital subject reproduces a hierarchy of 'the human' which – while often presented in the language of 'student-centredness', in fact serves to reinforce privilege based on sexism, racism, homophobia, transphobia and ablism. Rendering the 'student body' invisible, the diversity of actual student bodies is hidden from view. I suggest that a posthuman framing serves to 're-embody' and render visible, the moving, breathing, complex, diverse student bodies sitting in the classroom, walking the halls, handling books, writing notes and sitting at their computer screens.

The 'Tyranny of Participation'

The detail and the fine grain of day-to-day actions and embodied practices of students in the university is, I would propose, somewhat under-researched and under-theorized. While there is a literature of ethnographic work on what students actually do day-to-day, it is fair to say its findings are not used as the basis for mainstream discourses or approaches to pedagogy concerning students in the university. Arguably, the higher educational literature, and certainly policy discourses concerning students, tends to be undergirded by assumptions of how students *ought* to be, and how teachers might create the conditions for a particular type of student subjectivity, and concomitant activity to come into being, both in the classroom and in digital settings. The construct of 'student engagement' is an example of this which has become widespread in higher education circles, and I would argue this is used as a proxy term for a range of student activities and behaviours which describe how students approach their time at university. The term itself is relatively neutral, and as such I find it helpful as a broad concept to cover both orientations and actions. However, the way the term is used in the literature and in policy discourses is often not neutral or descriptive, but is instead – I argue – somewhat normative and ideological. Kahn (2013) provides a helpful analysis of how the concept is used, also pointing out that it is weakly theorized in the literature. I attempt to critique the term here and propose an alternative conception. It is important to point out from the outset that the term is also used somewhat differently across the literature. There is a valuable strand of research and development work, particularly in the US, which focuses on 'student engagement' in terms of broad participation in university and campus life, focusing not only on the classroom or on digital engagement, but also on involvement with volunteering, university societies, sports, and so on (e.g. Barkley 2010, Dunne & Owen 2013, Quaye & Harper 2015). This type of engagement has been found to be an important factor in promoting diversity, inclusion and retention of students. This is important, but is not the focus of this chapter. Instead I turn my attention towards how the term has been used to describe and imagine student engagement specifically in educational processes, in the classroom, online and in undertaking independent study. Student engagement was defined as follows in an influential UK review:

> Student engagement is concerned with the interaction between the time, effort and other relevant resources invested by both students and their institutions intended to optimise the student experience and enhance the learning outcomes and development of students and the performance, and reputation of the institution.
>
> Trowler 2010: 3

What I find noteworthy about this definition is that it is explicitly aspirational in the use of the term, the aim is to 'optimise the student experience', 'enhance the learning outcomes' and interestingly, to 'enhance ... the performance, and reputation of the institution'. Trowler elaborates by using Coates' (2007: 122) definition, which provides more detail on what 'good' student engagement ought to consist of, listing the following features:

- active and collaborative learning;
- participation in challenging academic activities;
- formative communication with academic staff;
- involvement in enriching educational experiences; and
- feeling legitimated and supported by university learning communities.

This 'wish list' – it might be argued – is uncontroversial. It appears to describe a positive state of affairs, and as such appears benign, even unassailable. However, I would suggest that its apparent 'innocence' is, in itself, a sign of the presence of a powerful, yet subtle ideology of what a student 'ought to be'. The use of language associated with *activity*, *collaboration*, *communication* and *community* is striking throughout the definition. Once again, these appear to be positive. However, it is worth reflecting on what unites all of these – they involve an almost exclusive emphasis on *observable interaction with others*, presumably via interlocution, or by means of semi-public online engagement via online written contributions. In her discussion, Trowler characterizes approaches which encourage this type of engagement as 'progressive', unlike what she calls 'traditional' approaches, which focus on subject content, and are implied to be retrograde.

Returning to the notion of 'the student body', it appears that a particular type of 'active' embodied engagement is encouraged. This may be explicitly rewarded, such as in the practice of awarding part of the grade for classroom participation, in which asking questions and taking part vocally in class discussion gains credits, while silence or reticence leads to lower grades. Coates (2007) also discusses a range of 'engagement styles'. 'Intense' refers to students '... highly involved in university study' (Coates 2007: 132–133). 'Collaborative' refers to students engaged in university communities outside class, '... interacting with staff and other students' (Coates 2007: 134). The tone is approving. However, 'independent' engagement is described as follows:

An independent style of engagement is characterised by a more academically and less socially orientated approach to study ... Students reporting an independent style of study see themselves as participants in a supportive learning community. They see staff as being approachable, as responsive to student needs, and as encouraging and legitimating student reflection, and feedback. These students tend to be less likely, however, to work collaboratively with other students within or beyond class, or to be involved in enriching events and activities around campus.

Coates 2007: 133–134

What is interesting about this definition is that lack of interest in collaboration is presented as a negative. The final 'passive' form of engagement is unambiguously portrayed as problematic:

... it is likely that students whose response styles indicate passive styles of engagement rarely participate in the online or general activities and conditions linked to productive learning.

Coates 2007: 134

While Coates may well have a point about disengagement, it is worth noting that collaborative activities appear to be framed here as the *only* ones 'linked to productive learning'. The four-part model is effectively a hierarchical typology, with 'intense' framed as the most desirable, and 'passive' the least.

In a more recent paper, Kahu (2013) critically reviews the literature on student engagement, and propose that it is a 'meta-construct', whose nature is less than clear. She identifies four perspectives on student engagement in the literature; *behavioural*, focused on teaching practice; *psychological*; which focuses on the internal processes of the individual; *sociocultural*, which considers the sociocultural context; and what she calls a *holistic* perspective, which attempts to cover all these aspects (2013: 758). She reviews the historical development of the behavioural perspective, pointing out its roots in quality assurance methodologies (Kuh 2009a), particularly the assumption that measurement of student engagement could function as a proxy for educational quality (Kuh 2009b). The National Survey of Student Engagement (NSSE), and its successor the Australasian Survey of Student Engagement (AUSSE) rely on this behavioural perspective in their measurements. It is claimed that these constructs are based on strong empirical evidence (Kuh 2001). However, Kahu points out that there is disagreement in the field, raising concerns that the definitions are overly broad, and lacking in theoretical justification. There is also a dearth of research evidence to establish predictive validity to these constructs in terms of student outcomes. She points out further problems, such as the validity of student responses, the lack of recognition of disciplinary differences, and the emphasis on behaviour over thinking and emotion.

The *psychological* perspective, she argues, addresses some of these issues. This is a perspective which she points out is particularly dominant in the schools sector. In addition to focusing on behaviour, the focus is also on 'self-regulation' (e.g. Fredericks, Blumenfeld, & Paris 2004). This perspective takes into account elements such as student emotion, pleasure in learning, and motivation. Kahu points out that this perspective has been criticized for lack of clarity in definitions, (e.g. Jimerson, Campos & Grief 2013). She also highlights the disadvantages of situating engagement within the individual. The sociocultural perspective, in contrast, emphasizes the social context and how it impacts the student. This strand of the literature focuses on themes such as alienation (e.g. Mann 2001) and exclusion of non-traditional students (e.g. Thomas 2002). Other work has focused on engagement of 'the whole person' (e.g. Dall 'Alba & Barnacle 2007), active citizenship (e.g. Barnett & Coate 2005), and effect of commodification of education (e.g. Smith 2007).

Kahu then reviews work which has attempted to pull together all of these perspectives, such as the qualitative perspective such as that offered by Bryson and Hand (2007). Although this work provides a welcome focus on emotion, Kahu points out that it falls into the trap of failing to disaggregate between engagement and its antecedents, such as student expectations. Zepke, Leach and Butler (2010) have also proposed a holistic model, taking in a range of research perspectives, which although comprehensive, also suffers from problems of definition, scope and categorization as highlighted in Kahu's critique. Kahu then goes on to propose her own conceptual framework, which aims to encapsulate various aspects in the literature, embedded within a sociocultural framing. Her categories are both structural, and psychosocial influences, which feed into and influence student engagement, leading to proximal and distal consequences (Kahu 2013: 768). Kahu's critique is a very helpful ground-clearing exercise, and her proposed conceptual framework goes a long way toward disentangling the various uses of the term.

This focus on student engagement has had a major influence on assessments of student 'satisfaction' with higher education, and has influenced the design of national student surveys in the UK, and beyond. This in turn, has led to a desire on the part of universities to exhibit or work towards this type of 'active learning', resulting in an emphasis on interactivity in particular, as a marker of engagement, as I have argued elsewhere (Gourlay 2015a). This leads to several effects. One is that a very substantial element of what it means to be a student – independent study and solitary reading and writing – becomes somewhat hidden from view, and de-emphasized. This also encourages the view that silent or reticent behaviour in students is somehow problematic, with students being characterized as 'passive', as we saw above. The same view may be seen in digital engagement, in the focus on learning analytics of observable and traceable evidence of online activity (e.g. Ferguson 2012), discussed in chapter 8. Online engagement without the production of written text, or observable contribution, is commonly referred to as 'lurking', and tends to be viewed negatively. This, I would argue, encourages a form of potentially superficial student performativity, in which unseen knowledge practices such as reading and thinking, which are central to learning, become relegated to 'preparation', the logical end-point of this stance being the 'flipped classroom', as discussed in chapter 4. The message that maximizing interaction equals 'good teaching' also infuses the advice and training given to new lecturers. As argued elsewhere (Macfarlane & Gourlay 2009. Macfarlane 2017), this can lead to a normative push for a very particular approach to 'teaching and learning'.

Learnification, Connectification

A strong emphasis on interactive work, as the activity to be prized above all others in higher education, can lead to a stance in which both 'teaching' and 'lecture' become dirty words. This, I have argued (Gourlay 2015b), may be associated with a form of anti-intellectualism, by positing academic expertise as inherently repressive towards students. As discussed in relation to MOOCs later in this chapter, this may appear to be a radical and liberating move away from fixed hierarchies of authority in higher education, and may in fact achieve this goal, but if it is applied indiscriminately, and taken to its logical conclusion, may lead to negative effects. One of these is the resultant positioning of the provision of academic intellectual knowledge, or content, as intrinsically inferior to interaction. If learning is seen as arising primarily via interaction, then teaching is not only challenged, but is rendered fundamentally problematic. This can be identified as an example of what Gert Biesta (2010) calls 'learnification', a process by which in education, the teacher's role has shifted towards that of a facilitator (Biesta 2012). He argues for the reinstatement of the importance of content, and the teacher-student relationship, in a context in which the language used to describe education has become suffused with terminology which supports this 'anti-teaching' ideology:

> ...including the tendency to refer to teachers as facilitators of learning, to teaching as the creation of learning opportunities, to schools as learning environments, to students as learners and adults as adult learners, to the field of adult education as that of lifelong learning, and to the very idea of education as that of 'teachingandlearning'—which I deliberately write as one word, as this is how many people nowadays seem to use it.
>
> Biesta 2012, 37

Although Biesta is focusing on schooling, his valuable critique may also be applied to contemporary higher education, where the same type of discourse proliferates. He mounts a challenge to dominant social constructivist notions of learning, but in seeking to reinstate the teacher-student relationship, his remains arguably a humanist stance, which does not take account of the sociomaterially situated nature of learning.

In a recent work focused specifically on higher education, Macfarlane (2017) presents a strongly-related challenge to what he sees as a coercive culture of performativity, which views silence and reticence as problematic. He argues for academic freedom for adult students, in what he calls 'freedom to learn'. In a wide-ranging critique, Macfarlane points out the effects of the contemporary focus in higher education on 'employability' and 'learning gain', which he argues lead to a focus on 'skills' and dispositions required by the neoliberal employment market. The skills he identifies are interaction, teamworking, reflection and 'self-regulation'. He argues that adult students should be able to choose how to engage, and characterizes several widespread practices in higher education, such the taking of registers and compulsory attendance, as infantilizing. He also raises questions about what he sees as the oversimplistic and judgemental binary between 'active' and 'passive' students discussed above, making the same point about the pathologization of student silence, reticent or indeed privacy, and also highlights the pressure placed on students to demonstrate behaviours in accordance to the ideology of 'active learning', he argues, represents an injustice. He advocates:

> ... the freedom to engage in higher education on a voluntary basis and according to individual learning preferences. Using such things as attendance registers of class contribution grading or requiring compliance with normative values ... are not conducive to student academic freedom. These things introduce restrictions, and soft forms of indoctrination, rather than freedoms. The freedom to learn needs to be understood as both a negative right not to have certain freedoms taken away from students and as a positive right to enable them to exercise freedoms that will promote their personal growth as independent thinkers.
>
> Macfarlane 2017: xvi

Macfarlane identifies what he considers to be a 'hidden curriculum' in contemporary higher education. This term, as he points out, was coined by Jackson (1968) to describe the ways in which particular values, dispositions and forms of behaviour are inculcated into students in schools. In Jackson's analysis in the late 1960s, these focused on behaviours in children such as punctuality, obedience to teachers and cooperativeness. This curriculum, he argues, propagates a set of implicit social imperatives governing what is considered 'good' behaviour in students, and also beyond behaviour, what is considered acceptable in terms of students' dispositions and attitudes, which they are required to explicitly display. He also suggests that 'student-centred' practices may appear to undermine the degree of control exercised over students in traditional 'teacher-centred' classrooms, crucially, he asserts that the current model is equally focused on student compliance. The compulsion to interact and engage in groupwork is just as rigid, in his view, as the stricture to listen quietly in class in previous generations. Macfarlane argues that students should be regarded primarily as scholars, not customers:

> They are autonomous adults who have chosen to further their education for a variety of reasons. Yet their primary identity as novice scholars is being submerged beneath a new identity as a managed customer, one of several so-called stakeholders that higher education institutions seek to satisfy and placate. Ironically, beyond the rhetoric and marketing hype, this identity weakens rather than strengthens the rights of students as learners. They are domesticated, or made docile, in their roles as managed 'customers' and subject to constraints as learners rather than as adult member of an academic community.
>
> Macfarlane 2017: 2

Macfarlane links this to the notion of the *performative university*, which he uses to encapsulate the way governments' views of higher education as primarily a preparation for employment is shaping the values of universities themselves. He points out that the concept of 'academic freedom' is overwhelmingly used to refer to the freedom of academic staff, not students. He proposes the notion of *student performativity*, which he links to a broader 'audit culture' (Power 1994, 1997). He refers to Ball's (2003, 2012) concept of 'teacher performativity', which describes the regime of surveillance, targets and performance indicators which dominate both the schools and higher education sectors. He identifies three types of student performativity – *bodily*, *participative* and *emotional*. *Bodily performativity* he sees as being fulfilled through embodied attendance, *participative* performativity is demanded via interaction, and *emotional* performativity he sees as being demanded via what he calls 'confessional' pedagogies, such as reflective journals.

This chapter has set out a critique of contemporary notions of 'student engagement' in general, before turning to look at *digital epistemic practices*. This is a deliberate strategy throughout this book, as the ideologies and values of face-to-face higher education frequently form, I suggest, the base upon which digital educational practice is developed, despite claims that it is 'radical', 'transformative' or even 'revolutionary'. This section will explore how ideas about 'student engagement' are played out, and have influenced the development of a prominent innovation in digital education of the last ten years, MOOCs, which are free courses offered on the open internet. MOOCs have their roots in the Open Educational Resources (OER) movement, and the first MOOC was an online course named 'Connectivism and Connective Knowledge', which was offered in 2008, fully online and free to the public, by George Siemens at Athabasca University, Canada, and his associate Stephen Downes, of the Canadian National Research Council. Over 2,000 students enrolled, accessed the content via RSS feeds, and had the opportunity to engage in interactive discussions online using blogs and discussion fora. It is worth noting that this original MOOC was itself focused on online learning, advancing the construct of 'connectivism', which Siemens defines as follows:

> Connectivism is the integration of principles explored by chaos, network, and complexity and self-organisation theories. Learning is a process that occurs within nebulous environments of shifting core elements – not entirely under the control of the individual. Learning (defined as actionable knowledge) can reside outside of ourselves (within an organization or a database), is focused on connecting specialized information sets, and the connections that enable us to learn more are more important than our current state of knowing.
>
> Siemens 2005

Connectivism is based on several beliefs about the nature of education, which Siemens elaborates:

- Learning and knowledge rests in diversity of opinions.
- Learning is a process of connecting specialized nodes or information sources.
- Learning may reside in nonhuman appliances.
- Capacity to know more is more critical than what is currently known.
- Nurturing and maintaining connections is needed to facilitate continual learning.
- Ability to see connections between fields, ideas, and concepts is a core skill.
- Currency (accurate, up-to-date knowledge) is the intent of all connectivist learning activities.
- Decision-making is itself a learning process. Choosing what to learn and the meaning of incoming information is seen through the lens of a shifting

reality. While there is a right answer now, it may be wrong tomorrow due to alterations in the information climate affecting the decision.

Siemens 2005

The emphasis – as the name suggests – is on making connections, between people and ideas, and on currency, and the generation of new information. It is explicitly based on notions of learning in the digital age, and the potentials of internet technologies. Downes coined the term 'cMOOC' to refer to MOOCs inspired by this pedagogy. There is a strong emphasis in connectivism on participant interaction and collaboration, as opposed to expert instruction (Gourlay 2015a, Gourlay & Oliver 2018), connectivism positions itself as being a radical alternative to formal higher education, which is portrayed as hierarchical, oppressive and retrograde. This can be seen in Downes (2011), who characterizes OERs as 'free learning', 'edupunk'. He sets it out as follows:

> Edupunk, and for that matter EORs, are not and should not be thought of as the traditional educational model, where students are passive recipients of 'instruction' and 'support' and 'learning resources'. Rather, it is the much more active conception where students are engaged in the actual creation of those resources … this is exactly what corporations and institutions do not want edupunks and proponents of EORs to do, and they have expended a great deal of effort to ensure that this does not become the mainstream of learning, to ensure students remain passive and disempowered.

Downes 2011: 248

Proponents of connectivism seem to have taken the notion of the online network, with interconnecting nodes, and proposed it as a new and freestanding theorization of online learning, portrayed as entirely distinct from what has come before. However, although Downes is positioning himself in opposition to mainstream higher education and what he perceives to be its stifling and repressive nature, what is striking in this stance is paradoxically the *similarity* between the claims of connectivism and 'learnification' in higher education as discussed above. In both cases, the canon of previous knowledge, specialist expertise and teaching are viewed with suspicion, and cast as retrograde and antithetical to learning, or human flourishing. In both cases, the apparent potential of participants to generate knowledge *sui generis* via interaction is proposed as an alternative – connectivism takes this a step further by apparently rejecting the value of pre-existing content or knowledge altogether. Although they acknowledge the role of nonhuman appliances, the model – I would argue – remains intensely humanist.

This point is also made by Knox (2016), in an insightful critical study of MOOCs. He emphasizes the persistence of humanist assumptions, even in this supposedly radical educational approach and rejects narratives of 'transformation', instead highlighting how MOOCs serve to reinforce existing ideas:

> Significantly more powerful than the supposed revolution and disruption of the digital are the underlying assumptions about the human beings who take part; assumptions that govern the ways we understand and engage with technology, and also what we perceive the purpose of education to be. Rather than a story of upheaval or transformation, the MOOC is better understood in terms of the progress and enhancement of existing beliefs and commitments. In many ways, MOOCs have emerged simply as the latest in a long and established line of educational endeavours premised on the nurturing and refinement of a particular type of human being: one that thinks in a reasoned way, has a capacity for independence; and which shares these exclusive traits with all others assumed to be of the same species.
>
> Knox 2016: 2

Knox critiques connectivism, which he contends '... constructs a mask of personal empowerment and technology instrumentalism' (2016: 2), based on the assumption that participants want a 'Western' educational experience, and will spontaneously organize themselves into the type of communities conjured by Siemens and Downes. He points out the predominant focus and concern regarding participation in the context of MOOCs focused on, '... student involvement that has failed to meet expectation' and '... the perception of a largely silent and indifferent populace, surfacing briefly at the point of enrolment only to disappear behind the veil of inactivity as non-completion.' (Knox 2016: 89). He points out the normative aspect of how participation is expected and measured, leading to a hierarchy of participation which values 'active' learners and finds 'lurking', 'passivity', or silence to be a problem to be solved. He proposes that this undesirable participation is responded to as a form of 'contamination' of the community, which needs to be continually 'purified'. Rather than being an open and inclusive space, Knox argues that MOOCs use indoctrination to discipline their community members into a particular type of behaviour. He examines and contrasts the connectivist-influenced cMOOCs and the discourses surrounding them, and concludes that connectivism is equally normative in its expectations surrounding participation. Siemens stated in a blog post in 2010 that 'lurking = taking' – silence is regarded as not only unacceptable, but also unethical, against the 'law' of the community. As Knox points out, connectivism reifies the network to such an extent that the network does not simply facilitate learning, in this view the network *is itself learning*. Knox also analyses a YouTube video providing guidance to MOOC participants (Cormier 2010), which consists of five recommended steps – 'orient, declare, network, cluster, and focus'. The exhortation to 'declare' oneself immediate through posting online is notable, also the requirement to 'network'. Knox goes on to discuss the features of the 'personal learning network', which is seen as fundamental to MOOC participation, and argues that this evinces the highly individualistic nature of the whole endeavour.

Knox's critique is an insightful one, and it draws out a series of points which are pertinent to this chapter and the book as a whole. What is striking is the strong echoing of the same points discussed earlier in the chapter, with regard to the face-to-face classroom, and how students are expected to behave and perform. Despite claims to be radical and inclusive, it appears that MOOCs (both xMOOCs and cMOOCs) replicate and reinforce the same ideology. The student is expected to exhibit very specific behaviours, a performance of participation in which must be made visible in order for them to be accepted as a legitimate member of that class or 'community'. Once again, a somewhat superficial discourse of inclusion, interaction, community and 'belonging' masks what I suggest is a highly normative, disciplining regime which requires students to conform/ perform, or be regarded as deviant. As with the campus-based ideology, online in the context of MOOCs we also see what is essentially a neoliberal, humanist view of the human subject – autonomous, rational, and unencumbered by materiality, or the workings of power and privilege – despite the trappings of either corporate images of 'community', or the more self-consciously 'maverick' identity positioning of connectivism. As with the campus-based literature on 'teaching and learning', the realm of the digital also seems to be another arena onto which fantasies about higher education and the human subject can be projected, through – I argue – the coercion of students into carefully-coordinated and narrowly-specified performances of 'activity', a regime which I have characterized to as 'the tyranny of participation' (Gourlay 2015b), (an expression also used by Knox in his analysis). I have also proposed (Gourlay 2015c) that OERs and connectivism are based on what I have called a 'heterotopia of desire', following Foucault – an acting out of a utopian fantasy of education and the subject. Knox's analysis seems to provide further support for this critique.

What is also striking from a close analysis of MOOCs and the literature surrounding them (particularly in the case of connectivism) is the invisibility of content. As with 'learnification', there is a collapse into a reification of pure process, and a positioning of interaction, interlocution or posting online as *the learning itself* – the parallel expression 'connectification' could perhaps be coined to be paired with 'learnification' in the campus. Once again, although there is a somewhat obsessive focus on making connections, there is scant attention in this literature paid to the fact that these are primarily digitally-mediated textual practices, and little or no attention to the detail of *how* they emerge; crucial aspects to understanding this form of educational engagement. Again, interaction is simultaneously reified and made to stand for learning, and rendered oddly invisible, like the students themselves, who are somewhat erased as embodied humans, and only regarded as 'present' via a narrow band of prescribed textual linguistic performance. Knox concludes his discussion with a comparison of how the 'network' is conceived of in connectivism, in contrast with in actor-network theory, drawing on Bell (2010). He makes the point that the connectivist network is seen as the product of human agency alone, in which nonhuman devices are seen as merely storage facilities as opposed to agentive elements. He makes the crucial point that in an Actor-Network theory (ANT), '. . . the autonomous individual is *produced* through networked relations, rather than pre-existing as the originator of the arrangement.' (Knox 2016: 114).

An Interview with a MOOC

Viewed in terms of Adams and Thompson's heuristics, the MOOC as a set of digital epistemic practices can be interrogated further. Their sixth heuristic seems to offer potential, 'applying the laws of media'. They propose the following questions:

- What does a technology enhance? What human capacity is extended, enhanced, or amplified when this technology is used?
- What does a technology render obsolete? What human capacity is diminished, attenuated, or simply forgotten when this technology is used?
- What does a technology retrieve from the past that was previously obsolesced?
- What does a technology reverse into when used ubiquitously or pressed to an extreme?
- What radiated 'lines of force' does this technology put into play?

This heuristic is drawn from media ecology, with the concept of 'line of force' originating with McLuhan (1964: 15), referring to the ways in which media creates effects in society. As Adams and Thompson put it:

Every medium or lived technology is recognised as ecological. It dilates and contracts, infects and infuses human perception, action, and understanding, with potentially far-reaching implications and reverberations in our personal, social, cultural, and political lives.

Adams & Thompson 2016: 66

The questions above are based on McLuhan and McLuhan's (1988) 'four laws of media', which they use in the forms of tetrads to analyse technologies. Adams and Thompson provide an example of GPS technology, in this section I will use the same heuristic to examine the effects of a MOOC.

In order to do so, I browsed the EdX website, seeking a course which I felt was close enough to my interests that I might be motivated to join it. After a brief search, I found 'META101x: Thinking about Thinking', offered by the University of Queensland in September 2019 (EdX: 2019). It was commencing that day, and seemed suitable, so in the spirit of a casual browser, I decided to explore this course for the purpose of this chapter. I considered the ethics of this, and decided I would not take part in the interactive elements, as I was viewing the materials for research purposes. For this reason, I do not show screenshots showing participant names or posts, but will only provide a textual description of the elements I experienced, all of which were in the public domain. This section was written while browsing the course, switching between screens, in a two-hour period. It is not intended to be a criticism of this MOOC in any way, but simply an account of my experience of it, followed by analysis of it in terms of the heuristic discussed above.

The first page showed a small video screen on the right, with a photograph of a sunflower, and the instruction 'play video'. The video opens with classical music and 'bucolic' scenes of a verdant university campus. A white man and woman are shown from above sitting on the grass relaxing, and entwined as a couple. The camera cuts to two gargoyles (stone heads found on medieval buildings) on the wall of the overlooking university building. These are animated with the talking heads of two people, another white man and woman. In a clearly humorous tone, they comment on the students below, saying they should be getting on with their studies, not 'frolicking'. They then express that students need to learn how to think, but they don't listen to their advice. The man then suggests they should create a course to help the students with this. Then we see two different individuals (another white man and woman) sitting on the grass, talking about how hard it is to think clearly and critically. Then suddenly, a large, leather-bound book lands in front of them from above, with the title META. They open it and light shines from it, then it morphs into what appears to be an iPad screen showing the META101x course. End of video. The text on the rest of the page includes a brief text entitled 'about this course':

> What can we learn through philosophical inquiry that will help us to think with clarity, rigour and humour about things that matter? This course introduces principles of philosophical inquiry and critical thinking that will help us answer this question. Learn how we can use philosophical ideas to think about ourselves and the world around us.
>
> META101x: 2019

This is followed by a list entitled 'What you'll learn':

- How to think with clarity and rigour
- How to identify, analyse and construct cogent arguments
- How to think of solutions to the central problems of philosophy
- How to engage philosophical conversations with others about topics than matter

META101x: 2019

Scrolling down, I see the next section, 'meet your instructors', and I realize that they are the two individuals who were superimposed onto the gargoyles in the video. The next block of text offers me the opportunity to pursue a verified certificate from EdX for $99. The final element on the first page is entitled 'learner testimonials', and shows one highly positive recommendation. I proceed to enrol via a form. The next page I see is headed:

> 'Congratulations! You are now enrolled in Philosophy and Critical Thinking'.

Under that heading, I am invited once again to pursue a verified certificate. The full text is as follows:

> Pursue a Verified Certificate
> Highlight your new knowledge and skills with a verified certificate. Use this valuable credential to improve your job prospects and advance your career, or highlight your certificate in school applications.
> Benefits of a Verified Certificate
>
> - **Official**: Receive an instructor-signed certificate with the institution's logo
> - **Easily shareable**: Add the certificate to our CV or resume, or post it directly on LinkedIn
> - **Motivating**: Give yourself an additional incentive to complete the course
> - **Support our Mission**: EdX, a non-profit, relies on verified certificates to help fund education or everyone globally

Below this, there is an option to 'audit this course', which advises: 'Audit this course for free and have complete access to all the course material, activities, tests, and forums. **Please note that his track does not offer a certificate for learners who earn a passing grade.**' I click on 'audit this course'. The next page begins by asking me to 'set a course goal by selecting the option below that best describes your learning plan'. Arranged as buttons, the options are 'earn a certificate', 'complete the course', or 'explore the course'. I decide not to choose just yet, but scroll down to read the welcome:

Welcome

Hello and welcome to META101x – a free online introductory course about Philosophical and Critical Thinking. Thinking well is important. This course is a celebration and exploration of our ability to think and hence to philosophise. We look at how thinking in certain ways allows us to frame and approach some of the biggest questions that can be asked – questions about how we can know about the world and ourselves, how we can understand identity and change, even what it means to be thinking in the first place. We start with the basics of argumentation and slowly build from there. We ponder the characteristics of a good argument and how to identify one. We'll cover deductive and inductive inferences and social knowledge. At the same time, we'll explore some philosophical conundrums like whether or not our reasons for believing something need to be grounded on earlier beliefs, and the connection between thinking, our minds, and our brains.

The next part of the screen is entitled 'How to navigate through the course'. Three ways to 'enjoy the course' are suggested, in the form of three 'tours' that '… you can shape for yourself'. These are the 'Promenade Tour', which is illustrated with a photo of tourists on a seaside promenade taking photos. I am invited to 'enjoy a leisurely stroll' through the basics. I am told that my 'guides will prepare intellectual snacks' and will 'point out … ideas'. This 'tour' comprises videos with short questions to test my understanding. It concludes with the statement 'we hope you enjoy your stay'. Next is the 'Dilletante's Tour', which 'provides the extra service the discerning philosophy student deserves'. This includes 'enlightened commentary crafted in-house', an 'exclusive range of in-depth interviews with some of the world leading philosophical minds'. This is illustrated with a photo taken in what appears to be the first-class cabin of an aircraft, with a pair of feet in socks propped up in front of a TV screen. Thirdly, the 'Catacombs Tour' is offered for 'the serious philosophy student'. I am invited to 'plumb the depths' of philosophy and 'wander down a dazzling array of links'. This is illustrated by a photo of a Lego figure which appears to represent the movie character 'Indiana Jones'. Below this, there is 'additional information', which includes a link to the syllabus, guidance about a 'notes' feature, a link to a demo EdX course. Towards the bottom of the page in a box, the following text is displayed:

> UQx acknowledges the traditional custodians of the land upon which this material was created, Australia's First Peoples, and pays respect to their histories, connections to land and continuous living cultures.

Below this, the course outline is shown. It consists of an introduction and four modules, plus extended interviews with philosophers. The final element of this page is a button at the bottom, inviting me to 'learn about verified certificates'. I go on to discover that this button appears on every page of the course. I move on to the course introduction, which begins with 'G'day and welcome to META101: Philosophy and Critical Thinking!'. I'm invited to 'join' (four names). The first two are the names of the instructors, I assume the other two are also instructors on the course. There is a video entitled 'course introduction'. The static image shows a white man sitting on the grass with a white woman lying with her head on his lap in what appears to be a somewhat sexualized relationship. On the right of this image, there is a transcript of the opening video I already watched in which the instructors, as gargoyles, criticize these students for 'frolicking'. I click on the video and discover it's the same one. I scroll down and find I am invited to 'say g'day!' to students 'from all over the world'. There is a moderated forum below, where participants have posted messages saying hello and introducing themselves. The next section shows videos of students addressing the question 'Why do philosophy?'. The static image is of a young white woman. I skip on to the next section, which features professors addressing this question. At the top of this page, the following text is shown; 'OK, so philosophy classes and seminars seem pretty interesting. Maybe even fun. Maybe.' There is a static image of an older white man on the video screen, and a list of ten names with links below, eight male, and two female, the female names shown at the bottom of the list. I decide to skip these videos at this point. The next page shows another forum where participants comment on their motivations for doing the course.

There are several points that can be made about the introductory pages and module of this MOOC. The first is the clearly light-hearted tone adopted. It opens with a humorous video, and the tone is 'friendly' and informal from that point onwards. Approaches to the course are presented as options, using the language and imagery of tourism, with the potential participant positioned as a commercial client selecting between different products. Although this is no doubt also intended to be fun, the way it positions the participant is worthy of attention. The invitation is to be served, or guided, in various ways. Links to texts are a 'dazzling array'. It is also worth noting the situated nature of the cultural references throughout. The visual setting is the home university, and opens with the trope of a couple 'canoodling' on the grass, which arguably may be culturally unacceptable for some potential participants. Australian slang ('g'day') is used, which is likely to make the course seem accessible and informal to Australian students, but may be less transparent to others. The use of the image of a physical book – a hardback 'tome' which is seen as landing on the ground and then morphing into a website, is also interesting. It appears that the creators of the course have chosen the image of an 'old school' book to indicate authority, even in this fully-online setting. However, the overall message seems more focused on how philosophy can be 'fun'. The repeated exhortations to sign up for the verified certificate ($99), are a frequent reminder that EdX is also a commercial operation, even if it is a non-profit.

I move on to module 1. The first page shows the instructors outdoors in matching T-shirts, with the word 'philosophy' in the centre, and a speech bubble above saying 'what part of "know" don't you understand?'. I decide to skip ahead, and a few pages later I see an image of the male instructor, with the female instructor as a tiny figure transposed on the screen and dressed as a fairy, with wings, wearing a tiara, a pink dress and cape, holding a wand. I stop exploring at this point, as I find the image sexist. The rest of the course is structured into videos, followed by quizzes and discussion fora. The instructors provide commentary while the 'experts' are featured in videos.

Turning to the McLuhans' tetrad, and their 'four laws' of media, this MOOC may be analysed as follows, the baseline comparator I am using here is the face-to-face university course (see table 1).

Although I have referred to a specific MOOC, it seems fair to assert that this analysis would apply to other MOOCs, if based on the same elements of talking-head video broadcasts, online discussion boards, and quizzes. Analysed in terms of the critique offered earlier in the chapter, the ethos of 'learnification' does seem to be apparent in various aspects of this MOOC. The importance of individual motivation is emphasized, although this sits rather uncomfortably with the emphasis on credentialing and career enhancement, used in the justification for opting for the verified certificate. There is a somewhat infantilizing tone throughout, with much emphasis on 'fun'. Complex concepts are 'tested' by use of simple

Table 1

Enhances	Reverses into
Control over of sequence, element, and duration of engagement.	Course as a range of products of options, to be selected from.
Access from any location with internet access.	Alternatively, course as a range pre-specified tours to be chosen and enjoyed.
Broadcasts of TV documentaries made for lay viewers interested in academic topics.	Written academic texts, presented as only for the more 'serious student'.
TV lectures given by experts.	Participant academic writing.
Quizzes used for 'fun'.	Verbal interaction and co-presence.
Retrieves	**Obsolesces**

quizzes, reminiscent of material for younger learners. Any impression that philosophy may be serious and difficult is avoided. The instructors adopt a joking, 'matey' tone throughout, and seem at pains to avoid any impression of hierarchy, dressing up in 'silly' costumes and matching T-shirts, for example. The status of expertise is a confused one in the MOOC in this regard, as this performance of informality sits alongside more conventional tropes indicating authority; the weighty 'tome' falling from the sky, and the menu of (predominantly older white male) expert videos. 'Connectification' is also apparent, in the frequent invitations to contribute to online discussion boards, although the extent to which these lead to meaningful discussion is negligible. Arguably, what we see here is an elaborate performance of these twin educational ideologies, in an assemblage which seems to assume/position the 'default' participant as a young white Australian, an ingénue who is likely to be intimidated by philosophy, with a low boredom threshold and in need of frequent entertainment, but one who would like to obtain a certificate in order to advance his or her career. The instructors perform rather like youth TV hosts, and the academic texts are very much kept in the background as for 'serious students' only, ready to 'plumb the depths' of the catacombs; an image of danger and mystery, unlike the 'fun' promenade or the luxury of the 'bespoke' dilettante tour. Again, it is not my intention to strongly criticize this MOOC; it works very well on its own terms, and is indeed kind of 'fun'. My task here is rather to point out the various profound ways in which it differs from a face-to-face university course, how it exemplifies the ideologies I have described above, and also to illustrate what – in terms of the 'Laws of Media' – has been lost in this 'transformation'.

Presence

The previous chapter explored and critiqued the ways in which students are expected to behave and 'be' in the contemporary university, both face-to-face, and digitally. It made the point that apparently innocuous, or ostensibly positive notions such as 'active learning' and 'connectivism' may in fact distort educational practices, and can render them into a form of mutual performance, which is more concerned with the expression of a particular ideology than with the pursuit of learning. I placed an emphasis on the embodied nature of educational practice, and suggested that students' bodies, and engagement online, are both governed by an ideology of performance. In this sense, I suggested that they are required via bodily/linguistic conformity, to animate and express a particular form of 'the university'. I examined how this dynamic is played out in digital education in a discussion of the set of *digital epistemic practices* on one MOOC. This chapter looks in detail at another site of epistemic practice, the lecture, and to examine how the history of the lecture and contemporary discourses surrounding it have shaped contemporary digital epistemic practices.

I have chosen to focus on the lecture for several reasons. Firstly, because it arguably represents the prototypical educational encounter in the university setting. As we will see, its roots stretch back to the very origins of what we now call the university, and it is a ubiquitous feature in all higher education systems, in some shape or form. I argue that this ubiquity is no accident, and that there are features of the lecture which can account for its longevity, and also its persistence. Another reason I am drawn to analyse the lecture is that it is, in the contemporary period, often held up as an example of all that is retrograde, stultifying, elitist and 'teacher-centred', and is also frequently positioned as such, in comparison with the more allegedly dynamic and 'transformative' potentials of the digital. Developing the theme which I started in the previous chapter, I speculate on what it is about the lecture that leads to such virulent criticism, and why it appears to be a 'lightning rod', or a gathering point around which educationalists can express a particular form of virtue and identity, strengthening the 'learnification' stance expressed via a support for 'active learning'. I spend the first part of the chapter focusing on the 'traditional' campus-based lecture; as with the previous chapter, my analysis of digital epistemic practices flows from an analysis of the 'face-to-face' setting and its practices. I begin by reviewing work which has provided a valuable historical perspective, drawing on the work of Norm Friesen in particular, and pay particular attention of Friesen's application of Goffman's analysis of the lecturer's 'selves'. In doing so, I focus on two aspects of the lecture, *co-presence* and *ephemerality*. I argue that these represent the essence of the lecture, and I question the assumptions commonly made in the contemporary period about the notion of 'audience', 'listener', 'silence' and 'passivity' in lecture settings. I propose that by casting the students present at a lecture as 'passive', inert listeners, a fundamental category error is committed in terms of the subjectivities of the students themselves, the subjectivity of the lecturer, and the nature of the encounter. I develop this point by arguing that this leads to a miscasting of the lecture as essentially a broadcast event, and contend that even the most apparently 'traditional' and supposedly 'teacher-centred' lecture is in its essence intensely interactive, due to co-presence and ephemerality. I develop this point by extending the notion of 'interaction' beyond interlocution, to take in the commitment, the energy and interchange of focused co-presence. I argue that the casting of students as passive and inert 'audience' members elides this, and in doing so also denies/obfuscates the essentially and necessarily embodied nature of the 'face-to-face' encounter.

I go on to explore how the influence of digital technology has already altered the lecture in terms of both co-presence and ephemerality. I caution that the apparently 'logical' conclusion of the inclusion of digital technology is to lose both of these essential features. I illustrate this with a discussion of the *digital epistemic practices* of a 'flipped classroom', the online input element of which is essentially a broadcast event which *resembles* a lecture, but is *not in fact a lecture* in the terms I have proposed. Instead, I argue that it is a spoken event which is stripped down to the pure transfer of a fixed and pre-prepared text. I extend the analysis by arguing that the flipped classroom model is an extreme example of the ethos of *learnification*, which 'wears the clothes' (as with 'active learning') of 'student-centredness', and therefore functions as an extended and orchestrated performance of that ethos. Once again, I argue, the students are required through their bodily and linguistic performances, to enact a profoundly humanistic, social constructivist ideology, which paradoxically regards the primary site of texts, learning and higher education to be the human, while simultaneously seeking to elide the importance of bodily co-presence, and temporal ephemerality. The human (in this case the student) once again is simultaneously placed 'at the centre' of educational processes, but is also, in a profound sense, not required to be present, except to enact a very particular type of cultural performance. I will conclude that, as with 'active learning' more broadly, this serves to distort the nature of unfolding practice, concealing aspects which are not readily observable, or that do not fall under the accepted category of 'active'. I argue in conclusion that a posthuman/materialist analysis provides a more insightful and nuanced lens on the practices of the lecture and the subjectivities it conjures, drawing once again on Adams and Thompson's 'interview' heuristics.

History of the Lecture

Friesen (2017) provides a fascinating historical review of the lecture, focusing on what has persisted in the forms that higher education takes, as opposed to what has changed. He begins by refuting the notion that schooling is antithetical to learning, stating:

> This circle begins with education being painted as hopelessly artificial, stifling and outmoded – arguments that have natural resonance. Next (or simultaneously) demands are made for radical change or even revolution. Ultimately, though, these calls end up having little or no effect. Despite this fact, new reformers and critics rise up, along with the newest technologies and the latest findings in physiology and neurology. What finally materialises however is not a silver bullet for education, but instead the repetition of a clear pattern: calls for change repeated over decades and centuries that lead to great expectations – and to ultimate disappointments.
>
> Friesen 2017: 6

He highlights the prevalence of the notion of the lecture as 'mere information transmission' across different theoretical traditions:

> Cognitivists, who believe the mind works like a computer, and constructivists, who emphasise the construction of mental representations, both see the lecture and the textbook as mere information transmission. They understand reading a textbook or attending a lecture to be actually discouraging deep processing or active knowledge construction. But it is not so simple. A lecture is much more than an information dump, and a textbook is not just inert content.
>
> Friesen 2017: 7

He points out that the lecture forms the basis of many highly popular contemporary educational forms, such as the MOOC, the Technology, Entertainment and Design (TED) talk, and short 'ignite' presentations, and he highlights the popularity of 'lecture capture'. He reminds us that the history of the lecture (and the textbook) are '... not marked by convulsive moments, sudden impacts or revolutions' but instead '... follow the contours of broader and more gradual cultural and social changes.' (2017: 8), likening the process to that by which a river forms its banks. He refers to the French historian Fernand Braudel's concept of the '*longue duree*', a focus on slow, meandering change, in which social affairs may even appear to be motionless. This type of thinking is central to Friesen's project, where he chooses not to look at rapid change, 'transformation', or 'revolution' in education and media, but instead focuses on what has changed most slowly, or appears to be almost still. As he points out, 'Both the lecture and the textbook began and developed as a means of preserving knowledge, word-for-word, from its original, sacred or ancient source.' (2017: 11). He emphasizes the role of remediation, in which new media build on previous forms, and the central position of the lecture, stating:

> It could even be said to serve as a kind of nexus point for educational change and continuity. Different media and educational formulations and possibilities are constantly being reconfigured around the lecture, and these configurations have the power in turn to adjust the function and character of the lecture itself.
>
> Friesen 2017: 110

He points out the many contemporary criticisms of the lecture, reminding us of the commonplaces which are used to denigrate it, such as 'chalk and talk', and the adage that the 'sage on the stage' should be replaced by the 'guide on the side'. He reminds us that the lecture was also critiqued by Lyotard (1984) as likely to be obsolete in the future, as he predicted students would access resources directly from libraries and computers. Friesen reviews Laurillard's (2001) classification of the lecture as narrative or discursive, alongside print, video or DVD resources, all of which she categorizes as 'non-interactive'. She regards the lecture as a form focused on dissemination of information in a transmission mode, which she rejects as an obsolete remnant of historical tradition. However, Friesen points out the contemporary and enduring popularity of the lecture format.

The predominance of these online videos, particularly the importance of instructor-produced videos for the MOOC, puts us in an ironic situation: the latest educational and technological innovations are being used simply to create and disseminate copies of one of the most archaic pedagogical forms.

Friesen 2017: 112

Focusing on the spoken nature of the lecture, Friesen suggests that the lecture '... can be most effectively understood as bridging oral communication with writing, rather than an obstinate form of primitive residual orality.' (2017: 112). He reminds us that the lecture in the medieval period took place in a situation of extreme textual scarcity, therefore the early lecture was less about disseminating knowledge, and more focused on the preservation of texts, and '... rescuing a written cultural heritage from irretrievable loss and decay.' (2017: 113). Teaching and study were also seen as acts of preservation and continuity, rather than creation of new knowledge. Before the printing press, books existed only in rare handwritten form, which were difficult to preserve, lectures therefore provided a means to maintain these vulnerable texts across generations.

The medieval meaning of 'lecture' comes from the Latin *legere*, to read, or to read aloud (2017: 113), and lectures at that time consisted of the dictation of an authoritative text. The words were not seen as originating from the lecturer, but from the material book itself. Some books were even designed to fit on the podium (*cathedra*), and some were written in *scriptio continua* without vowels, and needed vocalization to be deciphered. Friesen points out that extemporizing one's own ideas was not part of the process, the lecturer at that time was more of a conduit, or channel. He quotes the media theorist Friedrich Kittler, who draws a comparison between the medieval library and contemporary digital storage devices:

> Most European universities came into being as extensions of former monasteries or cathedral schools. Therefore, they possessed from the outset a library full of Latin manuscripts. This very wealth not only guaranteed the famous translation studiorium transporting classical antiquity to the High Middle Ages, but also constituted a kind of hardware, a storage device just as precious as our hard drives.

Kittler 2004: 245, in Friesen 2017: 114

Whole books were heard by the students, and the lectures were at times labelled *dictate ad calamum*; read at a pace suitable for full transcription. 'Lecturers were functionally comparable to conduits through which voices of the past could speak.' (2017: 116). The era of the printing press changed this context, from a paucity of texts to relative availability. However, the lecture remained central, as books were still rare and costly. Over time the role and function began to change as Friesen describes, as lecturers began to add their own gloss, which was written into the margins of manuscripts by the lecturers. Friesen cites Clark (2006), whose study into the origins of the research university reveals a gradual shift away from dictation, towards free commentary. Friesen concludes that the introduction of the printing press did not in fact cause an abrupt change in practices surrounding lecturing and note-taking, instead the emphasis is on continuity and gradual shifts in practice.

In the final part of his historical review, Friesen focuses on the latter years of the eighteenth century, and in particular the German professor Johan Gottlieb Fichte, who was recorded to be the first to lecture without an official set text (Clark 2006), which Clark characterizes as '... the ultimate break with the sermon.' (Clark 2006: 410, in Friesen 2017: 119). At this point, the height of the Romantic period, the spontaneous, spoken word was valued over the written word, which Friesen reports Fichte saw as '... all but dead' (2017: 6: 119). Fichte regarded the *Geist* – the spirit, thought or intellect – as the source of the self, created in action. As Friesen puts it, 'According to his own philosophy, Fichte can be said to have produced *himself* as a self-producing process through his articulations at the lectern.' (2017: 121). Fichte explores the relationship between the spirit and letter as follows:

> I set before you a product, into which I believe I have breathed a few ideas. But I do not give you the ideas themselves, not can I do so. I give you the mere body. The words which you hear constitute this body. Taken in themselves, my words are no more than empty noise, a movement in the air that surrounds us. You place a meaning in these words for yourself, just as I place a meaning in them for myself.
>
> Fichte 1993: 201, in Friesen 2017: 122

Friesen draws a link between Fichte's philosophy and modern-day constructivist psychology, which emphasizes individuals constructing knowledge 'for themselves'. Both Romanticism and constructivism privilege the notion that learning is naturally-occurring, and individualized, based on the experience of the lone human individual; Friesen points out the irony of the current-day critique of the 'sage on the stage' being regarded now as the enemy of education, based on constructivist principles. Fichte privileged the spoken word over writing as the best way to invoke 'spirit', with an emphasis on emotion and the ignition of 'fiery sparks' in the souls of the students (Fichte 1993: 198–199).

The next major development was the work of Wilhelm von Humboldt, and his establishment of the Humboldt University of Berlin, which came to serve as a model for universities in the US and Canada. Crucially, at this time the emphasis moved towards not simply the preservation or reproduction of knowledge, but the creation of new knowledge through scholarship. For Humboldt, lecturing was seen as a site for the generation of new ideas, alongside research. This vison of the university was a hopeful, even idealistic one. However, Friesen ends his review with Nietzsche's somewhat bleak characterization of the university as a soulless 'culture machine' (*Bildungsmaschine*). Friesen attributes Nietzsche's cynicism to the contemporary introduction of electromechanical media, which in Nietzsche's lifetime were the typewriter, telegraph and phonograph. Regarding these technological innovations, Friesen argues '... none of these forms made the lecture obsolete ... they were ultimately influential in its being recast from a spontaneous authorial expression to a much more calculated performance, aiming only at the illusion of spontaneous expression.' (Friesen 2017: 125). He goes on to analyse the nature of the lecture from the twentieth century until now, focusing on the influence of recording technologies, radio and film, focusing in particular on the notion of the lecture as a form of performance. Discussing the advent of the televised lecture, he highlights the paradox that the broadcast lecture, while reaching a much larger audience than the live version, is experienced as a more intimate, one-to-one event by the individual viewer, who is likely to be alone or in a small domestic group. He also draws attention to the need for speakers on TV to receive training on how to appear in close-up, effectively acting training. He draws a comparison with the early days of online education, when the idea of using professional actors to deliver internet-based lectures was considered, a suggestion also raised at the time of the more recent introduction of MOOCs.

Friesen considers that this focus on performance has come about as a result of the lecture becoming 'theatricalised' (2017: 132), and turns to the work of Erving Goffman to explore this notion in more detail, in particular Goffman's 1976 work 'The Lecture'. Crucially, Goffman views the self as essentially performative, and also multiple. Different selves are brought to bear in the lecture, as he sets out:

> At the apparent center will be the textual self, that is, the sense of the person that seems to stand behind the textual statements made and which incidentally gives these statements authority. Typically, this is a self of relatively long standing, one the speaker was involved in long before the current occasion of talk. This is the self that others will cite as the author of various publications, recognise as the holder of various positions, and so forth ... And he is seen as the 'principal' namely, someone who believes personally in what is being said and takes the position that is implied in the remarks.

> Goffman 1981: 173, in Friesen 2017: 133

This is the academic self which Goffman characterizes as 'textual', although Friesen points out that these days that self may also be expressed via video, images and audio. However, the main role for the textual self in Goffman's framing is in the preparation of the lecture. In order to deliver the lecture, another self is required, the self as 'animator'. Goffman defines this self as '... the person [who] can be identified as the talking machine, the thing the sound comes out of.' (Goffman 1981: 171, in Friesen 2017: 133). This 'talking machine' self also responds to the situation in the lecture as it unfolds, provides asides, and uses a form of speech Goffman calls 'fresh talk', which he defines as follows:

> In the case of fresh talk, the text is formulated by the animator from moment to moment, or at least from clause to clause. This conveys the impression that the formulation is responsive to the current situation in which the words are delivered.
>
> Goffman 1981: 171, in Friesen 2017: 133

Goffman identifies three forms of spoken words in the lecture context – *memorisation, aloud reading* and *fresh talk*, and regards a lot of what appears as fresh talk is in fact an illusion of spontaneity, actually reading aloud, made attainable by media, advance preparation and notes. Friesen argues that this creation of a 'fresh talk illusion' through theatrical techniques is fundamentally different to the 'sparks' described by Fichte, the spontaneous creation of new knowledge while lecturing prized by the Romantics. Friesen points out the strong echoes of Fichte and the Romantics in the contemporary advice to TED speakers – that they should be 'passionate' and 'ignite sparks' in the audience, but also paradoxically that they should practice their performance until it is at a highly polished state of illusion. However, he also underlines the ways in which the medieval, Romantic and postmodern configurations interleave in contemporary lectures, with elements of all three being used.

Friesen's analysis is insightful and highly useful in opening up the ways in which the lecture has evolved over the centuries. However, I would suggest there are a few questions which arise out of the analysis of Fichte, the Romantics, and Goffman's model of the 'fresh talk illusion'. One relates to the concept of *genre* (Swales 1990), which Swales defines as follows:

> A genre comprises a class of communicative events, the members of which share some communicative purposes. These purposes are recognised by expert members of the parent discourse community, and thereby constitute the rationale for the genre. The rationale shapes the schematic structure of the discourse and influences and constrains the choice of content and style.
>
> Swales 1990: 58

Swales' concept of genre has been applied predominantly to the written word in academic contexts, and the construct is not without its detractors. However, it reminds us that forms of communication – in terms of linguistic, semiotic and stylistic choices – do not appear fully-formed and *sui generis*, but are historically and socially framed, and are strongly governed by social and institutional expectations about how they should be enacted or performed. Gitelman defines genre as:

> ... ongoing and changeable practices of expression and reception that are recognisable in myriad and variable constituent instances at once and across time. They are specific and dynamic, socially realised sites and segments of coherence within the discursive field.

Gitelman 2014: 2

Applying this concept to the case of the 'spontaneous' lectures of the Romantic period, it seems unlikely that they were uninfluenced by social expectations and genres of 'successful' public speaking known to the lecturers of that time. These are likely to have included religious sermons and exegesis, in addition to other forms of vocal public performance such as theatre or storytelling. Evidence may be scant as to the exact nature of these lectures, but it seems likely that they would have absorbed some influences from these forms, which are designed to capture listeners' attention, and also to persuade, entertain, or even enchant. This analysis can also be applied to contemporary audience expectations according to the setting and medium. Television tends to generate an expectation in the viewer of slick, expertly-performed entertainment, in a way that the lecturer in the traditional lecture theatre traditionally does not. The same argument may also be made for video, whether viewed on TV, or online. The device itself creates expectations about the nature of what is viewed, and also positions the listeners in a fundamentally different way from the lecturer in the setting of the university, where the listeners are students and participants in a way that the viewer of a lecture online is not. I will return to this point towards the end of the chapter, in my analysis of the flipped classroom.

The point about genre also leads us to the socially-situated nature of lectures. Historically, vocal performers in genres such as sermons, political speeches, storytelling, announcements, theatrical performances and lectures have tended predominantly to be men with social capital. For this reason, the cultural expectations surrounding vocal performance are not 'neutral' in terms of structural power and individual subjectivity. Likewise, the concept of 'charisma' cannot be separated from sex, sexuality, class, ethnicity, ableism, and the reproduction of power, in terms of the amount (or lack) of authority that is imbued in the individual, their bodily presence and vocal performance by their listeners, due to their embodied self and aspects of their subjectivity. This can be evinced, for example, by contemporary instances of systematic bias against women and black and minority ethnic lecturers in student evaluations; the adoption of the 'animator' self may feel risky, in comparison with relative institutional safety and clarity of the 'textual self' for lecturers who do not have high degrees of social prestige. Therefore, I feel it would be helpful to complement Friesen's media analysis, by bringing in more attention to linguistic and social context, and also the importance of embodiment. In doing so, I will review a study which applies Goffman's ideas, using an ethnographic analysis of vignettes from lectures which 'break the frame'.

Theatre

Thesen (2007), like Friesen, highlights critiques of the lecture, such as that of Bligh (1971), who denigrated the lecture as being focused on the imparting of information, as opposed to problem solving, and Barnett (2000), who states that the lecture '... freezes the hierarchy between lecturer and student, removing any responsibility on the student to respond' (2000: 159). She seeks to challenge this assumption, looking at the lecture through the lens of ritual studies, also taking as her starting point the work of Goffman (1981), in particular his observation that all interaction is governed by shared frames, at the level of micro interaction in daily life, through to large and formal institutional occasions. Like Friesen, she draws on Goffman's analysis of the lecture, in which he points out that while the lecture is ostensibly a text, it '... allows a cover for the rituals of performance' (1981: 194), with the lecturer using their embodied presence to communicate with the audience through aspects of performance such as stance, movement, vocality and asides which are not available in a written text ('fresh talk' as discussed above), as evinced by the large body of work on multimodal semiotic resources (e.g. Kress & van Leeuwen 1996, Archer 2006). Thesen makes the thought-provoking point that this is of particular importance in postcolonial settings, where oral performance has been predominant, in contrast with the dominant literate traditions of the colonizers. She highlights the term lecture *theatre*, and asks us to consider the lecture as a cultural, as opposed to solely educational event. As she puts it:

The tension in lectures, the struggle between the strong coding of authority, single expertise and routine transmission on one hand, and performance hat introduces meanings related to physical presence and students-as-audience on the other hand, suggests that lectures are a fertile site for exploring meaning that conventional approaches to the examinable curriculum will not bring to the fore.

Thesen 2007: 35

She refers to what Bell (1992) calls 'ways of acting', and what McLaren (1993) calls 'interactive states'. The emphasis is on *lived practices*, placing the body at the centre of meaning. She mentions the possibility in the lecture for what Bell calls 'mute' form of activity which the student can access, which she sets out as:

... an important point in a 'contact zone' with its asymmetrical power relations. For students arriving at university with such different backgrounds, there is some value in being able to experience symbolic access, and to be able to observe and receive, as one can in a lecture, rather than having to produce language in spoken or written forms, where your accent, control of the English language, handwriting, or familiarity with technologies such as ICTs, will immediately mark you.

Thesen 2007: 40

Thesen's study uses the notion of ritual as an 'unfolding process' (Thesen 2007: 38) to place an emphasis on embodiment, performance and symbolic meaning in a series of 'liminal moments' (e.g. Turner 1974/1982) in lectures in a university in post-apartheid South Africa. As she puts it:

Ritualisation is not concerned with the more mundane, rational, instrumental means-and-ends functions, such as delivering up-to-date information, or helping students orient to the examinations, although those functions are undoubtedly important. It draws attention instead to the cultural politics of the situation, how (sub) communities and categories are created with feelings of belonging or alienation, how lecturers may perform to an audience, to impress, play with, charm, shock, seduce, or delight students, invoking strong feelings of affinity or distance.

Thesen 2007: 38

The emphasis here is on the co-creation of unfolding meaning, with participants adjusting frames of reference. Her analysis focuses on two instances where lecturers deliberate 'break the frame' and create liminal moments, via unexpected behaviour. However, I would suggest that this analysis is also of relevance when considering more conventional embodied practices in lectures.

She challenges the grounds on which lectures have been 'written off' as antithetical of 'student-centred' learning paradigms, and primarily authoritarian, and argues that lectures should be interpreted in terms of orality and performance, as opposed to literacy. In conclusion, she makes the following point about the influence of the digital:

> It is important to ask what place we have made for students to have face-to-face contact with expertise and authority. Ironically, the rise of the 'new media' may perhaps strengthen, rather than weaken, the meaning and semiotic potential of lectures. As the online environment gets drawn into pedagogy and assessment, and with the increased 'textualisation' of academic work, for both students and lecturers, this performative face-to-face aspect may be kept alive.
>
> Thesen 2007: 49

In a later paper, Thesen (2009) extends her analysis of lectures, discussing what she calls 'sites of intense co-presence' (Thesen 2009: 391), emphasizing the term 'engagement' as opposed to 'learning'. Drawing on social semiotics derived from the linguist Halliday (1978), she focuses on language as a resource for meaning to be used in the 'interest' of social actors, alongside nonverbal semiotic resources, as discussed in the previous paper. She emphasizes how the live co-presence of lecturer and students in fact leads to learning which is co-constituted, as opposed to uni-directional and hierarchical, as lectures are often characterized. She also draws on Bakhtin (1981), again on Goffman (1981), and on Bauman and Briggs (1990) who have all variously theorized engagement as dialogic and performance-oriented, arguing that '. . . central to meaning is the anticipation of a response – a judging, feeling, audience, whether this audience is present or not' (Thesen 2009: 393). This analysis brings to the fore the body, and again she refers to ritual studies. She considers the ephemerality of these live encounters, and whether they can have a life beyond their unfolding.

In seeking to explore how these moments may 'live on', and how meaning is distributed across time and space, she utilizes the concept of *entextualisation* (Bauman & Briggs 1990, Blommaert 2005). This is defined by Blommaert as:

> . . . the process by means of which discourse is successfully decontextualized and recontextualised, and this made into a 'new' discourse. In every phase of the process, discourse is provided with new metapragmatic frames.
>
> Blommaert 2005: 252

For Bauman and Briggs, entextualisation is intensified by performance. They argue that:

To decontextualize and recontextualise a text is thus an act of control, and in regard to the differential exercise of such control, the issue of social power arises. More specifically, we may recognise differential access to texts, differential legitimacy in claims to the use of texts, and differential values attaching to various types of text.

Bauman & Briggs 1990: 76

Thesen (2009) analyses one of the 'liminal' moments of lecturer performance featured in her earlier paper, with an emphasis on how the 'fleeting moment' centred on the body and co-presence was untextualized, and re-emerged in blog discussions between students at a later stage. She makes the point that the digital allows meaning to be more radically distributed across semiotic sites, giving different identities and possibilities for interpretation (e.g. Kell 2006), in a process in which as she puts it '... authority is reinflected with successive crossings' (Thesen 2009: 400). Thesen's study seems to complement Friesen's analysis, by drawing close ethnographic attention to performance and the body. Here – I propose – we see foregrounded the importance of co-presence, performance and ephemerality, as aspects of the lecture which have persisted throughout the long period covered in the historical review. In the final section of this chapter, I will apply Goffman's framing to an analysis of a contemporary approach to lectures influenced by digital media, the *digital epistemic practices* implicated in 'the flipped classroom'. I will then once again augment the analysis drawing on Adams and Thompson's heuristics for 'researching a posthuman world'.

An Interview with the Flipped Classroom

In recent years, the 'flipped classroom' has become vaunted as a pedagogic approach which is claimed to be innovative, or even 'revolutionary' in terms of challenging alleged hierarchies and power relationships in education, by placing students 'at the centre' of activity. With reference to higher education, this paper will examine these claims, and will challenge the assumptions underlying them, by an interrogation of the claims underlying the construct of 'active learning', through the lens of Biesta's 'learnification' critique. I will conclude that the 'flipped classroom' is the logical end-point of a performative culture of education, which seeks to conflate observation interlocution, participation, engagement and learning into one observable construct. I will argue that this leads to a reintroduction of the tenets of behaviourism in the guise of 'student empowerment'. Applying Goffman's framing, I will argue that the pre-provided online 'lecture' is not in fact a lecture; it is performed drawing exclusively on the 'textual self'.

The 'flipped classroom' is an approach which has attracted a great deal of attention in higher education in recent years, and has been proposed in some quarters as a preferable replacement for 'the traditional lecture'. The defining feature of the flipped classroom is that it separates the process into two stages. The first is focused on providing the students with 'input' in advance of the live face-to-face class, usually supplied in the form of a pre-recorded video lecture and other reading material, to be accessed online in the students' independent study time. The live class is then devoted entirely to interactive group work, which is intended to deepen student knowledge and understanding of the 'content' already supplied online. The flipped classroom has been linked to work in the 1990s which began to question the value of the 'traditional' lecture. King's (1993) paper 'From sage on the stage to guide on the side' was highly influential in introducing the idea that class time should be used for student interaction, as opposed to lecturing. King opens the paper as follows:

> In most college classrooms, the professor lectures and the students listen and take notes. The professor is the central figure, the 'sage on the stage', the one who has the knowledge and transmits that knowledge to the students, who simply memorise the information and later reproduce it on an exam – often without thinking about it. This model of the teaching-learning process, called the transmittal model, assumes that the student's brain is like an empty container into which the teacher pours knowledge. In this view of teaching and learning, students are passive learners rather than active ones.
>
> King 1993: 30

It is worth bearing in mind that this paper is somewhat 'of its time', and may have represented radical and useful ideas at that juncture in the field. However, the series of statements above, which are somewhat simplistic and contestable, are set down as indisputable fact. King goes on to draw explicitly on social constructivism, in order to make an argument for a model which '... places students at the centre of the process' (1993: 30). Interestingly, she describes the student as follows:

> In the constructivist model the student is like a carpenter (or sculptor) who uses new information and prior knowledge and experience, along with previously learned cognitive tools, (such as learning strategies, algorithms, and critical

thinking skills) to build new knowledge structures and rearrange existing knowledge.

King 1993: 30

It appears to be taken as read in King's argument that this must take place in verbal interaction, as opposed to while listening to a lecture. The lecturer's new role is set out as follows:

> Such a change can entail a considerable shift in roles for the professor, who must move away from being the one who has all the answers and does most of the talking toward being a facilitator who orchestrates the context, provides resources and poses questions to stimulate students to think up their own answers.

King 1993: 30

These ideas have arguably become part of the educational mainstream in subsequent decades, but it is worth taking a close look at what is actually being stated here. The lecturer is not simply being asked to provide an opportunity for students to discuss content or ideas already provided, but she should expressly *not* 'have all the answers'. Lecturer expertise is cast here as a problem to be solved, in an echo of 'learnification' and 'connectification' discussed in previous chapters. The lecturer's voice is also portrayed as a problem; instead she should 'orchestrate the context'. Perhaps most strikingly, the students should 'think up their own answers', these are presumably regarded as superior to those the lecturer can provide. King then goes on to provide advice on how to promote 'active learning', emphasizing that '... students must use their words and experiences – not regurgitate the text or lecture' (1993: 30). This point is also of interest; not only is the lecturer's voice seen as potentially contaminating, but so are the words heard in a lecture, and the academic text/content itself. King goes on to recommend a series of pair and group work tasks, which of course may be used profitably to stimulate student discussion and thought, the intention here is not to argue against interactive pedagogy, which has an important place in higher education. However, what is of relevance to this chapter is the list of *prohibited* elements discussed above. It appears that in order for 'active learning' to be brought about, the most urgent task is to *remove* elements which are regarded as problematic; the lecturer's voice and academic texts.

This paper and others like it may be seen as ideological precursors to the present-day flipped classroom. Tucker (2012) provides an account of a US high school (Woodland Park High), where Jonathan Bergmann and Aaron Sams, two chemistry teachers, were struggling to allocate sufficient time to re-teach students who had been absent from class. Bergmann and Sams went on to popularize the term, but, the notion of the 'inverted classroom' was proposed much earlier, by Lage et al. (2000). Bergmann and Sams '... bought software which allowed them to record and annotate lessons' (Tucker 2012: 82), and Tucker relates how these online materials were also popular with students who had not missed class:

> ...soon, Bergmann and Sams realized they had the opportunity to radically rethink how they used class time ...With teacher-created videos and interactive lessons, instruction that used to occur in class is now accessed at home, in advance of class. Class becomes the place to work through problems, advance concepts and engage in collaborative learning. Most importantly, all aspects of instruction can be rethought to best maximise the scarcest learning resource – time.
>
> Tucker 2012: 82

Tucker relates how Bergmann sees the advantages of this approach, which he states allows him to interact with all the students in class and provide more support for weaker students, although he does not elaborate on how the class time was organized. Bergmann and Sams published a book aimed at school educators (2012), entitled: 'Flip your Classroom: Reach Every Student in Every Class Every Day'. The description of the book on Amazon.co.uk reads: 'It started with a simple observation: students need their teachers present to answer questions or to provide help if they get stuck on an assignment; they don't need their teachers present to listen to a lecture or review content.' This is noteworthy, as it is clear that when Bergmann and Sams refer to 'reaching' students, they mean via verbal interaction, it is also worth noting that the initial impetus for Bergmann and Sams was a remedial one, driven by a lack of time to offer repeat classes for non-attending students. Tucker goes on describe the video-making practices of another teacher, Andrea Smith. She creates short videos, which she refers to as 'the director's cut', with a clear reference to the world of cinema. In another early publication, Roehl et al. (2013) provide a review of the literature at that time. They open the paper by stating:

> A sense of urgency to adapt to Millennial learning preferences is heightened as educators increasingly struggle to capture the attention of today's students. Unlike previous generations, Millennials reared on rapidly-evolving technologies demonstrate decreased tolerance for lecture-style dissemination of course information (Prensky 2001). Incorporation of active learning strategies into the classroom is critical in order to reach Millenial students.
>
> Roehl et al. 2013: 44

It is worth pointing out that Roehl et al. use as their warrant for this claim an article published by the journalist Marc Prensky (2001), which has subsequently been discredited as an opinion piece without adequate substantiation. It is also interesting to see the expression 'reach the students' used once again here. Roehl et al. go on to argue for '... a learner centred paradigm' on the basis of the argument presented above regarding 'Millennials', in addition to setting up a dichotomy between lectures – portrayed as focusing on 'surface' rote learning, versus 'deep learning' leading to understanding, to be attained via 'active learning'. They then describe various pedagogic strategies which can be used. As with the King (1993) paper, these papers present no doubt engaging activities and ideas for teaching, but also set out various premises for 'active learning' and the flipped classroom as undisputed fact, which is problematic. 'Challenges' are acknowledged, but the basic notion that the flipped classroom is an improvement on the 'traditional' lecture is not questioned. Repeatedly, the notion of not using, or 'freeing up' 'valuable class time' on lecturing is also raised as a further justification (e.g. Milman 2012: 9) and efficiency (e.g. Enfield 2013: 14).

The notion of the flipped classroom arguably takes the idea of 'purifying' the classroom with the removal of academic expertise to its logical conclusion, by (in many cases) providing the students with online 'talking-head' video lectures to be viewed in advance at home, with class time devoted entirely to interactive tasks. This is reminiscent of Knox's (2016) 'contamination' in the context of MOOCs. In this regard, viewed in terms of Goffman's lecturer 'selves', the textual self and animator self are no longer intertwined in the performance. The video lecture is recorded in advance, therefore the lecturer has no need to respond to a live audience. She may use 'fresh talk', but this is likely to be added as a stylistic feature, more likely than ever to be an example of Goffman's 'fresh talk illusion', or viewed through the lens of genre, in effect a formulaic simulacrum of a live lecture. As such, the 'animator' self is silenced in the online lecture element. It might be argued that this represents – in its essence – a return to the medieval model of recitation, in that the lecture is seen as an opportunity for the transmission of pure content alone. The co-presence of the lecturer is seen as dispensable (or even problematic) for this reason, acting as a conduit only. This can be seen with even greater clarity in flipped classroom models which use textual input only in advance; the lecturer is dispensed with altogether. The live class is organized in such a way as to deliberately decentre the lecturer, whose role is to facilitate student activity. In this regard, it appears that the human, embodied, spontaneous co-presence creating a 'spark' in Fichte's terms is deemed unnecessary. This move can be linked back to the phenomenon of 'learnification'

(Biesta 2012) discussed in chapter 3; in the case of the flipped classroom, elaborate arrangements are put in place to resolve the 'problem' of the lecturer and academic expertise by removing her altogether from any co-present teaching, instead relegating her to an information conduit, by means of a format which may exhibit some of the features of a lecture, but has been stripped of any of the advantages of co-presence, ephemerality, responsiveness, dialogue and spontaneity. The lecturer's voice is constrained, and Goffman's multiple selves are reduced to one. This absence is regarded by proponents of the flipped classroom as one of the primary advantages of the model, the teacher is once again cast as a damaging figure.

Adams and Thompson (2016: 40) suggest the following questions for the heuristic 'listening for the invitational quality of things':

- What is a technology inviting (or encouraging, inciting, or even insisting) its user to do, think, or perceive?
- What is a technology discouraging (or constraining, or even prohibiting) its user from doing, thinking, or perceiving?
- What prereflective 'conversations' (van Lennep 1987) or gestural 'correspondences' (Ingold 2012b: 435) unfold between human being and a technology and/or their material surround?
- What kind of scaffolding is a technology explicitly or implicitly offering to frame thinking, intensify perception, or enhance action?

Their focus is more on objects in their use of this heuristic, while I would like to apply it to a more complex set of practices, the flipped classroom, looking at the whole technological assemblage. In the previous chapters, I have taken a reflective approach as suggested by Adams and Thompson, in order to provide insights into my own experiences of educational technologies. However, in this case I do not have that opportunity, and therefore will base my analysis of the flipped classroom on information about an example from the public domain. I acknowledge the limitations of this analysis, and do not seek to make claims as to participant viewpoints or feelings in response to the experience, instead seeking to address the questions above with a discussion of what is known about the pedagogical/ mediatic arrangements, and the intended engagement of students.

I will analyse an example from the literature on the flipped classroom, taken from Enfield (2013). This example was chosen, as a reasonable level of detail was provided as to the sequence of activities, in the context of Multimedia students at a US university, and video material were available online. I will quote this in full, as I would like to look at each step, in turn:

The Flipped Classroom model of instruction was implemented in two sections of ctva361 (50 students in total) during the spring 2013 semester. To facilitate this, 40 lessons were created to provide students with instruction outside the classroom. 38 of these lessons were instructional videos (13.5 hours in total) created by the instructor, and two of the lessons were assigned readings. Quiz prep questions were provided along with each lesson. The learning process generally followed the same sequence. First, prior to class, students were expected to watch two to three video lessons (approximately 1 hour of video). Second, during class, a short quiz was given. This quiz was created from a subset of the quiz prep questions to encourage students to complete the assigned lessons and to provide the instructor daily formative assessment. Third, after the quiz, students were provided in-class activities to reflect on, discuss, and practice what they had learned. These activities were often teacher led demonstrations. Because students were expected to already know the content, the instructor was able to rely on students (by calling on individuals) to explain what to do to complete the task. Other times, the classroom activity was not teacher-led; instead, students (sometimes in small groups) completed an assigned task while the instructor provided individual guidance as needed. Regardless of how the in-class activities were structured, they often provided students with a variation of the tasks they completed when watching the video providing opportunity for practice and transfer of learning to new situations.

Enfield 2013: 16

The author also provides a link where the videos and quizzes can be viewed on the open internet, which is another reason why I selected this example. My methodology for this analysis was to watch the video, and pause it every couple of minutes in order to write this description. Lesson 1: 'html files and web browsers' is just over ten minutes long, and opens with the voice of Jacob Enfield over a screencast of his computer. He welcomes us, then demonstrates how students should proceed by demonstrating how to use a text editor. While doing this, he types in text and changes the format. He then shows us how to change from rich text format to plain text, also how to display html code. He goes on to show how to save a file in the right format to create an html page, open it in various browsers, and mark it up using html. Throughout the video, he is progressing through various steps on his computer, describing what he is doing as he goes along. He finished by saying 'that was the first lesson, I look forward to seeing you next time'. In his paper, Enfield states that his intention was for students to work along with him while watching the video. Interestingly, he also states that he made his own videos rather than directing students to the commercially-produced ones they had access to, in order to prove to them that he knew the content himself. He also states that he continued to provide 'stand and deliver' classes (Enfield 2013: 16), as he felt this was what the students expected in terms of value in their education. He reveals that he made the videos without a script or editing, so they each took several takes to get right. He estimates that the 13.5 hours of video material with questions took around fifty hours of preparation. Like the example given above, he mentions the problems posed in the past when students had missed classes and he had to repeat explanations in class time. I then moved on the click on the questions for lesson 1, these are the following:

Lesson 1 Questions
What does HTML stand for?
Name a basic Text Editor that may be used to create html files? on MAC: on PC:
In most programs, what is the shortcut key combination to save? on MAC: on PC:
Name three popular web browsers: 1.
2. 3.
Are html files displayed the same by all web browsers?
Is it possible to view the html code for any webpage on the Internet?
Is it possible to edit the html code for any webpage on the Internet?

This was as far as I could go personally with my experience of this flipped classroom, using what was available online. In terms of the questions posed by Adams and Thompson (2016) above, I felt the video technology 'invited' me to watch, listen and copy. In order to do all of these simultaneously, it discouraged me from continuous listening, as I needed to pause the video occasionally. It also discouraged me from speech, as I was alone at the time, and asking questions, as it the teacher was not co-present and the presentation was a recording. The voice of the instructor was friendly and relaxed, which I felt 'invited' me to take part and try the online tasks. It enhanced action in the form of procedurally following what I could see the instructor demonstrating. Overall, it felt closer to watching TV than being in a classroom.

Returning to the 'interview' questions set earlier in the chapter:

- What is a technology inviting (or encouraging, inciting, or even insisting) its user to do, think, or perceive?
- What is a technology discouraging (or constraining, or even prohibiting) its user from doing, thinking, or perceiving?
- What prereflective 'conversations' (van Lennep 1987) or gestural 'correspondences' (Ingold 2012b: 435) unfold between human being and a technology and/or their material surround?

- What kind of scaffolding is a technology explicitly or implicitly offering to frame thinking, intensify perception, or enhance action?

I felt the online materials in this case mainly invited me to watch, listen and familiarize myself with the procedural steps being demonstrated. I did not feel actively discouraged from any particular activity, but any additional action would have felt concurrent, and unrelated. I did not find it easy to make notes while watching. In terms of gestural 'correspondences' and relationships with the material surround, as I was watching the video on my laptop, it felt reminiscent of solitary entertainment, such as YouTube. The scaffolding of the structured lesson overall explicitly invited me to understand the series of steps in the sequence which would be required, should I decide to use html code to make a website, so it had the feeling of a private mental rehearsal space. It has to be borne in mind that I did not take part in the following interactive element of the flipped classroom experience, and so only experienced the first 'input' stage. Also, it is worth noting that the 'lecturer' spoke in a manner which included 'fresh talk', despite the fact that he was recording it in a solitary setting, over multiple takes. However, this – I suggest – was an example of Goffman's 'fresh talk illusion'. The lack of co-presence and ephemerality resulted, for me, in the video exhibiting the characteristics of a broadcast, not a lecture in the historical sense discussed in this chapter. It seems that sometimes people do need to be in room together, at the same time – talking, listening and thinking together.

5

Interfaces

In the previous chapters, I have focused on educational activities, and student engagement, critiquing what I regard to be the unhelpful humanist-based notion of 'active learning' and its resultant effects, in the face-to-face setting and also in the world of digital education. In this chapter, I turn my attention to *texts* associated with higher educational processes, and *artefacts* used for the production and interaction with texts, such as books, pens, paper, digital devices, screens and so on. As with chapter 4, I begin with a review of how these have formed part of higher education throughout history, again drawing on Friesen. I then go on to examine how they have been regarded and conceptualized, and how they are described in the contemporary period. I pay particular attention to the broadly-used concept of the device or artefact as 'tool', particularly in terms of the digital, and mount a case against this, arguing that to characterize the artefact as a tool, is to once again place the human at the centre of the conceptual model of education, rendering essential nonhuman elements of the process as inert and secondary. I also critique this stance from the point of view of the subjectivities it conjures, arguing once again that it both isolates the human to some kind of freefloating essence, which is the antithesis of a materialist understanding of subjectivity and epistemic practice as it unfolds. I conclude by once again deploying Adams and Thompson heuristics, to 'interview' the VLE. The chapter will critique mainstream conceptions of digital devices in particular, but before doing so it will review the history of the tablet and book in higher education, making the argument, based on Friesen (2017), that there is direct continuity between these technologies of inscription, as opposed to a 'radical' break with the advent of digital technologies. The centrality of textual practices to the university will be explored, in terms of the materiality of the environment, the detailed enactment of practices themselves, and the subjectivities of students and academics.

A History of Textual Media in the University

Friesen also provides a very comprehensive review of writing and textual media throughout the history of education. Throughout his review, the theme of continuity is apparent:

> From the perspective of the *longue duree*, the story of the tablet as an educational technology or medium is certainly not the story of sudden technological or instructional breakthroughs or of unforgettable disruptions and changes. Instead, over the millennia, what remains important is the act of inscription and reading, and beneath it all, the stable bedrock of written language.
>
> Friesen 2017: 10

He begins by describing the *edubba'a*, or tablet houses of ancient Sumer in 2500 BC, in which boys learned to write on clay tablets using a reed stylus. He cites lapidary evidence that these tablets were used for copying of symbols, and also for dictation exercises, approaches still used today in the teaching of writing, and also that the evidence points to a teacher leading a 'class' of pupils, and also to the use of a 'curriculum' to develop student writing and ability to complete a range of tasks. Friesen provides further historical examples from Hebrew and Chinese language education, and concludes that the history of writing instruction should not be seen as a series of breakthroughs or radical innovations, but instead the historical record shows a consistently systematic approach to instruction and practice which remains remarkably similar across the centuries and disparate cultural settings. As he puts it:

> Whether in ancient Nippur or Beijing, or some 40 centuries later in New York or Bogota, reading and writing are skills reproduced from one generation to the next through carefully constructed and recognisably patterned physical arrangements and temporal sequences of instruction and practice. The forms, practices, and sequences of inscriptive instruction, in other words, appear as viral and tenacious and writing systems themselves.
>
> Friesen 2017: 34

He also provides a detailed overview of the history of the book. He begins by reminding us of the media theorist Marshall McLuhan's (1972: 429) point that *techne* – or 'craft' has been ignored and therefore undertheorized over the millennia by philosophers. McLuhan's interest was famously in the technical 'medium' of communication, rather than the 'message' as somehow separate. Friesen sets out to investigate the question of how the writing medium works 'with us' (2017: 69). He refers to Milton's characterization of books in the seventeenth century as having a '... potency of life in them to be as active as that soul was whose progeny they are' (Milton 1644: 4, in Friesen 2017: 70). For Friesen:

> On the one hand, the book for Milton is something material, a preserving container, a vial. In this limited sense, books are indeed inanimate or 'dead things'. But they are so much more: the hold 'a potency for life', which is 'as active as that soul was whose progeny they are'. The book, in other words, brings together two dimensions: the physical, material reality of the medium and the living world of ideas and events the medium can contain. So, the book, like its living human author, is both physical 'container' and active mental 'content'. A familiar combination of flesh and spirit, body and soul.
>
> Friesen 2017: 70

Friesen accounts for the lack of interest in media as stemming from the tendency of media to perform a 'disappearing act' (2017: 70), becoming invisible to the reader or viewer, while the content is foregrounded. Moving on to consider digital media, he characterizes it as a 'metamedium' (2017: 73), containing a range of media – textual, spoken and visual. He points out the tendency in commentaries surrounding media to place them in opposition – in particular orality versus print. In contrast, he regards them as in a relationship of interdependence, citing Barton's work on classroom literacy practices, and what he calls 'talk around texts' (Barton 2007: 179, in Friesen 2017: 74). He goes on to discuss the status of the physical book and its relationship to knowledge through history. He also refers to Knorr-Cetina's (2001) *epistemic object* discussed earlier, or what Foucault characterized as an *episteme*, '... a way of knowing, of understanding and verifying reality and truth.' (Friesen 2017: 76). He asks, recalling Nietzsche 'How is this reading "tool" working with us on our thoughts? ... What in other words, does it mean that the book is in a sense the embodiment of Western knowledge?' (2017: 77).

Friesen connects this with the Romantic-era rejection of the book as mediated, in favour of the immediacy associated with feeling. He highlights the Latin phrase '*tabula rasa*' – meaning blank slate, drawing a comparison with how the mind may be viewed by Empiricists, something with potency and the potential to both contain and to communicate meaning. Referring to the writings of Locke (1700) and Berkeley (1734) regarding the book's status as physical object and also carrier of ideas, he points out the book's '... capacity to act as an interface between physical and mental' (Friesen 2017: 79). The book is cast here as at the intersection of the immaterial and material. However, unlike a webpage, it is a clearly demarcated, self-contained static, physical object with a beginning and an end.

Book as Interface

He goes on to develop the notion of the book as *interconnecting interface* (2017: 81). The term 'interface' is more commonly used to refer to the meeting of two systems in the digital context. He quotes Bazin, who describes it as follows:

> The circuit of the book in the form it has eventually taken ... regulates the subtle dialectic between particular and universal, consensus and pluralism, private reader and citizen ... the book sets the stage for a trilogy – author, book, reader – based on the separation of roles and a stability: on the one hand, the author, on the other, the reader, each exchanging their singularities through the stable, reliable, and published 'interface' of the book.
>
> Bazin 1996 159, in Friesen 2017: 81

Emerson also provides an in-depth exploration of the concept of the interface in textual practices and media. She defines it as:

> ... a technology ... which mediates between reader and surface-level, human-authored writing, as well as, in the case of digital devices, the machine-based writing taking place below the gloss of the surface.
>
> Emerson 2014: x

She characterizes the interface as a threshold, which not only opens up space, but also conceals the workings of digital technologies via a 'glossy', transparent surface. She argues that an overemphasis on the transparency of an interface renders devices '... appliances for the consumption of content instead of multifunctional, generative devices for reading as well and writing or producing content' (Emerson 2014: xii). Friesen then turns his attention to education, focusing on textbooks in particular, arguing that the book also has a dual nature; a physical object, but also a kind of 'vial' with potency. Textbooks have been criticized as clichéd, but Friesen points out that Kuhn (1962) wrote approvingly about their ability to communicate science in a pedagogic context. Friesen regards the textbook as an essential element of education, and proposes it as a 'middle point'. With reference to Kuhn, he sets out how textbooks allow students to work through simplified problems within the established paradigm of the field, thus re-enacting the process of discovery that established it.

As he points out, early textbooks were closely interrelated to the lecture, which functioned as a scriptorium where a text was annotated; as discussed in chapter 4. Friesen provides two historical examples of 'textbooks' before the word was coined. The first was *Zhou Bi Suan Jing* (Cullen 1996) from the Zhou dynasty of China, a compendium containing 246 practical arithmetic problems, structured as a dialogue, the second is Euclid's *Elements* (Heath 2013). As with the example of Sumerian tablet-based writing instruction, powerful similarities can be observed between these early volumes and the textbooks used today. These include careful visual design and economy, organization into a collection or compendium, reflective of ways of thinking, as opposed to books produced by a single author. They are structured in such a way as to facilitate repeated reading or study. Another feature of the *Zhou Bi Suan Jing* is its form of dialogue which contextualizes and dramatizes the content, based on spoken interaction. Friesen argues that dialogue is also present in textbooks more broadly, and is only apparently supressed by print. He argues that it was the Protestant Reformation, as opposed to the printing press, which lead to some of the major developments in education of the period, in particular the call of direct access of the people to the 'truth' of God's written word. Martin Luther identified risks of factionalism and divisions due to differing interpretations resulting from lay people reading the bible directly, therefore the 'pre-existing educations genre' of the catechism – using pre-set questions and answers – was adapted for the purpose of interpreting its contents in a manner tightly controlled by the church. Friesen points out the similarities in organization and layout between the catechism and textbooks, in addition to dialogue and exposition.

Crucially, the catechism addresses the reader as 'you', giving the rhetorical effect of spoken dialogue, which Althusser proposed had the effect of positioning the readers as 'Christian religious subjects', through what he called *interpellation* or hailing (Althusser 1984: 48). The readers' subjectivity is then interpellated, or brought into being, by the question-and-answer format, in a process by which the text and their verbal responses designates their place in the world. He describes the subsequent historical development as 'secularising the catechism' (1984: 100), in which the catechism became a template to be used for schooling. Similarly, the focus was on mass indoctrination and uniformity, plus minimal preparation or expertise on the part of the teacher – the voice of the teacher was identical with the voice of the text, which was used effectively as a script for an oral performance. However, there was a reaction against the rigidity of this practice, and a move to use one's own words in order to escape from the absolute authority of the text. At this time, the popular educationalist Pestalozzi (1889) began advocating for a move away from recitation, through the development of the 'inductive' textbook, which involved working from the specific and subjective, towards the abstract and general. As Friesen suggests:

Although the term 'interaction' is generally reserved for engagement with computers or other sophisticated digital technologies, it is clear that textbooks have long been used to script teaching and learning activities in ways that prefigure instructional software. Like some of the most basic instructional computer games, the interaction may exist only on the level of call and response – or perhaps better, stimulus and response. Or the interaction may be much more sophisticated, responding to the student's own typed or spoken words. Either way, this form of student interaction has been developed and refined in textbooks for hundreds of years. And these methods are still in evidence in contemporary textbooks.

Friesen 2017: 105

Friesen concludes with an examination of a modern Psychology textbook, pointing out the contemporary emphasis on 'self-talk', of 'self-explanation', and internal feedback loops, as opposed to interaction with others. He traces this to the work of Bandura focused on 'self-regulated learning', which aims to improve student cognition and performance in tests. The focus here is on the inculcation of a different kind of subjectivity, 'A postmodern self (which) is an optimally self-regulating and self-optimising one ...' (2017: 108).

Like the book, when understood as an epistemic metaphor, the textbook can be said to be a container or 'vial' that encloses its own specific 'potency of life'. This potency, however, is one that is thoroughly pedagogical. Through its lively images and formatting, its interactive problem-solutions, questions, guides, and prompts, the textbook does not so much bring its authors experience or ideas to life as it vivifies the originality and (re)discovery of the dominant paradigm.

Friesen 2017: 109

Having reviewed the history of the book in higher education, the next section will explore the status and nature of what has arguably become a primary site for academic reading, writing, and interaction in the contemporary digital university, the VLE.

An Interview with a Virtual Learning Environment

VLEs, more commonly known as Learning Management Systems or LMSs in the US) such as Moodle and Blackboard have become widespread across higher education in digitally-resourced settings, and are now a requirement for all modules and courses at many universities. Weller (2007) refers to Brown and

Jenkins' (2003) finding that at that time, 86 per cent of respondents in their study reported they had a VLE at their Higher Education Institution. As such, they have come to be seen as a 'normal' part of student engagement, mostly intended to be used as an aid to digital epistemic practices of independent study outside class. Weller refers to them as '... something of a Trojan horse that has slipped into most institutions almost unnoticed' (2007: 2). He quotes the definition provided by the UK government Joint Information Systems Committee (JISC), who define the VLE as '... the components in which learners and tutors participate in 'on-line' interactions of various kinds, including on-line learning' (JISC 2000). Weller's own definition is '... a software system that combines a number of different tools that are used to systematically deliver content online and facilitate the learning experience around that content. The role of educators in this world is to facilitate dialogue and support students in their understanding of resources.' (Weller 2007: 5).

VLEs are commonly used as digital repositories for slides, files and other resources which may be those presented in the lecture, or may also be used to provide additional study materials. They also have a range of interactive features such as discussion boards, in addition to quizzes and a variety of other elements which lecturers and students can use. The VLE is normally used from the outset of a course, often before the first lecture, for example to provide the timetable, administrative information and links, and possibly reading lists or slides provided in advance. It may be populated with all the material in advance, or added to in stages as the course progresses. Lecturers and students access it via desktop computers, laptops and personal handheld devices. This technology has been used in universities for around twenty years, and is so widespread in the contemporary period that it is no longer referred to as 'innovative', as it once was. It might be argued that it has become somewhat transparent to users, and taken for granted. As such, it is an artefact, or *digital epistemic object* which merits further investigation.

One of the most noteworthy aspects of the VLE is the way it is used in terms of textual practices in face-to-face, campus-based courses. As discussed in the previous chapter, the lecture remains an important element of higher education, and as I have argued earlier, is essentially a spoken, ephemeral, co-present encounter in a particular time and space. However, the lecture does not exist in isolation from epistemic textual practices surrounding it. As we have seen, in the past the lecturer as speaker and the manuscript were entangled in complex ways in terms of voice, textual synthesis and performance. As such, there has never been a period in the mediatic history of the university in which the spoken lecture has existed in isolation from handwritten or printed texts, present both prior to and after the lecture itself. The lecture has tended to be held in a specialist setting, with a lectern, and possibly a board of some kind, and an arrangement of seats to allow the listening audience to take part. In this regard, the lecture has always been posthuman, in the sense that it has always entailed this entanglement of human and nonhuman actors in order to emerge.

However, the advent of digital media has altered and complicated the picture in a range of ways. Lecturers are likely to research and write digitally in preparation for a lecture or lecture series, using the internet and word processing, or other applications. They are also highly likely to use digital slideshow applications such as PowerPoint, to be displayed during the spoken lecture. This has become commonplace, but in fact was at the time of introduction a major change in the mediatic conditions of the lecture. Although overhead transparencies or photographic slides were available before PowerPoint, they tended to be used if a visual image was to be focused on, such as a map, diagram or photograph. In contrast, slideshow applications such as PowerPoint are commonly used to present text or other material. This text usually consists of 'bullet points' summarizing the main points being made by the lecturer. The students read these on a screen while listening to the speaker. Interestingly, the size of the screen is likely to be larger than the pre-digital blackboard, which was at a human scale or could be rotated in order to allow the lecturer to write on it. As such, the lecturer in the past was able to spontaneously write or draw on the board as required, while talking. Again, this is likely to have been used when diagrammatic information, or perhaps equations or similar, were required. The central form of communication was the lecturer's voice, and students would listen and take handwritten notes during the lecture. PowerPoint, however, supplies written text on the screen to the students before, during and after the lecture, depending on how it is used. If the students have a printed or electronic copy of the slides, they may perceive that this constitutes the lecture notes, and may either take no handwritten notes of their own, or may add to the notes already supplied by PowerPoint. As such, it functions rather like summarizing subtitles.

Adams (2006) examines the implications of using PowerPoint for knowledge dissemination, in particular the ways in which it reshapes knowledge. She draws on the work of Tufte, who asserts that PowerPoint does not support a cognitive style consistent with higher-level analytical thinking, and '... elevates format over content, betraying an attitude of commercialism that turns everything into a sales pitch', arguing that PowerPoint '... disrupts, dominates, and trivializes content' (Tufte 2003). She also refers to Turkle, who characterizes PowerPoint as '... a product of the cultural assumptions of the Western corporate boardroom' (Turkle 2004: 102). She quotes Apple, for whom new technology '... embodies a form of thinking that orientates a person to approach the world in a particular way.' (Apple 1991: 75). Adams seeks to explore what forms of thinking, modes of knowing and habits of mind are privileged via the use of PowerPoint. Compellingly, she refers to Dreyfus and Spinosa's observation that a cathedral, as an 'architecture of experience' (Adams 2006: 390), solicits meditativeness (Dreyfus & Spinosa 2003: 346). In a similar way, she sets out that '... all objects invite us to extend or change our relationship to the world' (Adams 2006: 390). She cites Illich, who, with reference to modern technologies, urges us '... to listen to what objects *say* rather than do' (Illich 1996: 64). Adams suggests that all objects can be heard as 'invitations', and also refers to Turkle's characterization of PowerPoint as '... not just a tool but an evocative object that effects our habits of mind' (Turkle in Coutu 2003).

She points out that PowerPoint was originally designed for the Western corporate setting. She describes how the software invites the author to add a title to each slide, plus bullet points as a default. She points out the ease with which the user can 'fall into' using this default setting, and links it to the notion of 'habits of mind' (Adams 2006: 394). She reminds us of the Latin root of habit, *habere*, meaning to hold, have, or possess (2006: 394), and proposes that 'Taking hold of an object, we also take up residence in it; we *inhabit* it, but it also inhabits us' (2006: 394), via what Merleau-Ponty calls 'knowledge in the hands'. In the case of PowerPoint, the author is encouraged to write short phrases as opposed to full sentences, and begins to 'think in slides' (2006: 394). This, she argues, forecloses other forms of knowledge. She applies McLuhan and McLuhan's (1988) *Laws of Media* also used in chapter 3 with reference to MOOCs, to PowerPoint. The four questions posed by the McLuhans are:

- What does [the medium] enhance or intensify?
- What does it render obsolete or displace?
- What does it retrieve that was previously obsolesced?
- What does it produce or become when pressed to an extreme?

McLuhan & McLuhan 1988: 7, in Adams 2006: 396

The resulting tertrad is as follows (see table 2).

She goes on to suggest that various forms of *pointing* are at the heart of PowerPoint use, drawing a comparison between these acts of pointing and language itself as a system of signification, stating that:

Table 2

Enhances		Reverses into
Pointing	Pointlessness	
Bulleting, point form	Insignificance	
Outline	Incoherence	
Hierarchical, linear thinking		
4:3 rectangular, flat display		
monologue		
Plato's cave	Overhead projector	
Rhetoric in the academy	Writing on the board	
Sales pitch	Note-taking	
Kiosks	Divergence, digression	
Cole's notes	Narrative	
Wall art	Complex tabular data	
	Conversation	
	Socratic dialogue	
Retrieves		**Obsolesces**

(Adams 2006: 397)

A thing does exist in a meaningful sense until it is signified, that is, an object has no significance until it is pointed out, at, or to. Our most basic communicative technology, language, may be understood as a sophisticated pointing device. Words themselves are not the actual things they name, rather words point to things ... as such, naming evokes or calls a thing into existence. Pointing, whether accomplished with a finger or through the extension of some pointing instrument – linguistic, artistic or otherwise – brings things to attention, and thus to significance.

Adams 2006: 398

There is a tendency for students to perceive the content of the PowerPoint slides as the only important information salient to the lecture. It fragments and also simplifies ideas and knowledge, and makes it difficult to represent certain complex forms or extended narratives. She likens the frame of the PowerPoint to a camera viewfinder, which focuses on one area by not focusing on the rest. She also explores Barthes' (1981) notion of the *studium* versus the *punctum* with respect to PowerPoint. Barthes, in his consideration of photographic images, set out that most photographs are *studium*; they are representations which objectify their subject. In contrast, for Barthes, *punctum* penetrates the ordinary to evoke a particular mood. The presence of punctum 'returns subjectivity to the object' (Adams 2006: 400). For Barthes, a photograph with punctum '... annihilate[s] itself *as medium*, to be no longer a sign but the thing itself.' (Barthes 1981: 54, in Adams 2006: 400). Adams suggests that PowerPoint is devoid of punctum, and therefore unlikely to provoke students' interest. She points out the type of embodied response to PowerPoint, in particular that the students' hands, while watching a PowerPoint slideshow, are idle, as note-taking has become obsolete. It is interesting to speculate how this may have effects, in terms of Goffman's lecturer selves discussed in chapter 4.

She then looks at PowerPoint from the perspective of Borgmann (1984), who contends that modern technology has the effect of hiding processes by which things are produced from view. PowerPoint slides are a *product*, which needs to be procured by the students from the teacher. The process of knowledge-in-action by which the teacher produced is occluded. However, she does concede that '... each slide has the potential to trigger the embodied insights of an experienced practitioner in the immediacy of the now. This punctum, evocative capacity can "save" a PowerPoint presentation from being merely a product.' (Adams 2006: 401). However, she warns that the use of what she calls 'devices of expediency' (2006: 401) may serve to 'short-circuit' enactments of knowledge. She goes on to make the crucial point that while listening to a lecture, the student is conducting a 'listening conversation', a form of dialogue, albeit silent; this contrasts with the notion of teaching as 'delivery'. However, with PowerPoint, the students' attention is divided between the slides, and the lecturer's speech. It also closes down what is unplanned, emergent or unexpected. She also makes the point that PowerPoint leads us away from the material and tactile, towards the virtual, giving the example of studying apples either by showing images of them on slides, or handling them. This is the difference between pointing and touching. She suggests that teacher presence can counterbalance the totalizing and dematerializing effect of PowerPoint, but overall there is a tendency for it to '... diminish both substance and human substance' (2006: 406). The point is also made that PowerPoint tends to homogenize and 'level off' information, eliding detail. She cautions that this has led to a '... disappearance of the diverse flora and fauna of knowledge forms native to specific disciplines' (2006: 406).

In a follow-up study, Adams (2010) looks at university teachers' experiences of using PowerPoint, basing her analysis on Heidegger's (1951) 'Building Dwelling Thinking' and 'The Thing' (1949). She interviewed twelve lecturers, conducted observations of undergraduate teaching, and reflected on her own use of PowerPoint. She used a hermeneutic phenomenological methodology (Van Manen 1990/1997) to create 'lived experience descriptions'. She points out how the teacher adopts two different *embodiment* relations with PowerPoint, first composing the presentation, then presenting it. As she describes:

> In performing this preparatory work, the teacher is sitting in her office with computer, screen, keyboard and mouse; texts and papers litter the desk. Her screen shows numerous windows open: a web browser, email, a Word document, as well as PowerPoint. Occasionally her eyes wander from the screen, and stare thoughtfully through her office window into the distance. She turns back to the PowerPoint window, pulls her keyboard a little closer, nudges her mouse and continues working.
>
> Adams 2010: 5

Adams describes how 'inhabiting' PowerPoint frames the lesson planning world, a 'world of surface and interface' (2010: 6) with a rectangular window and invitations to click to add text, click to add notes, etc. Her aims and her inscriptions are intertwined and enmeshed with those of the software. As she puts it, 'The teacher-technology relational boundaries blur and a hermeneutically rich but "silent" corporeal rapport sets in.' (2010: 6). In her data, a teacher reports how he composed and refined a PowerPoint slideshow, in terms of arranging 'points' showing the main points of a section of a textbook. She highlights how the software has 'technologised' how the knowledge is shaped, collapsing complex or extended narrative or argument to bullets. She then provides a description of the teacher giving a PowerPoint presentation in class, which involves 'configuring a televisual (screenic) space' (2010: 6). The lights are switched off and blinds drawn, and the student take on the role of spectators, in a space analogous to a cinema. The teacher in the study reports that his style of speaking changes when presenting PowerPoint, becoming more oratorical, and less dialogic. The slide 'speaks' and so does the teacher, the dialogue, Adams suggests, is between them. PowerPoint, however, also constrains. Its 'finished' quality is reported by one teacher in the study as being a barrier to improvisation or a change of direction. She quotes Howells, who describes the shift in attention brought about by PowerPoint:

> From the moment I walk into the lecture theatre I feel the pressure from my students to line up my thinking with their PowerPoint notes, without which they seem to be lost. I usually succumb to connecting them to the screen rather than to myself, each other, and the subject matter. In giving precedence to the object of PowerPoint, where the slides take on language and world of their own ... students may subconsciously be encouraged to zoom out of the teacher's presence in favour of the rectangle on the screen.
>
> Howells 2007: 139

The balance of communication and attention is drawn away from the embodied figure and ephemeral human voice of the lecturer, and towards the pre-prepared digital text on the screen. Instead of the board being used as a form of visible 'margin' for the lecturer to add spontaneously to the central spoken performance, as in the previous technology of the chalkboard. Instead, the impression is more that this has been reversed, and that the lecturer's voice is marginal to the screen and digital text. As such, the sense of ephemerality and co-presence is diminished, and I would argue with reference to the previous analysis of the lecture and flipped classroom, the ontological status of the lecture is fundamentally altered as a result.

A similar analysis can be applied to the VLE, which is intimately intertwined with PowerPoint, as the repository where slide decks are uploaded as products, to be accessed by the students. This has a range of effects. One of these is temporal, as having the possibility of providing students with access to the slides in advance of the lecture, and after, it therefore blurs the sense of the lecture as a temporally bounded co-present spoken event, and also blurs the point at which it can be said to begin and end, in the sense that it 'takes place' in one specific location. The lecturer's voice becomes more performative and ritualized as a result, as described by Adams. The appearance of the VLE home screen is arguably reminiscent of an entertainment website such as Netflix. The modules which the student has access to are represented on the screen as small rectangles, which may be selected. Within each of these, various menus are displayed, and students may 'browse' (itself a word associated with shopping), and download PowerPoint slide decks in a manner similar to shopping online. The PowerPoint slideshow at this stage of its trajectory, has been converted into a fixed and complete commodity to be obtained.

The VLE has also changed the way in which students interact with reading texts. Pre-VLE and electronic journals, students were required to buy books, or visit the material setting of the library, move around and find texts, and either physically take them home, or more recently, photocopy them. The emphasis was on texts as print literacy artefacts, epistemic objects which needed to be obtained, owned and handled. In contrast, the contemporary VLE allows the lecturer to supply the students with digital texts which can be downloaded and read on screen, or printed, which is vaunted as highly convenient and flexible.

It is worth deconstructing the name – Virtual Learning Environment – in order to understand the assumptions behind the nature of this particular piece of educational digital technology. First 'virtual'. This is defined by the Oxford English Dictionary as 'not physically existing as such but made by software to appear to do so', or 'carried out, accessed, or stored by means of a computer, especially over network' (Lexico 2019). The first definition is interesting when applied to the VLE. Firstly, it is not strictly the case that online texts do not exist physically, as there is a physical substrate of hardware underlying them and texts such as online PDFs can be argued to be objects, although clearly, they are not 'physical' in the same sense as print texts. The use of 'virtual' here seems to echo the fantasies of online, disembodied and wholly nonmaterial 'magic' critiqued elsewhere in this book, and by commentators such as Emerson (2014). However, there is a further point worth making about this definition; that the VLE appears to exist due to software.

This raises several questions. The VLE is not a simulation of a pre-existing environment outside of the digital, as there is no equivalent. In this regard, there is no other ontological entity it appears to be; it only exists *as itself* online. There are components which may fit this definition; PDFs and Word document may be seen as 'virtual' texts which mimic the features of print texts according to this definition, but there is no 'environment' outside of the digital which the VLE could be said to simulate or recreate online. In this regard, the applicability of the term 'virtual' seems weakened. The second definition, 'carried out, accessed, or stored by means of a computer, especially over a network' (Lexico: 2019), seems at first glance to be appropriate to the VLE. However, this is also worth looking at more closely. The word 'virtual' is being used as an adjective to modify the noun 'environment'. An environment is not 'carried out' or 'stored', the element of the definition which seems most appropriate is 'accessed' – or better – 'lived in'. Again, this seems innocuous, as students and tutors do indeed access, or enter, the VLE 'by means of a computer ... over a network'. However, the notion that it is accessed by means of a computer implies that it is an entity which exists separately *a priori* to access, and somehow separately from the digital. Again, we see an underlying stubborn dualism in the language used. The next word in the term is 'learning'. It is not clear whether this is a noun or an adjective in the formulation. Does it mean the VLE is an environment for 'virtual (*adj*) learning', and if so, what would that consist of? The more commonsense interpretation would be that it is a 'virtual environment', for learning (*noun*). Once again, I would argue, we see the effects of learnification, abstraction and the elision of textual practices in this nomenclature. Although clearly the student should learn while engaging with the VLE, what they actually *do* is read and write texts, as the VLE is a profoundly textual *digital epistemic object*.

When students engage with the VLE, as with all digital texts, they do not do so in a rarefied virtual and nonmaterial 'bubble', despite the implications of the name and the discourses surrounding it. The *digital epistemic practices* are always embodied and situated in a material setting, which may be part of the university campus, but is likely not to be, given that VLEs are primarily used for independent study outside class time. As such, they are likely to be engaged with it in domestic settings, or transported via handheld devices. They are, in that sense, highly mobile. They are contingent on the physical operation of digital devices in and outside the university. They are likely to be intertwined with print texts, as students print off files, mark them up, and so on. In term of their interactive features such as discussion boards, they provide an opportunity for interactive engagement which is reminiscent of tutorial-based spoken discussion. However, unlike the face-to-face tutorial, which is characterized by co-presence and ephemerality, the VLE is textual, and arguably more performative as a result. Unlike a spoken utterance, which may or may not be remembered in detail by listeners, and is not recorded, a student contribution to the VLE is written, and so is visible and remains so for the other participants and the tutor. As such, it is inevitable that the nature of student contributions is likely to be less spontaneous, and tentative, than an idea expressed in a free-flowing spoken discussion. In this regard, the use of digital texts here in fact renders the ephemeral and emergent features of speech into a more 'complete', self-conscious and fixed textual performance. This is taken to its logical conclusion where student contributions to online discussions become part of the assessed element of the course. Their texts (in the form of comments) may be assessed for particular qualitative features, or for quantity, frequency and the degree of responsiveness and interactivity with others. Once again, whether this is 'learning' is open to contestation. It would equally be argued that, under the guise of apparently 'student-centred' digital activity, students are in fact being required to enact and perform the 'active' subjectivities already discussed in chapter 3. This in fact formalizes what was previously informal, and is likely to limit student comfort with risk-taking, alongside once again positioning reticence as deviant, in the form of 'lurking'. In this regard, the VLE can be critiqued as a technology of surveillance, which is used to discipline students into a very particular form of digital textual performance. It is common to ask students to 'reflect' on their learning on VLE discussions boards, and relate the content of the course to themselves in some way. As I have argued elsewhere (Macfarlane & Gourlay 2009), reflection may appear to be highly personalized, but can in fact be used as a disciplining practice, corralling participants into a narrow band of acceptable ways of expressing their subjectivity. It may also be used to quantify student engagement in terms of the frequency of logins and length of time spent on the VLE.

Adams and Thompson propose the following questions for the heuristic 'discerning the spectrum of human-technology-world relations':

- What kinds of human-technology-world relations does this technology engage?
- Embodiments? Hermeneutic? Alterity? Background? Others?

Applying Adams and Thompson's fifth heuristic may allow us to gain further theoretical purchase on the nature of the VLE from a posthuman perspective. As with elsewhere in the book, I will describe my own engagement with the VLE Moodle, in order to explore these questions. I will also extrapolate from this to explore how the VLE invites certain types of human-technology-world relations for the students.

I had been on sabbatical for a year, and before that was not teaching for a long period as I was in the role of Head of Department. For these reasons, I had barely looked at Moodle for several years. In this respect, this account really is to a large extent from the point of view of a near-newcomer, as the format has changed a great deal since the last time I taught a module using it. Consequently, although I had used an earlier version extensively to teach a module fully online, I did not have to work very hard to 'make the familiar strange' for this analysis. In order to open Moodle, I open my web browser and go to 'Favourites', where I placed it the week before. It is represented there by an orange square with a capital 'M', and the text 'my home'. I double click on this and a new window appears, it is the login screen for UCL Moodle. I have it set up on my laptop so I only need to click once on the 'username' empty box and my username and password are inserted. My username is a collection of letters and numbers. I don't understand how it has been derived as I was given it by the university. The password is represented by a series of dots, so it cannot be seen. This is to prevent an observer nearby from seeing my password, so it is designed in response to other human embodied presences which may be nearby and have the intention of using my login credentials for their own purposes. I think I know the password, which has to be a certain length with numbers and other characters, but as I have it automated in this way for all my login screens for the university (the library, the intranet, the finance system, HR), it is a fairly frequent occurrence that I forget it and cannot produce it on another machine. I have contracted the job of 'remembering' this password to my laptop, and when I am isolated from that close and daily symbiotic entanglement, I cannot perform this function alone without my nonhuman partner.

I log on to Moodle, and another window appears. The UCL logo is prominent. The screen is arranged into blocks and squares. On the right, there is the following text 'Looking for late Summer Assessments 18/19?'. Under this there is a photo of a young white woman who appears to be sitting in an exam. She is holding a pencil in her hand and looking at what appears to be pad of paper, so appears she is writing. She has a glass of water, which confuses me as I don't think students are provided with glasses of water when taking exams at UCL. I then deduce that this is a stock photo. This sidebar makes me think I am looking at a version of Moodle for academic staff. There is also a strip running along the top, under the main log, entitled in capitals MOODLE NEWS. It has a series of four headings which are cycling, in the style on an online news website. These are all concerned with facilities related to the VLE itself, or the enrolment system. I click on one which is entitled 'Known Issue: Using Turtinin assignments?'. I click on this and a new window appears, showing a wiki entitled 'UCL Moodle Guides for Staff'. So far, I am still getting the impression that this is a version of Moodle for academics. However, there is a menu bar running along the top which include drop-down menus for 'Staff Help' and 'Student Help', so I then assume it is some sort of hybrid or adapted version of the student Moodle, or generic version for all users. Underneath this, I see my 'Recently Accessed Courses', and below these 'Course Overview'. Each one is represented by a rectangle with a different colour and pattern, the code number of the course, and its name. I have access to courses from three programmes, so at first, I wonder if they are colour-coded accordingly. However, it does not appear to be the case, and I deduce the colours and patterns are randomly assigned. However, I then notice one course has a photo instead of a coloured pattern. The photo shows the left hand of a white person over a keyboard, with an apple placed on a pile of Post-it notes. The Moodle course is related to academic writing, so I assume it is a stock photo intended to represent this activity. My set of 'courses' on Moodle is in fact a mixture of credit-bearing modules related to the various courses which relate to my role, and more general functions. There is a Moodle 'course' devoted to my academic department, which is used for news and updates. There is also a course for a programme handbook, and another focused on research ethics at the Institute of Education. It becomes apparent that the word 'course' is being used in different way from the sense of academic module. Instead, it appears it is also a term used within Moodle to describe the units of organization. I have twenty different 'courses' on display, which is a larger number than I expected, but that is due to this breadth of focus. I begin to see that Moodle is now not only used for the academic courses, but seems to be a hybrid online space which is also used for general information for students and staff. I want to focus on academic modules, so click on one of these. I have access to this module but do not teach on it – due to one of my management roles – it is a module which is conducted face-to-face, and also uses Moodle. The new window opens up, and I see a series of drop-down menus along the top. These appear to be at least partially standardized, and are entitled and set out left to right in two rows in this order: module summary, timetable, module content, information and digital literacies, assessment, attendance (which is greyed out), module evaluation, getting help, contact, reading group forums, and programme hub. 'Welcome' is on a black background, and 'programme hub' is on red, the others are on the same shade of green. Under these menus, the word 'Welcome' appears in red, followed by a more specific introduction to the module. Under these, there is a vertical list, each with a circle showing a graphic of three stylized human figures. These are various online forums. The first is a news forum, the rest are identified by the first name of the member of academic staff who is running that tutor group. I click on the 'News Group' forum. There is a vertical list of messages which have been posted by the programme administrator, the module leader, and a member of library staff. These consist of a range of messages, covering room changes, announcements about the course, and a welcome from the module leader. The module leader and librarian are represented by small photos of themselves which appear to have been created by them, the administrator is represented by a blank white graphic of a human figures, which appears when a user has not uploaded a picture. At this point, I notice to my surprise a sidebar entitled 'my tutees'. I am momentarily confused as I am not a tutor on this module. I then realize it is a list of my doctoral students. I am initially somewhat surprised that Moodle 'knows' this about me, although I also find it vaguely disturbing, and feel somewhat under surveillance – I do not regard Moodle as having anything to do with my doctoral supervision, which all takes place on Skype or face-to-face in my office. I also notice that one of my students who passed her viva a few months ago with no corrections is listed. I start to worry that there has been some sort of mistake on the system. The sidebar distracts me entirely from my perusal of the module. I tear myself away from this and go back to the module homepage. I click on 'Module Content'. There is a red circle with the text 'PDF', and the text beside it 'Welcome – pre-reading summary for day 1'. I click on this and find a PDF giving an overview of the required reading for the first four sessions of the course. These are mostly presented in the form of lists, with a statement that they are taken from the pre-reading e-book they had received in advance, also giving its title. There is one reference with a hyperlink labelled VIEW ONLINE. I got back to the Forums, and find a message posted by one of the tutors asking for Skype addresses from her tutorial group. It becomes clear that a Skype group tutorial is planned for later that day. One the same forum, students have posted with comments and queries about their upcoming assignments. At around this point, I leave the Moodle course, having looked at all areas available.

Returning to the questions from Adams and Thompson's heuristic, they ask:

- What kinds of human-technology-world relations does this technology engage?
- Embodiments? Hermeneutic? Alterity? Background? Others?

This three-part typology of human-technology relations, is taken from Ihde's (1990) work in the postphenomenology of technics. The *embodiment* relation entails the technological artefact having an ontology like an extension of the body, creating an 'intimate assemblage' (Adams & Thompson 2016: 59). They give the examples of cars, smartphones and pens. *Hermeneutic* relations apply where the technology must be 'read', such as in the examples of a thermometer, a map, PowerPoint and a book. The relation is also embodied and intimate and a linkage with the world is formed by the technology in the case of these technologies, which act as 'translators'. *Alterity* relations refer to a situation in which the artefact is perceived to be 'other', and where the technology does not comply, is not transparent, or appears to have its own will, such as a smartphone. This where the technology is not transparent, but is instead encountered as 'other'. The category 'background relations' describes technologies which work 'in the background', such as heating and big data analytics. Adams and Thompson also use the terms *interpassive*, relating this to education, giving the example of an *interpassive* interactive whiteboard, which acts on the teacher's behalf. Considering the case of the VLE in these terms, it appears to fit in a hybrid space between the category of *hermeneutic* relations, and *alterity* relations. In certain respects, it can be 'read' like a book, and it does 'form a linkage with the word', although in a rather different sense than a thermometer. As with a book, the 'world' is connected to via a series of texts, which are themselves representations. The embodied relationship is different, mouse or tracker pad is used, instead of the hands holding a book. However, the VLE also seems to exhibit features of *alterity* relations in the sense that is 'other', emergent, at times difficult to interpret, and behaves in ways which seem unpredictable. Using this heuristic appears to confirm that the VLE, while sharing some of the features of the book as *interface* discussed earlier in this chapter, inhabits a liminal space between two main categories of relationality with technologies. It is not-quite-textbook, not-quite-classroom, not-quite-social media. This, indeterminate status may go some way to accounting for its somewhat ambiguous, uncanny nature, as part in the *longue duree* of educational media of inscription in the university.

Wayfaring

The previous chapters have looked at students and their embodied meaning-making digital and analogue epistemic practices, the nature of the lecture in history and in the digital age, and the ways that artefacts of inscription and devices intertwine with humans in both online and offline. In each of these chapters, I have critiqued mainstream humanist assumptions about these aspects of higher educational process. In each one I have also made a case for a shift in how we understand the agency of nonhuman actors in epistemic practices in the university, moving the emphasis away from the human at the centre, with associated ideologies regarding lecturers, teaching, students and devices.

In this chapter I will turn my attention to texts once again. My focus here, building on previous discussions of the emergent nature of *epistemic objects*, will be that texts should not be regarded as inert paper objects, or images on screens, which merely contain information, but are instead agentive, mutable, lively, and mobile actors in the university, in both analogue and digital formats. I will explore this point with reference to the literature in linguistic ethnography on *text trajectories* and will focus on how analogue and digital texts arise, and also on how they move, behave and travel. I will augment these analyses by applying Tim Ingold's ethnographic and conceptual work concerning 'lines' and 'wayfaring', attempting to apply this concept to deepen our understanding of textual practices in the digital university. I will conclude that a posthuman reading of textual practices and text trajectories provides us with a fuller theoretical purchase of the agentic nature of texts in the contemporary university, looking at the nature of hypertext and 'hypereading' online, drawing again on Adams and Thompson's (2016) heuristics.

One of the key aspects of texts is that they are not static entities which 'magically' appear. Instead, they have histories. As we saw in chapter 5, textual practices in the university have evolved gradually over many centuries, and practices we may consider to be relatively new often have long roots in the past.

In addition to this connection with the past via practices and text types, individual texts also have a past, and complex connections with people, places, objects and other texts. They do not exist in isolation, and they do not stand still, but are agentive, fluid entities which are acted on, but also act on the world. In this chapter I turn my attention to a body of work which has studied the movement of texts in detail; this work does not refer specifically to the digital, but I argue later in the chapter that this type of analysis allows us to shed light on how digital texts move around and act in higher education, and via that, on digital epistemic practices themselves.

Text Trajectories

A body of work in linguistic ethnography has focused on the notion of *text trajectories*, and the related processes of *entextualization* and *decontextualization*. An early use of the latter two terms can be found in Bauman and Briggs (1990), in a theoretical consideration of the nature of poetics and verbal performance, (this paper was also discussed in chapter 4 in the context of Thesen's work on lectures). They point out that a verbal performance does not arise out of nowhere, but has a history and set of preceding 'speech events' leading up to it:

> ... a given performance is tied to a number of speech events which precede and succeed it (past performances, readings of texts, negotiations, rehearsals, gossip, reports, critiques, challenges, subsequent performances, and the like). An adequate analysis of a single performance thus requires sensitive ethnographic study of how its form and meaning index a broad range of discourse types, come of which are not framed as performance.
>
> Bauman & Briggs 1990: 60–61

They refer to the foundational work in philosophy of language on Speech Acts (Austin 1962, Grice 1975, Searle 1969, 1976, 1979), in which language use was identified as being social action, as opposed to simply an act of representation. An important concept in Speech Act Theory is that of 'illocutionary force'; the outcome of an utterance when spoken, what effect it has on the world. The key point they make is, 'The illocutionary force of an utterance often emerges not simply from its placement within a particular genre and social setting, but also from the indexical relations between the performance and other speech events that precede and succeed it.' (Bauman & Briggs 1990: 64). Put more simply, meaning does not arise exclusively through the content or syntax (grammar) of an isolated stretch of language, but it is much more complex, and is embedded in and emerges in interaction with larger units of speech events, frames, and participation structures in society. In this way, we can make sense of an utterance, as we have had experience of similar types of speech in the past and we have a set of social expectations surrounding how a speaker might speak, how we should respond and so on, such as in a lecture, for example.

Bauman and Briggs go on to present a detailed review of the development of this field of enquiry, to trace a shift away from the study of texts in isolation, towards 'the analysis of the emergence of texts in contexts' (1990: 66), citing Bateson's (1972) and Goffman's (1974) work on *frames* in particular, as discussed in chapter 4. In doing so, they challenge the conventional understanding of the idea of 'context', which is often taken to mean the setting in which speech takes place, moving instead towards a focus on text which '... starts with the narrative outside its enactment.' (Blackburn 1988: 49). Put more directly, they expand the idea of context to include interactions and events prior to the speech event. They argue for a more intertwined and dynamic conception of the relationships between text and context, moving away from a somewhat inert construct of text sitting in the 'container' of context, toward more dynamic conceptualization of the two in interplay. They propose a move from 'context' to *contextualization* (Bateson 1972, Goffman 1974, 1981) and also from text to *entextualisation* (Bauman & Briggs 1990: 68), placing the emphasis on these as processes, rather than viewing contexts and texts fixed entities. They consider some of the problems with the construct of 'context'; first that it becomes impossible to define what elements should be included or excluded, and secondly that '... positivistic definitions construe context as a set of discourse-external conditions that exist prior to and independently of the performance ... (which) also obscures the manner in which speech shapes the setting, often transforming social relations.' (1990: 68). It also reinforces the notion of meaning as pre-existing context in some sense. A *contextualization* reading sees contexts as emergent, arising through negotiations between participants in social interaction. They provide the example of meta-narration, in which a storyteller reaches out directly to the audience; this echoes Goffman's 'fresh talk' discussed in chapter 4. They also emphasize the role of audience in shaping performance. Crucially for this work, they point out that:

> Even when audience members say or do practically nothing at the time of performance, their role becomes active when they serve as speakers in

subsequent entextualisations of the topic at hand (e.g. in reports, challenges, refutations, enactments of consequences, and the like).

Bauman & Briggs 1990: 70

This echoes the analysis of the lecture in chapter 4. They go on to elaborate on the mirror concept of *entextualisation*, '... the process of rendering discourse extractable, of making a stretch of linguistic production into a unit, a text, that can be lifted out of its interactional setting.' (1990: 73). In linguistic anthropology, as they point out,

> ... performance is seen as specially marked, artful way of speaking that sets up or represents a special interpretive frame within which the act of speaking is to be understood. Performance puts the act of speaking on display – objectifies it, lifts it to a degree from its interactional setting and opens it to scrutiny by an audience. Performance heightens awareness of the act of speaking and licenses the audience to evaluate the skill and effectiveness of the performer's accomplishment. By its very nature, then, performance potentiates decontextualisation.

Bauman & Briggs 1990: 73

Although this work focuses on verbal performance, the construct of *contextualization* and *entextualisation* led to further work which focused on how texts move, change and mutate more broadly. Working in the same theoretical frame, Budach et al. (2015), in their introduction to a special issue of the journal *Social Semiotics* on 'objects and language in transcontextual communication', critique new literacy studies as having tended to study writing '... *in* context, rather than *across* contexts, with texts viewed as bounded and static entities.' (2015: 390). They also point out how objects and materiality have been neglected in social semiotics, despite the insights of work on multimodality (e.g. Kress & van Leeuwen 1996), and the recognition of the importance of objects as mediating tools (e.g. Scollon 2001, Scollon & Scollon 2003), as they put it:

> ... their role has been described mainly as a vehicle in the structuration, circulation, and re-distribution of discourses, rather than in their own right. This instrumental view of objects as an auxiliary device for the spread and re-contextualisation of discourse has blocked ways of considering objects more fully, and most importantly, the role and impact of their materiality.

Budach et al. 2015: 390

In the same issue, Kell (2015) cites Blommaert's (2014) claim that a 'sociolinguistics of mobility' has been achieved, but argues that the unit of analysis remains '... situated practices and meaning-making in bounded texts, contexts and entities.' (Kell 2015: 424). She takes as her focus not the movement of people, but the *movement of meanings*. Her question is 'What does the unit of analysis become when meaning-making is studied as it unfolds over time and across contexts which are not characterized by co-presence and mutual monitoring?' (2015: 425). She proposes the concept of *meaning-making trajectories* made up of contextualizing and resemiotizing moves, drawing on Bauman and Briggs (1990), but adding a dimension of focus on objects. She seeks to move the focus away from spoken language, towards meaning-making which is '... mediated across space and time through various types of text-artefacts and material objects' (Kell 2015: 425). She proposes that material objects constitute the 'joins' by which meaning is sustained across space and time. She identifies this as contributing to a turn towards materiality in our understanding of communication and notes Iedema's work on *resemiotisation*; how meanings draw on different semiotic resources as they shift across contexts (Iedema: 1999, 2001, 2003). She also critiques the notion of 'boundary objects' (e.g. Bowker & Star 1999) for being fundamentally based on a social constructionist understanding of the world, which '... puts human action first, and sees objects as only coming into existence when humans hail them for their purposes.' (Kell 2015: 428). She draws on a new materialist lens, such as that of Harman (2002) and Bennett (2010), who asks 'What if things really can, in some undetermined way hail us and offer us a glimpse through a window that opens, of lively bodies that are not just parsed into subjects and objects?' (Bennett: 2010).

This strand of work, I would argue, has much to offer in seeking to deepen our understanding of digital epistemic practices, as it recognizes the complexities of how texts arise, and how they interact with 'contexts' in a dynamic way, how they change, morph, cross boundaries, move around, and act on each other and on the world. This type of analysis has been applied to a range of texts, such as letters (Kell 2009), and call centre interaction (Woydack & Rampton 2016). I would suggest that it represents a powerful theoretical framing for the analysis of digital epistemic practices, given their complex and highly mobile nature. However, before discussing this in more depth, I would like to weave another strand of theory into my discussion, which I believe allows us further purchase on the topic at hand, by presenting a broader conception of the centrality of movement to human life. I will conclude the chapter with a discussion of how these ideas, taken together, might offer us insights into digital texts in higher education, illustrated with examples of hypertext and *hypereading*, drawing on Adams and Thompson (2016).

Gitelman (2104) refers to de Certeau's concept of the 'scriptural economy', what he characterizes as '... an "endless tapestry" of writing and writings that works as both discipline and myth: disciplines because writing is a form of socialization and control, and myth because writing accumulate with (that is, as) the weight of history itself.' She reminds us that the word 'document' comes for Latin *docer* – to teach or show. As she puts it:

> Documents are epistemic objects; they are the recognizable sites and subjects of interpretation across the disciplines and beyond, evidential structures in the long human history of clues.
>
> Gitelman 2014: 1

She rejects a unitary notion of 'print culture', and insists on a recognition of the specificity of media practices. Critiquing the idea of a clear division between 'print' and 'web' documents, she states:

> Better instead to resist any but local contrastive logics for media; better to look for meanings that arise, shift and persist according to the uses that media – emergent, dominant, and residual – familiarly have. Better indeed, to admit that no medium has a single particular logic, while every genre does and is.
>
> Gitelman 2014: 9

Gitelman goes on to examine the nature of the Portable Document Format (PDF) file:

> Whatever else they are, digital and (even more so) digitized documents appear as pictures of themselves. There is nothing simple here. 'A computer screen', Anne Friedberg notes, 'is both a "page" and a "window," at once opaque and transparent', a surface that nonetheless enables 'deep virtual reach to archives and databases', to local disk storage and the cloud.
>
> Gitelman 2014: 114

She delineates her task as follows:

> I am proposing, in short, that PDF technology imagines its users—that certain uses and conditions have been built in to the technology—at the same time that actual users continue to imagine and reimagine what PDF files are for, how and where they work, and thus what they mean. Only by taking account of these intersecting imaginaries can we understand the specificities of this digitally-mediated format or, indeed, of any technology.
>
> Gitelman 2014: 117–118

Of particular interest and relevance to this study is Gitelman's recognition of the co-constitutive nature of the relationship between the file and the user. She analyses the PDF in detail, focusing on it the measure of fixity achieved by the format. Like Friesen, Gitelman also takes a long view of history when considering the nature of the PDF, comparing them to the *paginae* of antiquity, which were presented on horizontal papyrus scrolls, or the typographical matter arranged by letterpress printers (2014: 119). With reference to Mak (2011), she argues that these are not pages in the sense of three-dimensional leaves of paper, but are the formal and visual conventions of a 'standard interface'. As she proposes:

> These pages can be read, then, but they can't be turned. It is in this sense that computer screens contain pages – think of web pages and Word files – of which page images form a special class and PDFs a specific variety.
>
> Gitelman 2014: 119

Exploring the roots and development of the PDF, Gitelman points out claims made that '... anything that can be done with a sheet of paper can be done with a PDF' (Webopedia 2005), these refer to actions such as printing, sharing, reading, filing, copying and archiving (Ames 1993). However, as she points out, 'These are the gerunds that animate the myth of the paperless office. Forget all of the other things you can do with paper, like folding, smelling, tearing, crumpling, shuffling, and wiping.' (Gitelman 2014: 128). She refers to Sellen and Harper's (2002) *The Myth of the Paperless Office*, where they argue that we use paper literally to '[get] *to grips with* information' and 'to fully grasp the meaning of the text in question' (Sellen & Harper 2002: 103, in Gitelman 2014: 128). They argue that '... no amount of wishful thinking will make PDFs into an equivalent, even if the cursor in many PDF readers sometimes takes the form of a tiny, grasping white hand' (2014: 128). She points out that a miniature virtual hand cannot 'get to grips with something' in the same way as a human hand can, and refers to White (2008), who proposes that cartoon hands '[act] as a kind of avatar or extension of the [user's] body'.

Interestingly, Gitelman points out that the hand-shaped cursor in Acrobat Reader does not represent the hand of the author, but that of the reader. She reminds us that:

> Hands have always figured within the readerly imaginary. They have also long been figured graphically on the page. Unlike the eye, brain, heart, of stomach (which wouldn't make much sense as cursors), hands are common in marginalia across the centuries.
>
> Gitelman 2014: 129

She gives the example of the 'manicule', the *nota* or *nota bene* image of a pointing hand which were commonly added to early modern books. The hand cursor in Acrobat Reader, however, does not point; Gitelman suggests its function is to give the message 'look here!'. As she points out, this movement depends on the movement of the 'unwatched and forgotten' actual hand of the user (2014: 130). Another feature of PDFs highlighted by Gitelman is that they encourage reading, without writing. They cannot be edited, and are designed for one-way information flow. As she argues:

> Work itself may have been 'given a voice' by the bureaucratized work processes of the twentieth century … but PDF technology has a reactionary, not a revolutionary, feel. It looks back toward the fixity of analog print artifacts and the division of labor between print publishers and their reading customers at the same time that it participates in the mystification of digital tools for an average user trapped in a 'friendly' environment where uses are parameterized, constrained to menu-indented tasks, and divided among discrete 'tools' and 'views'.
>
> Gitelman 2014: 131

In conclusion, Gitelman proposes the following:

> One might generalize that PDFs make sense partly according to a logic of attachment and enclosure. That is, like the digital objects we 'attach' to and send along with email messages, or the nondigital objects we still enclose in envelopes or boxes and send by snail mail, PDFs are individually bounded and distinct. Just as an email attachment must exist before the email message that makes it one ('Attached please find . . .'), so PDFs are already authored entities, understood as distinct from the written systems in and by which they are individually named and potentially manipulated and downloaded. The written system in question might be the web itself, a document management system created for a special purpose, a database, or any repository for storing digital files that has a query language and an interface for retrieving them. Using a file manager application to look on your own hard drive for a PDF is something like rooting through a filing cabinet, if you could ever root through files paying attention only to file names and locations, and not to things like thickness or signs of wear.
>
> Gitelman 2014: 133

Gitelman's analysis of the PDF emphasizes its fixity, in a sense its finality. The reader cannot interact directly with the text, cannot write into or on it or edit it. It separates reading and writing, and prevents authorship. This has implications for education, in arena where PDFs are commonly used, such as in the VLE. As discussed in chapter 5, the use of the VLE as a repository for PDF files and PowerPoint slides, is analogous to filling a filing cabinet. The readers may 'root around' in the VLE, but may only choose whole, predetermined files. The next section moves on to look at a very different form and conception of digital readership, in which – I argue – the reader and the text and co-emergent.

Lines

So far in this chapter, I have referred to fine-grained ethnographic work undertaken in linguistic ethnography, which has focused on texts and meaning-making, discussed and how that movement is intrinsic to their meanings and effects on the world. I have also looked at relevant work in media archaeology, considering the nature of digital texts. I would now like to weave in the work of Tim Ingold, in particular his work on *lines* and his notion of *wayfaring*. Ingold describes his work as 'a comparative anthropology of the line' (Ingold 2007: 1), and over two book-length works (Ingold 2007, 2015) offers a wide-ranging, eclectic, and highly original set of meditations on the nature of the line, and its importance for our understanding of the world and our place in it. It is beyond the scope of this book to offer a comprehensive review of his ideas, instead I will focus on the points which seem of greatest relevance to this study of texts in the digital university.

Ingold (2007) embarks on this investigation with an in-depth discussion on the nature of texts, writing and reading. He refers to de Certeau, who in *The Practice of Everyday Life* (1981), proposed the concept of writing a text as a form of colonization. As Ingold puts it, in this view of writing '... the text is an artefact – a thing fabricated or made – that is built where before there was nothing.' (Ingold 2007: 13). However, taking a historical view, he points out that this view is fundamentally at odds with the medieval view of scripture as something that *speaks* (de Certeau 1981: 136–137, in Ingold 2007: 14) – echoing points made earlier in chapter 5. Ingold proposes that in the medieval period, readers were, in a sense, '... using their eyes to hear' (2007: 14), and that written texts were regarded as primarily records of speech. He traces this back to Greek antiquity, where Havelock found that inscriptions had the quality of oral pronouncements, and artefacts could be perceived as in some sense having a 'voice' – he cites the example of a seventh-century pot discovered in Italy inscribed with 'Who so steals me shall go blind' (Havelock 1982: 190–191, 195, in Ingold 2007: 14). Additionally, as Ingold points out, reading at that time was not the silent and solitary activity we engage in today, but instead was accompanied by reading aloud. In monastic practice, the reader would murmur the words while reading or silently read along with the lips, known as *voces paginum*, the 'voices of the pages' (Leclerq 1961: 19,

Olson 1994: 183–185, in Ingold 2007: 15). He challenges the notion that the voices of the text were mere imagination:

> This division between the materiality of sound – its physical substance – and its ideal representation is however a modern construct. It would have made no sense in terms of a philosophy of being according to which ... bodily performance and intellectual comprehension are as viscerally linked as eating and digestion.
>
> Ingold 2007: 15

Here, reading is seen as a physical and embodied act; which I would argue is somewhat different from the rather rarefied notion of a text as 'transporting' the reader into a disembodied, dreamlike realm, particularly prevalent in discussions of digital engagement discussed above. He also highlights the role of writing and reading in remembering, and characterizes texts as '... pathways along which the voices of the past could be retrieved and brought back into the immediacy of present experience, allowing readers to engage directly in dialogue with them' (2007: 16). This strongly echoes the points made in the previous section about texts and their relationships to the past. Developing the notion of reading as movement, Ingold argues that in antiquity and the Middle Ages, readers were *wayfarers*, not *navigators*, making a distinction as follows:

> ... the navigator has before him (*sic*) a complete representation of the territory, in the form of a cartographic map, upon which he can chart a course before setting out. The journey is then no more than an explication of the plot. In wayfaring, by contrast, one follows a path that one has previously travelled in the company of others, or in their footsteps, reconstructing the itinerary as one goes along. Only upon reaching his destination, in this case, can the traveler truly be said to have found his way.
>
> Ingold 2007: 16

He argues that the text would have been regarded as a series of 'signposts' for the reader to find their way through a landscape of memory. He characterizes texts in that period as '... regions to be inhabited, and which one can get to know not through one single, totalizing gaze, but through the laborious process of moving around'. For him, a text is '... a journey made, rather than an object found' (2007: 17). In this analysis, he rejects the notion of reading as the act of a solitary and isolated intellect, but instead sees the reader as grounded in sensory immersion in the world, making their way. Again, the material nature of reading is emphasized and the embodied reader is brought into view, plus the idea of the text as incomplete and in interaction with the world, and with readers, is emphasized. He goes on to argue that the page has 'lost its voice' through print technology. His contention is that handwriting allowed the reader to follow the trajectory of the movement of the writer's hand, and argues that print technology has broken the 'intimate link' between manual gesture and graphic inscription. He sets out that printing is not *inscription*, but is *impression* '. . . of a pre-composed text upon an empty surface that has been made ready to receive it.' (2007: 27).

Although it is undeniable that the intimacy and direct visually-observable trace of the writer's hand is lost when handwriting is converted to print, I would argue that Ingold is presenting this as too strong a binary. Firstly, it is worth noting that while manuscripts of the medieval period were produced by hand, many did not resemble everyday handwriting as such, but instead were stylized, and relatively standardized in their presentation of text. Even if each had unique features, copies were widespread, such as in the case of illuminated religious manuscripts. Echoing Friesen in chapter 4, Ingold may have fallen into the trap of over-attributing to the printing press the effect of a complete 'rupture' in mediatic practices, when in fact the transition to print was more gradual. As Gitelman puts it, 'Far from being a simple precursor, manuscript stands as a back formation of printing.' Gitelman 2014: 7). It may be more helpful to think of the connection between an author's hand and the text for the reader as being a question of degree, and one of genre – a handwritten letter is likely to appear more intimate than an expertly-produced illuminated manuscript, although both are technically produced by hand. It is not clear why the trace of the hand itself (or its absence) is the only factor renders the reader a *wayfarer* or a *navigator*. It may be more helpful to consider a range of ways that a text can position the reader and allow different type of embodied movement and form of travelling along it, or through it.

Although he does not specify it, Ingold appears to be referring to printed and fixed texts in the form of analogue printed books, or other print material. He does not consider the nature of digital texts, which I will argue are somewhat different in terms of his framing. Although a digital text does not explicitly show the trajectory of the writer's hand, hands have nonetheless been at work to produce it, tapping on a keyboard, handling paper books, writing sticky notes, writing in the margins, and so on. The act of writing digital text remains intensely physical, and intertwined with the analogue, material world – the body has not been removed from writing, but is simply less directly evident in the finished text. It is true that the direct sense of the movement of the hands is not visible to the reader as with handwriting, but embodied action is still present, albeit under the surface of the text. For me, this does not entirely 'silence' the text, as Ingold proposes. Secondly, much of the digital text we read or interact with on screen is not in fact 'fixed' as he suggests for printed material, but is in flux, and is often open to direct intervention or dialogue, such as in wikis, interactive social media, online gaming, and so on.

In an in-depth exploration of the influence of digital media on how we interact with texts during an age she characterizes as 'the passing of print', Hayles (2012) differentiates between *close, hyper,* and *machine* reading. Hayles proposes *hyper reading* a term to describe the rapid, skimming and scanning that we frequently engage in while reading texts online, following hyperlinks and flitting around spontaneously, as opposed to reading a single text slowly from start to finish in *close reading.* I may be stretching the term beyond the use originally intended for it, but I would suggest that Ingold's notion of the *wayfarer* is highly suitable to describe the reader/writer of digital texts and media, given the lack of a fixed 'route' to be followed when researching a topic online, the highly individual and spontaneous nature of our journeys across the landscapes of the open internet in particular, and circuitous paths we take in order to read, gain knowledge and allow our own digital texts to emerge. Another relevant concept from Ingold is that of the *meshwork*, inspired by his consideration of natural phenomena. He defines the meshwork as:

> ...an entanglement of interwoven lines. These lines may loop or twist around one another, or weave in and out. This is what distinguishes the meshwork from the network. The lines of the network are connectors: each is given as the relation between points, independently and in advance of any movement from one towards the other. Such lines therefore lack duration: the network is a purely spatial construct. The lines of a meshwork, by contrast, are of movement and growth. They are the lines along which things become. Every animate being, as it threads its way through and among the ways of every other, must perforce improvise a passage, and in doing so it lays another line.
>
> Ingold 2012a: 49

He also introduces the concept of *knots*, which he defines as:

> ...places where many lines of becoming are drawn tightly together. Yet every line overtakes the knot in which it is tied. Its end is always loose, somewhere beyond the knot, where it is groping towards and entanglement with other lines, in other knots.
>
> Ingold 2012a: 49

He goes on to consider the nature of lines as abstractions, ultimately rejecting the notion that there are no lines in nature, instead positing that we should

'. . . treat line as a verb, and say that in the thing's growing – in its issuing forth, in its making itself visible . . . it *lines*.' (Ingold 2012a: 51). In the next section, I will attempt to apply these concepts to what I will call 'hyperwriting', using Adams and Thompson's heuristics, also drawn from Ingold's work.

An Interview with 'Hyperwriting'

Adams and Thompson propose the following questions, in order to investigate technology using the heuristic 'tracing responses and passages':

- *Co-responding*. How do human actors join with the things around them in co-response to what is happening around them? (Ingold 2012b)
- *Improvising Passages*. What kind of passages are being improvised as entities thread their way through the ways of others (human and material)? (Ingold 2012a)
- *Meshworking*. What lines of movement can be seen? What kind of knot-making (a temporary bringing together of human-technology energies) is going on? How are lines of movement (or becomings) being redirected? When do they loosen or tighten the knot? (Ingold 2012a)

This section will focus on another set of digital practices integral to the university and academic work, but one which is not normally regarded as a technology per se. The focus will be on academic writing in the digital university. This set of epistemic practices will be 'interviewed' using the questions and concepts above.

When a student engages in academic writing in the contemporary, digitally-mediated university setting, a complex set of agents, artefacts and technologies are intertwined, into a joint practice I will call *hyperwriting*. Hyperwriting is an embodied practice which involves movements of the hands, orientation of the body, movement of the eyes, and so on, while the student engages with the digital device and online resources. It also takes place in a particular material setting, which consists of artefacts such as chairs, desks, digital devices, pens, papers, and infrastructural elements such as electricity and Wi-Fi, as discussed in chapter 2. It involves reading and writing in a digital medium. This entails what Hayle's calls *hyper reading*, following hypertext and links online, in order to find texts, read them and follow on to find others. This may also include use of social media such as Twitter, again following links to other web pages and texts. It is a commonplace to say that online engagement of this nature is 'nonlinear', as opposed to the 'straight lines' interpretation of the word 'linear', characterized by the following of the horizontal rows of lines of text in a material book. However, if viewed in terms of Ingold's concept of *lines* in nature above, and in particular using the notion of line as a verb, the practices of hyperwriting may be regarded as profoundly linear in a different sense. The sociomaterial assemblage which has arisen for and through hyperwriting may also be seen as a *meshwork* in Ingold's terms, as opposed to a network. In these terms, a text may be seen as a *knot*; a contingent gathering of a mesh of lines which pre-exist the text, and also extend beyond it. In this sense, a text is not 'finished'. These lines are the other texts and voices which are woven in through hyperwriting. However, the metaphor of a woven fabric is not quite suitable, as it entails a cutting off of the threads, the digital text as a knot in the meshwork only appears to exist separately from the lines it consists of. Using the concept in another sense, the student hyperwriter could be said *to line* their way forward, up, around, back and through. The writer moves, and forms a *passage* in more than one way, in terms of fluid and individually-unique, unplanned movement through almost infinite web-based texts and sites, recalling Ingold's *wayfarer* without a map. A text is sometimes itself referred to as a passage. However, in another sense, the writer *passes through, makes a passage through*, a constantly shifting landscape of digital texts, material artefacts, and other humans.

Writing is often referred to as a *process*, a word which tends to be used to denote an emptiness, a route to reach what is substantive, in the form of *content*. However, it is worth considering the etymology of the word, which is derived from *procession*. A procession is not simply a movement for A to B, but is a movement infused with meaning. The *processing* is the meaning, not the route to it. With the notion of the writer as wayfarer, lining in a meshwork, I would suggest that insights into the richness, complexity and meaning of the *procession* of digital writing are revealed. It is, I suggest, no longer tenable to regard the text as a 'product' of writing, but is an emergent knot of lines which tangle in *hyperwriting*.

An example can be analysed by reflecting on the writing of this book. As described in chapter 2, I wrote this book on my laptop, which was entangled with a range of material artefacts such as Post-it notes, pencils, power supply wires and so on. It depended on infrastructural elements such as electricity and Wi-Fi. In that regard, it was sociomaterially complex, and involved a mixture of embodied and digital practices. However, this is not to suggest that the digital aspect of this process was straightforward or monodimensional. Instead, it was intricate, complex, and exhibited, I will argue, some of the features of Ingold's *wayfaring*, as discussed above.

A typical writing session would proceed as follows. I turn on the laptop early in the morning, probably around 6 am, after being woken up by the nuns in the neighbouring convent taking their wheelie bin out to the road. I can hear bird song, cars starting, bells, neighbours talking indistinctly, a burst of TV. The sky is still black. The machine makes its familiar 'musical' sound on being turned on, then I use the tracker pad to move the pointer to the top right of the screen, to check the battery levels. It is low. I lean under the nearby desk and find the power supply, which is in a tangled knot once again. I tease and pull at the wire until it is freed. I stretch up to plug it into the awkwardly high socket on the wall. I then notice the Italian adaptor plug is not there. I walk across the room and open the cupboard, where I find the adaptor. I walk back across the room and push the laptop plug into it, then plug it in. I then sit down and log in. I am in Italy, therefore one hour ahead of the UK. Due to this, I do not expect work email, but glance at the icon on the bottom left of my screen. There is a red number 1 showing on the blue square showing the white letter O. I click on the icon, and see that it is an email from a publisher in another time zone, sent overnight. It is soliciting me to join the editorial board of a journal. This company has written to me repeatedly, I have politely declined repeatedly. I feel a slight wave of irritation. I had spent a lot of time the day before 'clearing my inbox', and had felt a sense of satisfaction that my email was now 'tidy', and now this random message has messed it up. I navigate the pointer to my email signatures where I have pre-prepared replies for frequent emails. I click on the signature 'declining editorial invitation'. An automatic text is inserted which reads:

Dear Editorial Office Staff,

Thanks very much indeed for thinking of me for this, it's an honour. However, I'm afraid I am not in a positon to accept the invitation at this time, due to other commitments. I wish you all the best for the future of your journal.

Best Wishes

Professor Lesley Gourlay

Department of Culture, Communication and Media, UCL Institute of Education, University College London, 20 Bedford Way London WC1H OAL

I click on 'send' and then delete the email. I then move the cursor over the line of icons at the bottom of the screen, they become larger under it, seeming to rise up or expand in response. I clock on my web browser, and a smaller window appears layered on top of my email. In it, my 'favourites' are arranged in rows, each represented by a coloured square with a letter or a pictorial representation. I click on the website of an international newspaper, which I have online access to via the university in Italy where I work part-time. A window appears. This closely resembles the paper version of this publication, in terms of the colour, font, layout and general appearance. However, it differs in that it includes an advertisement running along the top of the masthead. The advert is static, but includes a button showing the text 'watch now'. I understand that if I click on that button, I will see a video advertising that company. I use my track pad to scroll down the page. As I do that, the whole page moves up in a long strip, reminiscent of a physical scroll, concealing the text at the top and revealing more text below. I can still see the edges of my email programme 'behind' it.

This is different from how I read the paper version of this paper, which I sometimes buy from the newsstand at the bus stop in the village square. With the physical paper, I need to use both hands and widen out my arms to open it and read its broad pages. I can't read it on the bus as it would encroach on fellow passengers' personal space. As the bus snakes down the switchback road to the university, I need to hold on with at least one hand. I need to fold up the paper and put it in my bag. However, with the digital newspaper, all that is moving are two fingers of my right hand and my eyes. Otherwise I am still. I am feeling a little sleepy and unmotivated to start work on the book, so I click on a story which interests me. Another window appears, showing a newspaper article with a photo at the top. It looks a lot like the one in the physical paper, except that under the photo and above the text, there is a row of icons. These consist of the 'flying bird' image of Twitter, the lower case 'f' of Facebook, the 'in' of LinkedIn, a small square with an arrow pointing upwards from in next to the word 'Share', and finally a simplified image of a bookmark next to the word 'save'. All of these icons give me the possibility of opening a social media platform directly, or choosing one of the first three or WhatsApp, in the case of the 'share' button, or placing the article in my 'bookmarks' list on the browser. The first four are present to allow me to place a link to this article on one or more of these social media sites. If I decided to do this, for example using Facebook, another window would open within that programme. A link plus image from the article would appear on my 'wall' of links, photos and messages I have written for my Facebook friends to access. I would then have the option of adding my own comment to the link to the article. My Facebook friends could then 'like' it, post an emoticon to represent their feelings in response to the article, or they could make a comment, which I and others could respond to. They could 'share' the link to their friends, continuing that process. I also have the option via this button to send a link to the article to 'anyone' using a gift token, or to other subscribers. I do not take any of these options, but am aware that they are possible, they are 'there'.

I will pause my account to take a step back and look at this five-minutes of activity in terms of the concepts discussed above. In terms of Ingold's concepts of lines and knots, we see examples already. The email was written, or at least sent, by a member of staff in a city in East Asia. There is no individual name provided in the signature, but human hands have been at work in some way. However, it appears to be a standard email, I have had exactly the same one before. I cannot tell how they found my name, it could be automated in some way, perhaps scanning sites like Academia.edu for academics working in Education. It cites one of my previous papers, but in a manner which makes it clear this paper has not been read – it has very little relationship to the focus of their journal. So, I assume some kind of automated process. This appears normal to me, if slightly irritating and intrusive. However, from a posthuman point of view, it is an example of a complex hybrid in terms of authorship. It seeks to masquerade as a personal email from one expert to another – praising my work and extending an invitation to join what is presented as a community of like-minded scholars. But I can see this is not the case, via the obviously template-like nature of the message, the incorrectly formulated salutation of 'Dear Gourlay', the repetitious nature of these messages which are always the same, the irrelevance of the journal, the fact that my repeated polite refusals have not stopped the flow of invitations. All the signs are that the 'author' is nonhuman, and my replies will not be read. But I persist in sending my polite reply, as I cannot be absolutely sure that there is no human correspondent present, and do not want to be rude if there is. I picture a hardworking and junior member of staff sitting in an office in that distant city. However, I am aware that many of my colleagues routinely block or delete these messages without ceremony. It appears I am caught between behaving as if my addressee is human, and therefore responding in what I consider to be an appropriate manner, or treating it as 'spam' which has been generated by an algorithm. There is a profoundly uncanny aspect to these type of written interactions, in which my 'interlocutor' is unknowable and multi-layered in terms of agency and authorship. This, I propose, is one feature of *hyperwriting*.

Moving to the online newspaper, even the perusal of one article reveals several important features. Unlike the paper artefact, there are links embedded in the text which would allow me to follow lines into other websites, other part of this website, or past articles. In this sense, what I see initially is a different type of surface to the paper page. It is an interface, or alternatively an apparently flat surface with is riddled with hatches or holes I can disappear down. These are not pre-prescribed, but are almost infinite in their possible trajectories. There are many possibilities for me to take this text and 'send' it moving into other online spaces for other readers. Readers can comment on stories and interact with each other. In this sense, the online paper seems to be an example of one of Ingold's knots – it has the appearance of stability, but it is contingent, timebound and changes through the day, looking mostly different the next day. This process is incremental, as stories move down the page, disappear or are replaced by more up-to-date news. The most popular stories are explicitly highlighted in a hierarchy. The laptop as a whole is constantly adapting what it 'shows' me, according to algorithmic interpretations of my likes, preferences, habits and it's understanding of my subjectivity in general, in ways which can feel intrusive, and disturbing. In this sense it is restless, emergent, and constantly on the move in a way that the crumpled copy from earlier in the week, which is now lying on the kitchen table, is not. The knot is made of a tangle of lines which extend out beyond the newspaper website. But these lines are not in existence until they are followed; they are emergent, and only come into existence when they are made by people following them by moving their hands over a keyboard, each pathway different, winding and unpredictable.

This can also be seen in process of online academic hyperreading and hyperwriting; the two are in fact entirely intertwined, and cannot be meaningfully separated. Finally, back in Italy, after some reading of the news website, following various lines and passages through the paper, and flicking over to Facebook to see if any of my friends in other time zones have posted, I notice the morning has become light outside, time has moved on and it's around 7 am. I have coffee. I feel it's time to get down to work, and start feeling a bit anxious and guilty about 'messing about online' instead of doing what I should be doing, writing my book while on sabbatical. I deliberately close the browser and email, in order to avoid the temptation of looking at them and being distracted. However, I remain aware that they are still present, a couple of clicks away. My 'wallpaper' on my laptop shows a photo of a close up of some black stones with water running over them, with a bright orange flower petal lying on top in the middle of the screen. I took the picture ten years ago while on holiday in South East Asia. I have changed it a few times, but always end up restoring it as my screensaver. I like the image, and find it calming and familiar. Layered over the photo, I have a vertical row of folders on the left of the desktop screen. The top one is entitled 'Posthumanism and the Digital University', and contains this document I am writing into now and a large number of PDF files of academic articles. I found each of those through a great deal of wayfaring online, and many long hours and complex journeys starting variously at Google Scholar, reference lists from other articles, the UCL university online library, and so on. They are now arranged in a neat alphabetical list, each now a tiny red and white square, with the author's name which I have usually had to add by renaming the file. They give the impression of order, or *a priori* principle. But they are not orderly, they are more like a harvest I have gathered through a great deal of foraging and hacking my way through the dense thickets of online journals, paths made even more difficult to forge due to the strongly interdisciplinary nature of this work, and the need for me to criss-cross some very different 'fields', with high hedges or fences standing between them. This text is similar. You as a reader are likely to be holding this in your hands as a paper book. But this book, I suggest, is a somewhat different example of Ingold's knot from the online newspaper. It may give the impression of boundedness. It has become a physical artefact you can handle. It has edges, weight, and is 'finished'. The enormous physical, virtual, temporal, mental and emotional set of lines, wayfaring, tangled and struggles that were involved in its production are hidden, stilled and tidied away. So, which is 'the book' and where is it now? Its ontology seems multiple and unclear.

Addressing the 'interview' questions:

- *Co-responding.* How do human actors join with the things around them in co-response to what is happening around them? (Ingold 2012b)
- *Improvising Passages.* What kind of passages are being improvised as entities thread their way through the ways of others (human and material)? (Ingold 2012a)
- *Meshworking.* What lines of movement can be seen? What kind of knot-making (a temporary bringing together of human-technology energies) is going on? How are lines of movement (or becomings) being redirected? When do they loosen or tighten the knot? (Ingold 2012a)

In terms of co-responding with other humans, my experience of 'hyperwriting' was complex. The most obvious example of interaction with other people seems to be email, which shows me a list of names of senders, and their messages authored sometimes just for me to read, often for many recipients. The example of the automated email was an interesting 'borderline' case, where it was unclear to me what the balance of machine and human agency was behind the email; the conventions of email are that they should be replied to if 'from' an individual, which was probably why I persisted in writing 'human' replies to what was almost certainly an algorithm-generated message. My passage felt like a mixture of navigation and wayfaring; I visited my 'regular' websites, but was aware of the possibility of straying off the path in endless ways, throughout. This possibly of wandering along improvised passages was in fact a problem at times, such that I needed to put in place various measures in order to avoid it, timeframes for writing, blocking browsing using a specialist app, and so on. The notion of meshworking seems generative here, my movements and passage-making online felt mesh-like, criss-crossing and emergent. I felt the manuscript itself was like Ingold's knot, and a tangle of many, many threads. I have in fact often used the metaphor of weaving threads to talk about academic writing, but the knot is even more apt, it seems. The knot of this manuscript has remained loose throughout most of the process, with 'tightenings' taking place at key moments when ideas seem to 'fall into place' (often to fall out again). One thread may loosen several others, unravelling what looked like a secure mini knot. Equally, a thread may suddenly gather others around it, in a formation rather like a ball of string.

In contrast, if I apply these same questions to my earlier foray into the VLE described in the previous chapter, the answers are somewhat different. In the Moodle course, I could see traces of other human actors (mainly the academic teaching staff) via the posts or other texts they had authored, the PDF files they had posted, and most noticeably via their forum posts, where I could see less formal texts, and in some cases, see the photos of the lecturers, who I know personally. The generic 'human head' icon, which shows when a participant has not uploaded a photo, gave the impression that the writer 'behind' it somehow was less important, or did not 'belong' in the VLE to the same extent as those who did have their photos identifying them and linking them to my knowledge of their embodied self. Overall, the impression was of *traces* of presence, of presence that had passed, as opposed to co-presence. The 'stock' photo of the student did not feel like a human actor in the same sense, instead I found it mildly alienating, as it appeared to be another example of a commonly used, idealized, stereotype of 'pretty white girl studying'. I felt very much as though I was 'improvising my passage'; however, I wonder whether that was simply an artefact of my being unfamiliar with that particular Moodle course. I suspect that once accustomed to it, if I were a student on the course, my passages through it would be rather fixed. There were no 'holes and hatches' of the type described in my process of using the laptop, instead I felt I was in an enclosed space. In terms of *meshworking*, the lines felt straight, as opposed to the sinuous ones discussed by Ingold. My movements were directly from point-to-point, purposeful and rapid. I did not wander, linger or rove around, as I did not perceive there to be paths to follow or make, apart from those provided. The academic articles posted as PDF files felt rather like 'knots', or gathering points. They formed the basis of the subsequent forum discussions, would also be discussed in the face-to-face class, and would also be written about by students in their assignment. Perhaps those reading, thinking, talking activities around the PDF knots in the VLE could be seen as 'loosenings', with the written assignments being new 'knots'; tied by the students, only to be loosened once again by the lecturers in the marking and feedback process.

It has to be noted that this was only one VLE course, and that there are many features available in the Moodle software package that allow for other types of activity, other paths to be followed or even forged. It is also worth noting that VLE courses are designed to teach students particular points, and allow them to attain pre-specified and agreed learning outcomes. Therefore, as part of an accredited programme of study, they need to be focused, selective, structured and clear. However, the abiding impression was one of *navigation* along predetermined paths, in a 'walled garden', as the VLE has been called, as opposed to *wayfaring* down side-paths and dense thicket in the 'forest' of the open internet, or even the shelves of a traditional library. This raises the question of – when the garden is too well-tended – what can be lost or inaccessible behind the walls.

Quantum

In this brief chapter, I venture into a more abstract area of recent ideas in the field, and attempt to relate them to my central project of the book. I will explore the notion of *quantum literacy*, taken from work in new materialism by Vera Buhlmann, Felicity Colman and Iris van der Tuin, as a further potential theoretical 'diffraction', which may help us to deepen our understanding of how meaning is made in the digital university. I will conclude with an examination of the 'Open Educational Practices' movement, as a potential example of an arena of digital practice which may be viewed profitably using this perspective.

Literacies

Before looking at recent work which has sought to develop these ideas in relation to literacy, it is worth noting that the concept of *quantum literacy* appears to have been coined originally by Whitehead (2001) in a paper which uses quantum physics as a metaphor applied to English education. Whitehead focuses on the influence of the observer in the construction of meaning, suggesting:

> Teachers of English can draw parallels with this concept in several ways. First, teachers can see themselves as observers who influence the construction of meaning. They do this through their questions, and through their cultural status within educational institutions and society. Similarly, readers as observers are never neutral. Beyond decoding and literal comprehension, they are opinionated meaning-makers. By acknowledging the influence of the observer, teachers acknowledge that the construction of meaning is idiosyncratic, that multiple readings produce multiple meanings.
>
> Whitehead 2001: 522–523

Whitehead also draws on Heisenberg's Uncertainty Principle to illustrate the importance multiple perspectives on and interpretations of a text, proposing that:

The utility of this second concept for teachers of English is that discourse may exist in multiple meaning-states simultaneously. These meaning-states seem to be available individually, rather than severally. Like subatomic particles, they are in a state of meaningful superposition, until a reader or writer makes one meaning conscious.

Whitehead 2001: 524

He also relates interconnectedness in quantum physics to literacy education, citing the 'stickiness' connecting particles which are not connected locally. He draws the following implication for teachers:

It suggests, for example, that all the potential meanings in discourse are connected and interconnected within a wider context, which includes the author who constructed them and the reader who deconstructs them. Separating discourse from society, the types of thinking that give it meaning and from readers who give it meaning, is consistent with the quantum concept of interconnectedness.

Whitehead 2001: 524

This paper does not appear to have been picked up in contemporary work on the theme, but is a strikingly prescient early attempt to bring ideas from the world of quantum physics to literacy education, arguing for 'quantum-consistent' teaching. The notion of *quantum literacy* re-emerges with Buhlmann et al. (2017), who, in contrast, draw explicitly on new materialist theory and seeking to work with Karen Barad's ideas, and those of other scholars of new materialism. They also reference the move away from Newtonian to quantum physics, and how it generates a completely different view of reality, in which the observer or measuring instrument cannot be meaningfully separated from what it observes or measures. In a journal special issue entitled 'Introduction to new materialist genealogies: new materialisms, novel mentalities, quantum literacy', they define *quantum thinking* as follows:

Quantum thinking is thinking that is inevitably situated and always already physically active. It is an active taking-measure that will have made a difference ... As such, quantum thinking is doing that is a dealing with measurements, a doing that generates data – data that can never entirely be singled out from the data with which it interacts.

Buhlmann et al. 2017: 49–50

They go on to propose *quantum literacy* as:

...a kind of disparate, distributive, and population-based cognitive faculty that is capable of expressing and addressing conditions, and hence grounds and reasons, to support all sorts of processes in terms of quantum thinking ... no insight can ever give an exhaustive account of what can, in principle be sighted within the probabilistic possibility-spectra that provide reason and support within quantum thinking.

Buhlmann et al. 2017: 50

Buhlmann et al.'s piece is ambitious, and sweeping in its scope. They seek to develop *quantum literacy* as a method with which to understand the effects of digitization on society at large. Their provocation is thought-provoking, but is perhaps not as precisely expressed as it might be. However, the concept seems to hold some potential in terms of the focus of this book. The challenge of this, is that the concept of quantum literacy is expressed in a way which is, to me, thought-provoking, but difficult to grasp. Their definitions are somewhat abstract, and couched in fairly dense theoretical terms. Seeking to relate this concept to the topic of this book, digital knowledge practices in higher education, is not straightforward. I will attempt in this section to draw out what I interpret the main points being made.

One of Buhlmann et al.'s central points is that quantum thinking is materially situated – it takes place in the physical world, and cannot be abstracted. Secondly, she defines it as 'an active taking-measure that will have made a difference'. As such, she is saying that quantum thinking acts on the world, as opposed to existing in a binary, separate from the 'objects' of thought. She also calls it 'a doing that generates data, that can never entirely be singled out from the data with which it interacts' (Buhlmann et al. 2017: 49–50). The 'thinking', which I take here to include all forms of analysis, consideration, discussion, measurement or viewing – is constitutive, as opposed to merely contemplative. If 'data' is interpreted broadly, as I interpret it here, it might be understood more broadly as referring to elements of knowledge, what can be analysed, or studied. Buhlmann et al. refer to quantum physics, in particularly with experimentation in quantum mechanics in which the act of observation of subatomic particles has an interactive effect on the particles observed.

Their definition of quantum literacy refers to a 'disparate, distributive, and population-based cognitive faculty'. It appears that their use of the term literacy as a *faculty* is closer to the sense of 'know-how' or familiarity, than a use of the term which refers to reading and writing per se. This appears to be a move away from an emphasis on the individual as the locus of literacy, and towards the idea of a scattered, fluid, distributed set of epistemic practices. Another element of quantum literacy is that it can never result in an 'exhaustive account ... of what can be sighted'. Again, I interpret this as a statement that it is analogous to the phenomenon in quantum mechanics, in which a subatomic particle's location can be predicted in terms of probability along a spectrum of possible positions, as opposed to being pinpointed in one location. The act of observation has a constitutive effect on the location that is recorded. To express it in less esoteric terms, they appear to be stating that data or knowledge is contingent on what is traditionally referred to as 'context' and also how it is observed or apprehended. Moving this closer to educational terminology, we could say that quantum literacy is a form of engagement such as study, analysis, discussion with/about data, knowledge, ideas, content or objects of study. This engagement is beyond the individual, and that engagement is in a reflexive or co-constitutive relationship with what is to be analysed, learned or understood.

Identities

In the same special issue, Stark (2017), explores the concept of *quantum identities*, she sets out how she sees the relationship between quantum physics and bodies as follows:

> Quantum physics disrupts the stagnancies of typically humanly recognized bodies. In quantum understandings, particles (classically understood as stagnant objects) also have wavelike properties, diffract, leap, and are quantumly entangled. The recognition of constant exchange, nonlinear togetherness, occupying multiple locations, and leaping shifts linear understandings of timespace, singularity and causality (Barad 2010: 248), allowing for the intra-active dynamism made up of many atoms/waves/energies/forces/identities that gather/ are-made-intelligible/show-interference-patterns differently when with differing (measuring) apparatuses of 'obstacles'. Maintaining the integrity of their measured closeness (identifications), accountabilities to marking bodies (performances) and agencies (multiple material-spatialised intersections), while always already participating in multiple movements, space(times), bodies at 'once'.
>
> Stark 2017: 69–70

Here, Stark seems to be making similar points to those of Buhlmann et al., particularly about the nature of quantum particles – they are not static, and appear differently when measured by different apparatuses. Again, she seeks to draw an analogy from this, discussing its relevance to the nature of political activism. However, her account of the entanglements of the human and nonhuman are relevant to the focus of this chapter:

> We are either always already cyborgs because 'we' are already in relation, inco(o/r)oration with multiple other 'things' dependent with each other: utilizing technologies of thought, medical technologies, or cell phones; electrons exchange, particles generate/die, 'we' ingest and incorporate 'each other'; from the smallest to the largest we are constantly temporary planes of palimpsests living upon and falling through each other. Or nothing of us is cyborgs because we are always already never separate – legibilised separateness being part of the phenomenological apparatus measuring such.
>
> Stark 2017: 73

Stark draws a link between the nature of quantum mechanics, and the nature of human life and sociomaterial processes. She, like many thinkers in the field, makes the point that we are enmeshed with technologies, suggesting we cannot be meaningfully seen as separate from them. She sees human subjectivities as planes of palimpsests – an interesting metaphor to deploy. A palimpsest is defined as:

> A parchment or other writing material written upon twice, the original writing having been erased or rubbed out to make place for the second; a manuscript in which later writing is written over an effaced earlier writing.
>
> Oxford English Dictionary Online

The human, as conjured by Stark, is then a *writeable* surface which is constantly overwritten. This is a complex notion, I take it to echo Buhlmann et al.'s point that the subject and object cannot be separated, but are in dynamic interplay with one another. Stark goes on to discuss examples of feminists of colour activism which she suggests exhibited these features, such as intersubjectivity, and lack of hierarchy in the movement. She likens these to what Barad described as '... a performance of spacetime (re)configurings ... more akin to how electrons experience the world than any journey narrated through rhetorical forms that presume actors move along trajectories across a stage of spacetime' (Barad 2010: 240, in Stark 2017: 75). Taken together, my interest is in whether and how these somewhat abstract, even apparently tenuous constructs might be related to a practical example taken from digital higher education. In the next section I will make a tentative attempt, considering the case of OEPs in digital higher education. In this chapter, and also the final one, I have chosen not to use the 'interview' approach, but to simply discuss these digital epistemic practices in more speculative terms, in the light of the ideas covered in the first part of each chapter.

Open Educational Practices and Entanglements

In seeking to explore this notion of quantum literacy in relation the theme of this book, I was drawn to an area of practice related to contemporary digital higher education – OEPs. I suggest that this disparate set of practices may exhibit – in broad terms – features which may be well-served by a quantum literacy analysis, and I attempt to explore its nature in Buhlmann et al.'s terms, in order to speculate as to whether this concept can provide us with further critical theoretical purchase and insight, considering questions of agency, subjectivity and performativity.

OEPs have emerged as an influential field of innovation and research in higher education studies, and more broadly in informal and community education over recent years. Cronin and McLaren (2018) provide a recent overview of the theoretical and empirical literature of the area, pointing out the range of conceptualizations at work in the field. Drawing on Lane's (2009) definition of 'open education' as '... encompassing resources, tools and practices to improve educational access, effectiveness and equality worldwide' (in Cronin & McLaren 2018: 127), they review the history of the movement, which is characterized by an emphasis on providing access to educational opportunities for those excluded from mainstream formal adult education, as evinced by the UNESCO definition, '... teaching, learning and research materials in any medium, digital or otherwise, that reside in the public domain or have been released under an open license that permits no-cost access, use, adaptation and redistribution by others with no or limited restrictions' (UNESCO 2012). The emphasis here is primarily on materials and access. However, as Cronin and McLaren point out, there exist more expansive definitions, such as the (2007) Cape Town Open Education Declaration, which states that:

> ...open education is not limited to just open educational resources. It also draws upon open technologies that facilitate collaborative, flexible learning and the open sharing of teaching practices that empower educators to benefit from the best ideas of their colleagues. It may also grow to include new approaches to assessment, accreditation and collaborative learning.
> Shuttleworth Foundation and Open Society Foundations 2007

This definition is broader, and expresses several values which are core to OEPs, such as those of collaboration, flexibility, sharing and participant empowerment. Cronin and McLaren go on to provide a detailed a review of several projects and frameworks focused on OEPs – some of which also mount an explicit challenge to mainstream formal education, in particular the role of the teacher, and approaches which are characterized as 'teacher-centred', with a desire to '... flatten the traditional hierarchy and change the balance of power in learner/teacher relationships' (McGill et al. 2013: 10). They also point out the explicit emphasis on social connections over content in the discourse of the related area of 'networked participatory scholarship' (e.g. Veletsianos & Kimmons 2012). Cronin and McLaren also review work taking place in the Global South at the University of Cape Town (e.g. Czerniewicz 2013, Czerniewicz & Naidoo 2013), where the focus is also on acknowledging the culture-specific pedagogical and epistemological cultural assumptions which might underpin a resource.

I consider this area of practice to be a potentially suitable for a quantum literacy reading for several reasons. OEPs are characterized by, as the name suggests, openness, and therefore, by extension, less-defined in terms of actual and potential participants than the conventional setting allows for, and in this sense, seem to accord with Buhlmann et al.'s notion of the distributive. They are typically resources and platforms which are digitally mediated, and freely available on the internet with an emphasis on personalization, as opposed to being only available to enrolled students or staff as members of a formal institution, so in that sense they are less controlled, patrolled and predictable than university-governed platforms might be, as with Stark's notion of lack of hierarchy. A further feature of OEPs is a strong emphasis on interaction, collaboration and participant-generated meaning and resource, reflecting its roots in social constructivist theorizations about education and learning. Again, this seems to echo – albeit loosely – Buhlmann et al.'s notion of knowledge (data in their terms) as an emergent entity, which is not *a priori* to observation/study/analysis, but arises from it.

However, it might be argued that the dominance of social constructivism in this area of educational practice may also lead to limits on how we might understand it, and also how OEPs might be developed in meaningful and engaging ways. In a previous paper, I critiqued one of the foundational concepts of the OER movement, 'connectivism', for a lack of theoretical coherence, and for overstating its radical credentials by mischaracterizing the nature of mainstream higher education (Gourlay 2015a, also Gourlay & Oliver 2018). My contentions included the point that – in some quarters – the OEP movement has been overly reliant on a fairly roughly-drawn and value-laden binary, which has sought to position mainstream formal higher education as inherently repressive, damagingly hierarchical, and limiting to the student or participant. Claims surrounding the 'transformative' potential of engagement with OEPs have been somewhat overblown, and I would argue that this is precisely as a result of a somewhat uncritical adherence to the assumptions of social constructivism as applied to education more generally, and also due to the limitations of that frame. Interaction and social connection are – I would contend – elevated to such a degree that the inherent value comes to be placed in interaction *in and of itself*, and this 'connectivism' may come to stand for learning, as opposed to being promoted as a means by which to learn. As such, I would argue that the theoretical base remains somewhat taken for granted and under-examined. Ironically for a movement focused on social justice and inclusion, this could (if applied in un-nuanced form) lead to new operations of normativity, in terms of what is valued in participant engagement. It might be argued that proactive production of text and other forms of contributions online, for example in a discussion format (like the production of prodigious speech in a face-to-face context), is itself culturally specific, and an approach based on this as a marker of engagement may in fact serve to favour already-privileged confident and forthcoming participants, encouraging a performativity of engagement through observable means, and could reinforcing privilege. Similarly, the attribution of the term quantum literacy may also carry with it a series of assumptions which are not value-neutral when transposed into an educational setting which is already heavily weighted with ideologies surrounding how students or participants should behave.

Educational 'content' is at times discussed in disapprovingly as retrograde in discourses of OEPs, particularly if supplied by a teacher, whose role tends to be presented as a problem to be solved, ideally via displacement. I have argued (Gourlay 2017) and in earlier chapters, drawing on the work of Gert Biesta and his concept of 'learnification', that although 'learner-centred' approaches may indeed be highly effective when used judiciously for a clear educational purpose, a strong version of this position as an exclusive methodology can lead to a less than helpful anti-intellectual stance, which may limit the applicability of the model – as the participants may not be in a position to generate adequate meaning without expert input and facts. The role of foundational and published texts becomes problematic if they are deemed to be agents of an undesirable hierarchy, generating a restrictive view of what constitutes an acceptable literacy practice. A further criticism could be made that the online nature of most OEPs, coupled with the tenets of social constructivism, may lead to a somewhat disembodied vision of the 'ideal participant', imagined to be engaging unproblematically in some kind of putative 'frictionless' online world, all the while untroubled by the complexities of social and material settings in which the practices emerge – although recent work in the Global South is mounting a strong challenge to this standpoint (e.g. Czerniewicz 2013). Cronin and McLaren's review reveals that – in practice – in addition to successes, a range of barriers have been experienced by practitioners seeking to implement OEPs. There are inevitably challenges to be faced in any educational innovation, but I would suggest that part of the challenge could reside the underlying theoretical model of social constructivism itself.

Returning to Buhlmann et al.'s definition quoted above, the features that they highlight in *quantum thinking* (to be investigated using *quantum literacy*) are that it is 'situated', 'already physically active', that it 'makes a difference', and that it generates data 'that can never entirely be singled out from the data with which is interacts' (Buhlmann et al. 2017: 49–50). First, it seems helpful to emphasize that engagement with OEPs is 'inevitably situated', as already insightfully acknowledged in the context of the Cape Town work and other scholars in the field. This may seem to be an obvious, or even facile point, but I would argue that a lack of focus on the particular and the nitty-gritty of *place* in all its senses, may have led in some part to unrealistic expectations in terms of participation in OEPs (as with other forms of digitally-mediated education). If the dominant notion of the participant is somewhat idealized, abstract, and also underpinned by a strong valorization of a particular type of 'active' engagement, then the actual participants in all their diversity of approaches to engagement may be lost from view, or their participation may not be recognized or valued. As such, the observation that quantum literacy must be 'already physically active' seems to add a helpful material dimension to the analysis. In mainstream conceptions, the sociomaterially situated nature of OEP participation and digital engagement more generally may be unseen, and therefore elided, along with the messy material entanglements with devices, time, space, mobilities, and the minutiae and demands of daily life around the screen. This aspect allows us to recognize the entanglements of human and nonhuman actors involved in this, as with all educational practices – grounding it in materiality and therefore moving away from the realm of digital 'magic'. Buhlmann et al.'s point that quantum literacy '... makes a difference' expresses that quantum literacy practices do not simply represent knowledge, but *intra-act* with it and through that intra-action, change it. This focus on making a difference through a circuit-like emergence of knowledge and meaning-making in human and nonhuman assemblages, seems a particularly apt way in which to characterize the distributed and emergent potential of OEPs. Their final point that quantum literacy generates data '... that can never entirely be singled out from the data with which is interacts' (Buhlmann et al. 2017: 50) also seems to capture the entangled nature of OEPs and the meanings and texts that emerge from it, where the borders between the meaning-making subject, the text and meaning itself are blurred, or perhaps non-existent.

In this regard, I would propose that quantum literacy might provide a useful alternative refractive theoretical lens on engagement with OEPs, as it seems to recognize some of its central features as a movement, while also demanding that more attention is paid to the particular, the situated and the material, which may help to avoid an overly-abstract or ideologically-driven vision of the participant as subject. It is important however, to bear in mind that this chapter is based on a brief definition of a much more complex and far-reaching philosophical concept of 'quantum writing' developed by Buhlmann in relation to the work for the philosopher Michel Serres (e.g. Buhlmann 2015), and as such, I fully acknowledge that I may have used it in a somewhat more prosaic and applied manner than intended by the author(s). However, caveats aside, it is interesting to speculate as to whether, and to what extent, the reading I have presented here of Buhlmann et al.'s concept of quantum literacy might inform digitally-mediated higher education more broadly. It provides a lens which allows for a sociomaterial perspective to be foregrounded, and which recognizes both the intra-agential nature of literacy and the entanglement with the nonhuman, while decentring the human individual as the primary site and focus of literacy practices. As I have suggested, it provides a potential counterpoint to the assumptions of social constructivism, which arguably dominate higher education, and in that regard, could be used to interrogate other forms of digitally-mediated literacy practices in higher education.

Document

Throughout this book, I have explored a range of relationships, entanglements, enmeshments and engagements with texts in digital higher education. I have looked at how texts emerge, move and act, and have considered how students and texts intra-act and co-emerge across a range of knowledge practices, both in 'face-to-face' and digital settings. In this chapter, I consider another proposed form of 'literacy' arising from a new materialist perspective, drawing on recent work in library and information science. This focuses on the nature of information and the document, exploring Kosciejew's compelling examination of the nature of documentation. I then move on to look at the case of learning analytics in higher education – as with the previous chapter, this is less of an 'interview' of a specific instantiation, and more of a discussion in broader terms. I look at critical work on learning analytics, particularly a sustained enquiry by Prinsloo on the nature of algorithmic decision-making, and the related concept of the *algocracy*. I conclude with the proposition that these processes of multi-dimensional surveillance, discipline and control lead to the creation of the student as document. I conclude the chapter with some thoughts on the implications of this for digital higher education more broadly.

Material-documentary Literacy

Writing from a new materialist perspective in library and information science, Kosciejew (2017) proposes the concept of *material-documentary literacy*, reminding us that one of the main functions of documentation is to materialize information. Following Coole and Frost (2010), he points out that 'information' is commonly regarded as being an abstract, dematerialized entity, and there is a distancing from its materiality. He provides an example:

> Much of the library and information science (LIS) literature tends to present information as different from its matter and to valorize it as superior to, or

at least more important and worthy of analysis and reflection than, its documentation – that is, its actual materiality and the inertia of its physical stuff.

Kosciejew 2017: 96

Kosciejew sets out to foreground the materiality of documentation, in order to '... help (re)configure our understanding of' information, as something not immaterial and intangible, but something material and tangible' (Kosciejew 2017: 97). He refers to Lehmann's (2016) notion of *material literacy*, where she sets out that '... art history is a field with a high degree of knowledge about materials, their characteristics, meanings, histories, agencies and effects.' He draws a connection between Lehmann's claims about materiality in art, to documents and practices related to them. He points out the role of documentation science in '... examining the materiality of documentation and the practices, processes and assemblages involved in the materialization of information.' (Kosciejew 2017: 98). In a manner similar to that described by scholars of *text trajectories* and the agentive nature of texts discussed in chapter 6, Kosciejew also focuses on how documentation science '... can illuminate bureaucratic tentacles that actually do, in a material sense, reach into and control ordinary lives, helping to ensure the effective functioning of governance and governmentality and to manage embodied subjectivities.' (Kosciejew 2017: 98). He emphasizes the centrality and ubiquity of documents to contemporary life, also suggesting that their very ubiquity and apparent banality causes us to be inured to them. He quotes Levy, who states that:

> ... here, right under our noses, too close and intimate to be seen clearly, are creatures that share with use the ability to speak. And we have created them. Some of them – books in particular – aspire to nobility and long life. Others, such as cash register receipts and personal notes, typically have a less exalted status and a shorter useful timeframe.

Levy 2001: 2

Levy also addresses the question of what makes a document different from another type of material artefact, categorizing documents as *representational artefacts*. Kosciejew points out that documents do not merely record, they are *constitutive*, again a point echoing those made by Kell (2006, 2015). For him, 'A document does more than reconstitute. It constitutes different things, such as ideas or entities and materializes them in order that they can be analysed, classified, placed, routinized, viewed, and used.' (Kosciejew 2017: 101). He cites Breit's (1951) example of the antelope as document. Breit asks us – in a compelling manner – to consider the case of an antelope which is captured in Africa, brought to Europe, put in a zoo and examined by experts, and also members of the public. She argues that the zoo in this case is effectively a laboratory in which the antelope is analysed, displayed and discussed like a document. As Kosciejew puts it, 'On its own, the antelope is just an antelope; however, when these material assemblages and components surround it, it becomes a document.' (Kosciejew 2017: 101). Breit refers to it as a 'catalogued antelope' (Breit 1951: 11), from which a series of secondary documents are derived. As Kosciejew puts it:

> Like the antelope in the zoo, each representation requires an assemblage of material things in order to stabilize and emerge; additionally, documentation helps constitute the animal for different institutions and their audiences. The more the antelope is documented, the more it becomes entrenched as something informative and factual.
>
> Kosciejew 2017: 102

He also reviews Buckland's (1997) framework of what constitutes a document, expanding the definition beyond printed texts, to take in other 'signifying objects' such as photos, art, film and audiovisual recordings – a point already well-rehearsed in the literature of multimodality (e.g. Kress & van Leeuwen 1996). Buckland proposes a framework for the definition of a document. The first element is materiality, for him the document must be a physical object. Kosciejew includes in this Frohmann's (2004) point that materiality is more than merely the object itself, but also includes '. . . institutions in which a document is designed, produced, and deployed; infrastructures in which it operates; actors who interact with and use it; and various kinds of relationships and practices it facilitates, obligates, or prohibits.' (Kosciejew 2017: 102). His next element is intentionality, in the sense that a document is an object which is intended to be read as evidence. For Kosciejew, this document must also materialize evidence and be part of institutional practice and routine, in order to be interpreted as standing as proof of something. Buckland's third qualifying component for a document is that it must be in some way processed, *made into* a document. As Kosciejew puts it:

> Processing is only one of many different and significant documentary practices necessary for the materialization of information; other documentary practices include deploying, reading, examining, analyzing, inscribing, circulating, and so on. A document, on its own, does not constitute information; practices with the document help facilitate this construction.
>
> Kosciejew 2017: 103

Buckland's fourth element relates to the object's phenomenological status, in that it must be perceived to be a document, and may be a document in one context, but not another (rather like Breit's antelope). Kosciejew also discusses Lund's (2007) framework for understanding documentation, the first element of which refers to the range of possible documentary forms. The second is document versus documentation; for Lund, a document is a specific instantiation of a form of documentation, such as a single particular book. Thirdly, Lund proposes the *doceme*, which forms part of a document, such as a photo in a book or a video on a blog. If the doceme is taken out of the document, '... it could change the document's properties and alter the document's contingencies and effects.' (Kosciejew 2017: 103). Kosciejew goes on to propose that in the field of library and information science, documentation has been neglected, and information has been regarded as more important. This has led, he argues, to a conceptualization of information as either immaterial, or at least separate from its material instantiation. He refers to Orom (2007), who argues that this shift towards information is a result of increased interest in digital technologies, and also the increased prominence of the concept of information processing in cognitive science. Orom argues that this emphasis has spread across society more broadly, including into the academic disciplines. He quotes Hjorland, contending that we should shift 'the object of study from mental phenomena of ideas, facts and opinion, to social phenomena of communication, documents and memory institutions.' (Orom 2007: 58, in Kosciejew 2017: 105), in particular the study of *informative material objects*. Referring again to Lehmann, he draws a parallel between history of art and library and information science, in that both have tended to occlude the importance of matter to practice.

In library and information science, several assumptions have been made about the nature of information, as elaborated by Frohmann. This first he identifies is the assumption of uniformity and universality, the idea that information is 'the same stuff' (Frohmann 2007: 7) regardless of the medium used to carry it or its content. Frohmann points out that information is in fact contextually contingent, 'Unlike information, however, documents are multiple, coming in many forms and materials, with various institutional, historical and cultural practices and properties.' (Frohmann 2007: 28, in Kosciejew 2017: 108). The second issue identified by Frohmann is the assumption of immateriality, discussed above. It is seen, he argues, as existing somehow elsewhere, 'indifferent to its vehicles' (Kosciejew 2017: 108). Again, he points out that information is in fact always embedded in particular contexts, and that documents are always materially instantiated. Thirdly, he raises the issue of assumptions around agency. Information practices are assumed to emanate from individual subject's consciousness, discounting the influence of nonhuman and separate autonomous agency. Frohmann concludes by drawing on Foucault's concept of 'power of writing' to better understand the process by which documents become 'things' which are autonomous and constitutive. In particular, he looks at how Foucault sees the power of writing as a documentary practice is used '... for the constitution of the individual as an analyzable case' (Kosciejew 2017: 109):

> These apparatuses and institutions depend upon a 'network of writing' in which masses of documents, coupled with systems of registration and documentary accumulation, help to record, classify, categorise, standardize, observe, and analyze individuals ... thus individuals are transformed into documents.
>
> Kosciejew 2017: 109–110

This final point – that the human can be rendered into a document – seems to have particular resonance for the project of this book, in various ways. The next section will discuss learning analytics, a controversial digital practice increasingly used in contemporary universities.

Learning Analytics and the *Algocracy*

Learning analytics is described as follows in the executive summary of a review document produced by the UK government agency JISC:

> Every time a student interacts with their university – be that going to the library, logging into their virtual learning environment or submitting assessments online – they leave behind a digital footprint. Learning analytics is the process of using this data to improve learning and teaching. Learning analytics refers to the measurement, collection, analysis and reporting of data about the progress of learners and the contexts in which learning takes place. Using the increasing availability of big datasets round learner activity and digital footprints left by student activity in learning environments, learning analytics takes us further than data currently available can.
>
> Sclater, Peasgood & Mullan 2016: 4

What is immediately of interest in this introduction is the mention of the 'digital footprint', which recalls the earlier discussion of wayfaring and pathways. However, in this case, the emphasis is on the documenting of the footprint, and the corralling of the student's steps, in contrast with Ingold's organic *wayfaring*. The document makes a case for the expansion of the use of learning analytics in UK universities, suggesting four main uses. The first of these to be listed is as follows, reproducing the bolded text:

As a tool for quality assurance and quality improvement – with many teaching staff using data to improve their own practice, and many institutions proactively using learning analytics as a diagnostic tool on both an individual level (e.g. identifying issues) and a systemic level (e.g. informing the design of modules and degree programmes).

Sclater et al. 2016: 5

It is worth focusing on the expression 'many institutions proactively using learning analytics' to analyse individuals, as well as at a systemic level. Taken as a form of surveillance rather than analysis, the word 'proactively' may be read as somewhat sinister. They go on to specify exactly how this quality assurance function can be achieved in the UK context of the 'Teaching Excellence Framework' (TEF), a state-run audit of teaching 'quality' in higher education. I have reproduced this in full, in order to analyse it in detail as the lead statement of rationale for the use of this form of digital surveillance of students:

In our response to the Higher Education Green Paper, we outlined how learning analytics could contribute to the Teaching Excellence Framework. In the first instance, we expect that learning analytics data could be used by institutions as part of their submission of evidence to support applications for the higher levels of TEF. In the medium term, we will explore with the sector whether learning analytics might be used to create appropriate new metrics. Similarly, we envisage learning analytics data will also be useful for institutions in demonstrating compliance with the new quality assurance arrangements being developed in England, which will require more regular review of outcomes and evidence of action taken by institutions to deal with issues.

Sclater et al. 2016: 5

What is striking is that the document opens with a justification for using learning analytics as motivated by the requirements of a state-run audit of teaching in the university sector. It also suggests that learning analytics might be used to inform future iterations of this audit exercise, incorporating – one assumes – a requirement that learning analytics data be included as a requirement in the future. The placement of this audit-driven element of the rationale in advance of any educational justification seems significant.

The authors then move on to present justifications that are claimed to offer potential benefits for students, referring to learning analytics as a 'tool' throughout. The second point is that it can be used 'As a tool for boosting retention rates' proposing that learning analytics may allow institutions to identify students 'at risk' of dropping out of university. It is then proposed 'As a tool or assessing and acting upon differential outcomes among the student population'. This focuses on the ability of learning analytics to 'monitor and assess the progress of sub-groups of students' who may be 'underperforming', the example given is BME (Black and Minority Ethnic) students. Fourthly, it is proposed 'As an enabler for the development and introduction of adaptive learning'. This is defined as '. . . personalized learning delivered at scale, whereby students are directed to learning materials on the basis of their previous interactions with, and understanding of, related content and tasks' (Sclater et al. 2016: 5). The use of the expression 'personalized learning delivered at scale' is noteworthy here. Learning is cast as an *a priori* 'thing', a product to be 'delivered'. The student is implicitly cast (once again) as both a customer, and also a recipient of a 'delivery'. The university is placed in the role of provider, arguably not even of a service, but of a product. The language used is clearly that of the market. What is also of interest, is that what will be delivered is 'personalized learning'. Again, the word 'personalized' is normally associated with the tailoring of a product to an individual's needs. This raises the question as to what the academic curriculum consists of, if it is to be 'personalized' to the needs or preferences of the student/customer. Finally, the phrase 'at scale' is worthy of attention. This presumably refers to the ability of learning analytics to be available to large numbers of students. The implicit comparisons seem to be that 'personalized learning' might have taken place through interaction with a teacher in a one-to-one or small group encounter, but the technology offers the opportunity to avoid this requirement. Academic staff and teaching are not mentioned, and again the impression is given that they are being treated as either dispensable, or problematic, in the context of an industrialized, large scale 'delivery' operation. Instead, it is stated that 'students are directed to learning materials on the basis of their previous interactions with, and understanding of, related content and tasks.' This begs the question one again of what the curriculum or required standards of learning are required in order to pass the assessment.

The report goes on to summarize cases internationally, where learning analytics has been claimed to have been used successfully to identify students who are seen to be struggling, using the use of the VLE as proxy for student engagement. There is some evidence presented (alongside unsubstantiated claims) that learning analytics had been effective, particularly in relation to low-performing or 'at risk' students. However, what is not discussed is how the pedagogic relationship between the teacher and student, where problems may have previously been identified and addressed by the teacher, has effectively been 'contracted out' to the technology, in response to massification of the system. It also shifts the locus of student engagement fully, or in large part, over to the digital setting of the VLE, requiring intensive engagement in that as a primary, or sole, marker of student engagement in general. Although this type of analysis may indeed have utility in identifying students who have disengaged, it would also render a student who chooses to work offline as deviant, or in need of remediation. As with the required face-to-face interlocution required in the classroom under the ideology of learnification, the use of learning analytics risks reproducing the same effect online, even more strongly, for example by making displays of interaction in VLE discussion boards a formal requirement.

Jandric et al. (2017), in their introduction to a journal special issue on 'learning in the age of algorithmic cultures', state that in education studies '... algorithmic cultures signal a shift away from the centrality of individual or social concerns and toward the complex relations between the human and nonhuman agencies that proliferate our digitally networked activities.' (Jandric et al. 2017: 101). Williamson (2017) provides an analysis of Lytics lab, a Stanford University facility which is focused on research and development in learning analytics, and also the Centre for Digital Data, Analytics and Adaptive Learning, owned by the commercial publisher Pearson. His focus is on ownership of the algorithmic techniques used to analyse big data, and in his analysis, he argues that these centres in particular have become 'methodological gatekeepers' in the field. Lytics lab is an academic research and development facility, while the Pearson centre is part of an a commercial 'edu-business'. Williamson argues that education data science has become a 'trans-sector enterprise', with ownership and power moving over to commercial vendors. He identifies a 'sociotechnical imaginary' (Jasanoff 2015), and defines these imaginaries as '... socially shared visions of technologically mediated progress, that have moved from single inspired individuals to much wider communities and fields of action.' (Williamson 2017: 107). He argues that educational data science is driven by such an imaginary regarding the future of educational research, leading to claims of a 'paradigm shift' towards a position which assumes '... the inherent truthfulness and unbiased, impartial agnosticism of numbers' (2017: 109). This goes hand-in-hand, he argues, with a disavowal of any need for educational theory, as the data are seen as able to 'speak for themselves'.

In the same special issue, Prinsloo (2017) also looks at this sociotechnical imaginary, framing his critique explicitly in terms of student surveillance. Prinsloo refers to Latour (2012), who proposes that, in relation to the design and development of technologies, '... unintended consequences are part and parcel of any action.' (Latour 2012: 25, in Prinsloo 2017: 139). Prinsloo explores our relationship to algorithms, comparing it to that on Frankenstein to the monster he created, following Latour 2012. He also references the 'claustrophobic maze' (Prinsloo 2017: 139) of Kafka's 'Trial' (1925), in which the protagonist finds himself trapped in a world with no way out, comparing this to a bureaucratic organization in possession of a large body of information about those within its ambit, such as a university using learning analytics. He refers to the concept of *algocracy*, coined by Aneesh (2006, 2009), in which '... code appears to have ... taken over the managerial function of supervision and guidance' (Aneesh 2009: 355). He also quotes Dahaner, who defines algocracy as '... an unorthodox term for an increasingly familiar phenomenon: the use of big data, predictive analytics, machine learning, AI, robotics (etc.) in governance-related systems' (Dahaner 2016). Prinsloo explores in his paper the conditions in which algorithmic decision-making may collapse into *algocracy*.

In educational settings, algorithms underpin learning analytics, as he reminds us. He quotes Williamson et al. (2014), who warn that:

> ... [the] algorithms that enable learning analytics appear to be 'theory-free' but are loaded with political and epistemological assumptions. The data visualisations produced by learning analytics – data dashboards as they are frequently described – also act semiotically to create meanings.
>
> Williamson et al. 2014

Prinsloo points out the prevalence of referring to algorithms in terms of human knowing and intentionality, by way of anthropomorphic metaphors such as 'knowing' or 'acting' (Dyjkstra 1985), and discussing them as if they had emotions (Gross 2017). Turning to education, he reminds us that algorithms should not be regarded as neutral technical entities, but are themselves both normative and political. As Kitchen puts it '... epistemological units, made to have a representational form that enables epistemological work' (Kitchen 2014: 19). He describes how human agency is encoded into them (Introna 2011), and how that encoding '... becomes part of organizational architecture and shapes/ informs/enacts decision-making that in turn shapes and informs human lives' (Prinsloo 2017: 143), in particular the power of algorithms to prioritize what is to be regarded as important, and what should be visible (Beer 2017a). He quotes Beer, who states:

> Algorithms 'govern' because they have the power to structure possibilities. They define which information is to be included in an analysis; they envision, plan for, and execute data transformations; they deliver results with a kind of detachment, objectivity and certainty; they act as filters and mirrors, selecting and reflecting

information that makes sense within an algorithm's computational logic and the human cultures that created that logic.

Beer 2017b: 97–98

Prinsloo sets out how increased digitization has combined with the proliferation of regimes of audit and quality, to lead to greater use of algorithmic decision-making in higher education. Learning analytics was introduced specifically to collect and analyse data on student engagement, particularly online, with the espoused intention to enhance teaching and learning in schools and universities. As Prinsloo states in an earlier publication, learning analytics is '... a *structuring* device. It is not neutral. It is informed by current beliefs about what counts as knowledge and learning, coloured by assumptions about gender/race/class/ capital/literacy and in service of and perpetuating existing or new power relations' (Prinsloo 2015, in Prinsloo 2017: 145). Prinsloo goes on to look in detail at two proposals relating to learning analytics, Dahaner's (2015) experimental framework, and an unpublished conference paper by Knox (2010). I will focus on Prinsloo's discussion of the latter, as it has greater salience to the subject of this book.

Knox identifies a typology based on what he sees as three types of surveillance of student learning; *panoptic, rhizomatic* and *predictive*. Panoptic surveillance involves elements of visibility and automation as a means by which to exercise discipline and control of student behaviour. Prinsloo does not provide an example from Knox, but describes the emphasis of this type of surveillance as being '... on automated, algorithmic decision-making processes to collect, analyse, and increasingly enact these analyses' (Prinsloo 2017: 149). In Knox's definition, panoptic surveillance '... reinforces and amplifies existing power structures by concealing control agents while exposing the observed' (Knox 2010: 4, in Prinsloo 2017: 149). Rhizomatic surveillance for Knox is based on the concept of the *synopticon*, (many watching the few), the *panopticon* (few watching the many), and *sousveillance* (many watching each other). These forms of surveillance are proposed by Knox as forming what he insightfully calls a 'surveillant assemblage' (Knox 2010: 9, in Prinsloo 2017: 149), and are regarded by Knox as both multidirectional, and also interacting. Thirdly, Knox identifies predictive surveillance, which is concerned with temporality, sorting and structuring. This mechanism leads to '... students' past experiences and performance (in and outside of education) determining their access to education, learning trajectories and the scope and intensity of the support they "deserve"' (Prinsloo 2017: 149). On the basis of these three frames, Knox proposes a typology of seven dimensions; 1) automation, 2) visibility, 3) directionality, 4) assemblage, 5) temporality, 6) sorting, and 7) structuring.

Prinsloo goes on to raise concerns also expressed by other critical commentators in the field, surrounding transparency and ethics with relation to this type of surveillance, in particularly these systems' lack of accountability (e.g. Dourish 2016, Diakapolous 2015). He concludes with four 'pointers', which he proposes as potential approaches to the complex challenges raised by learning analytics. The first proposal is that students should be informed about the surveillance systems they are subject to, should give their consent, and be invited to get involved in the decisions surrounding how algorithms affect their learning. He also advocates for critical engagement, surrounding questions of who or what stands to benefit from algorithmic decision-making. However, he also expresses the view that there is a need for education to collect information about students, in order to offer them appropriate learning opportunities. Finally, he issues a call for higher education institutions to ensure that ethical practices are adhered to and remain accountable. In his 'epilogue', he states:

> We have no choice. Amid the dangers and uncertainties regarding the unfolding of algorithmic decision-making and algocratic systems we cannot and should not recoil in horror as flee out creation. Our creatures, like Dr Frankenstein's monster, will follow us and demand an audience. Like Dr Frankenstein we have to face our creations even if this means Kafkaesque engagement where there is no clear exit or resolution to the tensions.
>
> Prinsloo 2017: 157

I would take issue with one aspect of the conclusion, by questioning the agency and responsibility attributed here. Are these 'our' creatures, and if so who is being conjured by 'we'? I feel the need to resist Prinsloo's 'discourse of inevitability' here, and feel it is still incumbent on critical scholars in the field to resist the fundamentals of this practice. These papers clearly highlight the problematic ethical and political nature of learning analytics. It is beyond the scope of this chapter to provide a full review of the copious further literature on the use of learning analytics, or to discuss its efficacy in terms of the claims made for it. Instead, what is of relevance here is the process by which learner analytics operates, and in particular – I suggest – how it both documents the student, and also renders the *student as document* in Kosciejew's terms.

The Student as Document

Throughout the foregoing chapters, I have critiqued some of the mainstream ideas about how students should perform in contemporary higher education, both in their embodied classroom practices but also their textual practices online. I have suggested that humanistic assumptions, alongside simplistic over-interpretations of social constructivism, have led to unhelpful implicit or explicit educational ideologies such as learnification and connectivism. What connects all of these critiques – I propose – is the thread of students being under surveillance and subject to ideological and normative force, and expected to exhibit certain types of behaviour and engagement in support of these ideologies. I have argued throughout that it is not sufficient for this behaviour to take place, in must also be observable, and ideally recordable. In addition to the approved 'teaching and learning' behaviours discussed in previous chapters, there are a range of other surveillance practices which have become prevalent in contemporary higher education, as Macfarlane (2017) points out. Returning to Kosciejew's analysis discussed above, it could be argued that the students themselves are datified through the processes of learning analytics and the *algocracy*. However, I would suggest, that this is not merely a process of documentation, with all the ethical complexities discussed by Prinsloo and others. I contend that its effect is more far-reaching, serious and fundamental – in that learning analytics, in my view, alters the very ontological status of the student, who is rendered – who unwittingly becomes – a digital document. The student's ontological status, her being, is in a sense contaminated, by this intervention, and she can no longer exist outside of the baroque entanglements of digital surveillance, rather like Breit's antelope in the zoo.

9

Conclusions, or, So What?

This book began by setting out that the perspectives of posthumanism could offer us fresh insights into how students and scholars read, write, communicate and gain knowledge in 'the digital university'. This perspective challenges the dominance of the individual human subject as the main source of action and agency, displacing or decentring the human. In doing so, other nonhuman actors are brought into view, and their contribution is more clearly recognized. The book has focused specifically on the effects of this perspective on how we understand knowledge practices in the university, in interaction with digital platforms and devices. I have argued that this area of academic practice has not received sufficiently detailed attention in the educational literature, leading to a predominant set of assumptions about how education 'happens'. These assumptions include, as I argued at the outset, an emphasis on the human subject as somehow 'freefloating' and endlessly agentive, in neutral 'contexts', and commanding a series of obliging digital 'tools'.

I have proposed, as other scholars have done, that this view of educational practices is inaccurate, and leads to a series of distortions which have far-reaching effects in terms of policy and practice, and indeed research itself. One of these is the contemporary preoccupation with 'active learning', and in particular observable interaction, which – I suggest – is a product of a strongly humanist conception of a decoupled, individual human agency. This emphasis has arisen from a laudable desire to empower students, and move away from what has been regarded as an overly hierarchical and 'teacher-centred' system. I do not seek to disparage the move to a more varied and interactive range of approaches to higher education in face-to-face and digital settings. However, my argument throughout the book is that 'active learning', and social constructivism, have become dominant to the point that interaction and activity have become ends in themselves, leading to an anti-teacher, anti-expertise stance. This position, as I have proposed, may appear to support the interests of students, and may be combined with apparently 'radical' or 'revolutionary' claims about the 'transformation' of higher education. Concurrently, a series of discourses surrounding digital technology in education have arisen which mirror this perspective. The digital has been portrayed as a means by which to be 'freed' from the constraints of the body, the material, and the temporal world. As I have argued, this encourages a somewhat utopian set of ideas, or even fantasies, to arise. Notions of 'transformation' are often evoked in claims about the effects of the digital on higher education practices and students. A predominantly humanist and constructivist ethos, when combined with these fantasies of the digital, seems to be intensified further. I have argued that this serves to reinscribe the notion of the autonomous, all-powerful, human subject who is somehow detached, or 'freed', from the sociomaterial world. This superficially seductive notion, I propose, is in fact underpinned by a deeply conservative, and normative neoliberal notion of an ideal human subject. This fantasy of the student or graduate is encouraged to be 'self-regulating', is autonomous, and self-reliant, and has mastery over their 'tools' and 'contexts'. I would suggest that this figure, while appearing to represent a radical break from the past, is none other than the post-enlightenment conception of 'man' at the centre of his universe. I use the male forms intentionally, as I would contend that this perspective conjures a fantasy 'human' who is implicitly assumed to be white, male, heterosexual, abled-bodied, and possessed of socioeconomic privilege. I would suggest that this reverberates with the patriarchal fantasies of transhumanism, with its focus on transcending the 'limits' of the body and materiality.

The project of this book has been to subject these assumptions to scrutiny, using a range of theoretical perspectives from several disciplines. In an attempt to sociomaterially 'resituate' digital knowledge practices in higher education, I looked at a series of digital technologies in turn, deploying Adams and Thompson's generative approach of 'interviewing objects' (2016).

In chapter 2 'Matter', I reviewed the contribution that new literacy studies have made to the process of situating knowledge practices, and argued that this could be helpfully augmented with a sociomaterial sensibility, which would allow us to 'surface' and see more clearly the complex nature of digital literacy practices, and their intertwined and entangled relationship with the material and the body. I explored this with a reflection on my use of my laptop, concluding that a fine-grained analysis of this practice revealed a close tangle of the digital, the material and the body which did not support the notion of the radically autonomous and straightforwardly agentive human subject, freed from the bounds of the physical. Instead, my account uncovered a complex mesh of actors at work, in a constantly emergent assemblage which seems to me to be the essence of posthuman.

In chapter 3 'Body', I turned my attention to how students are portrayed in mainstream educational discourses, looking in detail at the ideology of 'active learning'. I argued that this leads to a pedagogy of performativity, a collapse into pure process, and an over-simplistically negative stance towards teaching, educational content and expertise. Using the concept of 'learnification' introduced by Biesta in schooling, I proposed that this tendency is also evident in the higher education sector. Once again, I argued, the centring of the human serves to elide the actual texture and detail of how practice unfolds. I analyse an example of a MOOC in order to explore how this set of digital knowledge practices position the teacher, student, content and knowledge itself.

Chapter 4 'Presence' looked at the lecture, a practice which has become something of a 'lightning rod' in educational circles, frequently being attacked as obsolete and overly 'teacher-centred'. The discourse of 'the lecture is dead' has been intensified with the advent of digital technologies in higher education, alongside claims that there is no need for a face-to-face event on campus, now technologies can replace it and improve upon it. Drawing on Friesen's historical analysis of the history of the lecture, I moved on to focus on concepts of presence and absence, with reference to the work of Goffman and his notion of lecturer 'selves'. I proposed that the essence of a lecture consists of two elements, ephemerality and co-presence. I moved to 'interview' another digital practice which has been proposed as a candidate to replace the traditional lecture, the 'flipped classroom'. I argue that this approach regards the teacher and also educational content and disciplinary knowledge as problems to be solved, by removal or sidelining. This, ironically, leads us back to the medieval notion of the lecturer as conduit for a fixed body of knowledge, which is 'delivered'.

Chapter 5 'Interfaces' changed the focus to look at artefacts and objects associated with knowledge practices, in particular reading and writing. Again, drawing on Friesen's historical analysis, I critique the notion of artefacts of inscription and digital devices as 'tools', instead again arguing for an understanding of these as active and agentive participants in practice. I focus on the VLE.

Chapter 6 'Wayfaring' moves the focus back to texts, looking in particular at how texts move in various ways. I draw on the linguistic ethnography literature and theory on 'text trajectories' to explore how texts interact and act on human subjects and the world they are in. I then sought to connect these ideas with the work of the social anthropologist Tim Ingold, looking at his notion of 'wayfaring' in particular. This concept of the journey 'making itself' as an emergent entity in interaction with the path, as opposed to being pre-mapped and pre-specified, can be of utility when seeking to deepen our understanding of knowledge practices. I connected this motion of Katherine Hayles' notion of hyperreading, to suggest the construct of hyperwriting, to describe the practices of reading and writing online.

In chapter 7 'Quantum', I considered the broader concept of *quantum literacies* as proposed by Buhlmann, Colman and van der Tuin (2017). I went on to discuss its potential relevance to the area of OEPs, concluding that it may provide some valuable theoretical purchase on this complex and disparate collection of digital epistemic practices.

Finally, in chapter 8 'Document' I refer to pertinent work in library and information science on the nature of information, documentation and the document itself, in which Kosciejew made an important distinctions regarding the difference between information as an abstracted entity, as opposed to the document as a specific material instantiation, and also text which seeks to offer proof. He concludes, drawing on Foucault, to the notion of the human subject being rendered as document. I turned to critical work around the practice of learning analytics, which has pointed out the many ethical and political concerns surrounding this as technology of surveillance. I moved to a conclusion that learning and analytics, and the algocracy, have committed an act of ontological violence, by rendering students into documents, in a sector dominated by multiple forms of surveillance, normativity and discipline.

I have given this chapter the title 'Conclusions, or so what?', in order to explicitly return to some of the objections to the concept of posthumanism that I acknowledged in the introductory chapter, particularly criticisms that have been made of posthuman theory in relation to education. I'd like to return to these here, and then conclude the book by making a case for the potential utility of these perspectives for research in digital higher education practices, and education more broadly. One of these objections is that it is apolitical, and is not sensitive to the ongoing struggles of marginalized groups for recognition as 'fully human', with the same full rights accorded to those in positions of socioeconomic privilege. Although my focus throughout this book has not been to directly focus on those issues, I would argue that the challenge to humanism, transhumanism and simplified applications of social constructivism all serve to undermine and question the central, implicit positioning and portrayal of the 'prototypical', or 'default' student as human subject conjured by the education discourses, policies and practices. I would contend that an explicit focus on the minutiae of texts, bodies and materialities in digital higher education undermines these assumptions and fantasies of transcendence, and allows us to recognize the diversity of the real, moving, breathing, typing, reading and thinking 'student body'. Norm Friesen raised an important related criticism around where and how we situate agency, suggesting that the posthuman concept of agency distributed across nonhuman actors was – effectively – a 'cop-out', a shirking of our human responsibility to take ownership and act on the urgent challenges of contemporary higher education, around social justice, the importance of criticality, and so on. He is right, critical practice and 'speaking truth to power' need human decision-making, human voices, and human action. However, I would respond by suggesting that such projects and aspirations cannot be realized without an in-depth understanding of education 'in its becoming', as it unfolds and emerges. As I have argued, higher education as a sector is saturated with ideologies, imaginaries, fantasies, desires, conjured figures and – I propose – hidden operations of power, surveillance and control which are not aligned with these values of human (and nonhuman) flourishing, but instead may serve the demands of an increasingly marketized sector. Instead, even when well-intentioned, the presence and dominance of these ideologies limits the essence of the academy itself, and also curtails our ability as educational researchers and theorists to 'see' clearly what is happening on the ground, in the intricate, unobserved pathways and passages being forged, the threads being tied and unravelled, the meshwork in which students and scholars are entangled.

In conclusion, the question arises as to how – if taken seriously – this and other conceptual framings drawn from new materialism could inform higher education research and practice. The focus on the particular calls for ethnographic, slow, detailed work on practices 'on the ground', as opposed to ideological, and broad-brush assumptions about literacy practices and student engagement. In terms of educational design and practice, it necessitates a plural, multiple approach to student engagement which is sensitive to, and intra-acts with 'contexts'. The challenge for educationalists is to work meaningfully in the spaces opened up by these fresh perspectives on literacy research and education, in a manner which remains critical and incisive, while also seeking to deepen and extend the important work of inclusive and meaningful education. For me – despite the at times esoteric terminology and language – posthuman theory and research has the potential to be a profoundly practical, down-to-earth undertaking, and I hope that this book may have stimulated interest in 'improvising passages' to go down the pathways, explore the meshworks, and loosen the knots that it offers us.

References

Adams, C. 2006. PowerPoint, habits of mind, and classroom culture. *Journal of Curriculum Studies* 38(4), 389–411.

Adams, C. 2010. Teachers building dwelling thinking with slideware. *The Indo-Pacific Journal of Phenomenology* 10(1), 1–12.

Adams, C. and Thompson, T. 2016. *Researching a Posthuman World: Interviews with Digital Objects*. London, UK: Palgrave Macmillan.

Althusser, L. 1984. Ideology and Ideological State Apparatuses. *Essays on Ideology*. London, UK: Verso.

Ames, P. 1993. *Beyond Paper: The Official Guide to Adobe Acrobat*. Mountain View, C.A.: Adobe.

Aneesh, A. 2006. *Virtual Migration: The Programme of Globalisation*. Chicago, UK: Duke University Press.

Aneesh, A. 2009. Global labour: algocratic modes of organization. *Sociological Theory* 27(4): 347–370.

Anusas, M. and Ingold, M. 2013. Designing environmental relations: from opacity to textuality. *Design Issues* 29(4): 57–69.

Apple, M. 1991. The new technology: is it part of the solution or art of the problem in education? *Computers in Schools* 8(1/2/3), 59–81.

Archer, A. 2006. Opening up spaces through symbolic objects: harnessing students' resources in developing academic literacy practices in engineering. *English Studies in Africa* 49(1).

Austin, J. 1962. *How to Do Things with Words*. Oxford, UK: Oxford University Press.

Badmington, N. 2004. Mapping posthumanism: an exchange. *Environment and Planning A*, 36, 1344–1351.

Bakhtin, M. 1981. *The Dialogic Imagination: Four Essays*. In Holquist, M. (Ed.) (Translated by C. Emerson and C. Holquist) Austin: University of Texas.

Ball, S. 2003. The teacher's soul and the terrors of performativity. *Journal of Education Policy* 18(2), 215–228.

Ball, S. 2012. The making of a neoliberal academic. *Research in Secondary Education*. 2(1), 29–31.

Barad, K. 2003. Posthumanist performativity: towards and understanding of how matter comes to matter. *Signs* 28(3), 801–831.

Barad, K. 2007. *Meeting the Universe Halfway: Quantum Physics and the Entanglement of Matter and Meaning*. London, UK: Duke University Press.

Barad, K. 2010. Quantum entanglements and hauntological relations of inheritance: dis/continuities, spacetime enfoldings, and justice to come. *Derrida Today* 3(2), 240–268.

Barad, K. 2012. On touching: the inhuman that therefore I am. *Differences: A Journal of Feminist Cultural Studies* 23(3), 206–223.

Barad, K. 2013. Mar(k)ing time: Material Entanglements and Re-memberings Cutting together-apart. In Carlile, P., Nicolini, D. Langley, A. and Tsoukas, H. (Eds) *How Matter Matters: Objects, Artifacts and Materiality in Organisation Studies.* Cambridge, UK: Cambridge University Press, 16–31.

Barkley, E. 2010. *Student Engagement Techniques: A Handbook for College Faculty.* San Francisco, CA: Wiley and Sons.

Barnett, R. 2000. *Realising the University in an Age of Supercomplexity.* Buckingham, UK: Society for Research into Higher Education, Open University Press.

Barnett, R. and Coate, K. 2005. *Engaging the Curriculum in Higher Education.* Maidenhead, UK: Open University Press.

Barthes, R. 1981. *Camera Lucida: Reflections on Photography.* Trans. Howard, R. New York: Hill and Wang.

Barton, D. 2007. *Literacy: An Introduction to the Ecology of Written Language.* (2nd Ed.) Oxford, UK: Blackwell.

Barton, D. and Hamilton, M. 2005. Literacy, reification and the dynamics of social interaction. In Barton, D. and Tusting, K. (Eds) *Beyond Communities of Practice: Language, Power and Social Context.* Cambridge, UK: Cambridge University Press.

Bateson, G. 1972. *Steps to an Ecology of Mind.* New York, NY: Ballantine Books.

Bauman, R. and Briggs, C. 1990. Poetics and Performance: Critical Perspective on Language and Social Life. *Annual Review of Anthropology* 19, 59–88.

Baynham, M. 2004. Ethnographies of literacy: introduction. *Language and Education* 18: 285–290.

Baynham, M. and Prinsloo, M. 2009. *The Future of Literacy Studies.* New York, NY: Palgrave Macmillan.

Bayne, S. 2018. Posthumanism: a navigation aid for educators. *On Education: Journal for Research and Debate* 1(2) https://www.oneducation.net/no-02-september-2018/posthumanism-a-navigation-aid-for-educators/ [Accessed 29 January 2020]

Bazin, P. 1996. Toward Metareading. In Nunberg, G. (Ed.) *The Future of the Book.* Berkeley, CA: University of California Press, 153–168.

Beer, D. 2017a. Algorithms: the villains and heroes of the 'post-truth' era. 3 January [Blog post] *Open Democracy* https://www.opendemocracy.net/en/digitaliberties/algorithms-villains-and-heroes-of-post-truth-era/ [Accessed 29 January 2020]

Beer, D. 2017b. The social power of algorithms. *Information, Culture and Society.* 20(1), 1–13.

Bell, C. 1992. *Ritual Theory, Ritual Practice.* New York and Oxford, UK: Oxford University Press.

Bell, F. 2010. Connectivism: its place in theory-informed research and innovation n technology-enabled learning. *International Review of Research in Open and Distance Learning* 12(3).

Bennett, J. 2010. *Vibrant Matter: A Political Ecology of Things*. Durham: Duke University Press.

Bergmann, J. and Sams, A. 2012. *Flip your classroom: reach every student, in every class, every day*. Alexandria, VA: Association for Supervision and Curriculum Development.

Berkeley, G. 1734. *Three Dialogues between Hylas and Philonous*. London: Jacob Tonson.

Bhatt, I. 2017. *Assignments as Controversies: Digital Literacy and Writing in Classroom Practice*. London, UK: Routledge.

Biesta, G. 1998. Pedagogy without humanism: Foucault and the subject of education. *Interchange* 29(1), 1–16.

Biesta, G. 2005. Against learning. Reclaiming a language for education in an age of learning. *Nordisk Pedagogik* 25: 54–56.

Biesta, G. 2006. *Beyond Learning. Democratic Education for a Human Future*. Boulder, CO: Paradigm Publishers.

Biesta, G. 2010. Why 'what works' still won't work. From evidence-based education to value-based education. *Studies in Philosophy and Education* 29(5): 491–503.

Biesta, G. 2012. Giving teaching back to education: responding to the disappearance of the teacher. *Phenomenology and Practice* 6(2): 35–49.

Biesta, G. 2016. The rediscovery of teaching: on robot vacuum cleaners, non-egological education and the limits of the hermeneutical world view. *Educational Philosophy and Theory* 48(4): 374–392.

Blackburn, S. 1988. *Singing of Birth and Death: Texts in Performance*. Philadelphia, PA: University of Pennsylvania Press.

Bligh, D. 1971. *What's the Use of Lectures?* Harmondsworth, UK: Penguin.

Blommaert, J. 2005. *Discourse: A Critical Introduction*. Cambridge, UK: Cambridge University Press.

Blommaert, J. 2014. From mobility to complexity in sociolinguistic theory and method. *Tilburg Papers in Culture Studies* 13.

Borgmann, A. 1984. *Technology and the Character of Contemporary Life: A Philosophical Enquiry*. Chicago, IL: University of Chicago Press.

Bowker, G., and Star, S. 1999. *Sorting Things Out: Classification and its Consequences*. Cambridge, MA: MIT Press.

Braidotti, R. 2011. *Nomadic Theory: The Portable Rosi Braidotti*. New York, NY: Columbia University Press.

Braidotti, R. 2013. *The Posthuman*. Cambridge, UK: Polity Press.

Brandt, D. and Clinton, K. 2002. Limits of the local: expanding perspectives on literacy as a social practice. *Journal of Literacy Research* 34(3), 337–356.

Breit, S. 1951. *What is Documentation?: English Translation of the Classic French Text*. Translated and edited by Day, R., Martinet, R. and Anghelescu, H. Lanham MD: Scarecrow Press, 2006.

Brown, T. and Jenkins, M. 2003. VLE Surveys: A Longitudinal Perspective between March 2001 and March 2003 for Higher Education in the United Kingdom. UKISA. https://immagic.com/eLibrary/ARCHIVES/GENERAL/UCISA_UK/U051130J.pdf

Bryson, C. and Hand, L. 2007. The role of engagement in inspiring teaching and learning. *Innovations in Education and Teaching International* 44: 349–362.

Buckland, M. 1997. What is a document? *Journal of the American Society of Information Science and Technology* 48(9), 804–809.

Budach, G., Kell, C. and Patrick, D. 2015. Objects and language in trans-contextual communication. *Social Semiotics* 25(4), 387–400.

Buhlmann, V. 2015. Incandescent materialism, literacy in quantum writing. *Proceedings of the New Materialist Politics and Economies of Knowledge Conference*, Maribor, Slovenia.

Buhlmann, V., Colman, F. and van der Tuin, I. 2017. Introduction to new materialist genealogies: New materialisms, novel mentalities, quantum literacy. *Minnesota Review* 88, 47–58.

Callon, M. 1986. Some elements of a sociology of translation; domestication of the scallops and the fishermen of St Brieuc Bay. In Law, J. (Ed.) *Power, Action and Belief: A New Sociology of Knowledge?* London, UK: Routledge & Kegan Paul, 196–233.

Canagarajah, S. 2013. *Translingual Practice: Global Englishes and Cosmopolitan Relations.* New York: Routledge.

Carrington, V. 2012. 'There's no going back'. Roxie's iPhone: an object ethnography. *Language and Literacy* 14(2): 27–40.

Castree, N., Nash, C., Badmington, N. Braun, B. Murdoch, J. and Whatmore, S. 2004. Mapping posthumanism: an exchange. *Environment and Planning A* 36(8), 1352–1355.

Clark, W. 2006. *Academic Charisma and the Origins of the Research University.* Chicago, IL: University of Chicago Press.

Coates, H. 2007. A Model of Online and General Campus-Based Student Engagement. *Assessment and Evaluation in Higher Education* 32(2): 121–141.

Coates, H. 2010. Development of the Australasian Survey of Student Engagement (AUSSE). *Higher Education* 60(1), 1–17.

Collins, J. and Blot, R. 2003. *Literacy and Literacies: Texts, Power, and Identity.* Cambridge, UK: Cambridge University Press.

Coole, D. and Frost, S. (Eds) 2010. *New Materialisms: Ontology, Agency and Politics.* Durham: Duke University Press.

Cormier, D. 2010. *Success in a MOOC.* YouTube https://www.youtube.com/watch?v=r8avYQ5ZqM0

Coutu, D. 2003. PowerPoint, robomanagers and you: the growing intimacy of technology (interview with Sherry Turkle). In *Harvard Business School: Working Knowledge for Business Leaders* https://hbswk.hbs.edu/archive/powerpoint-robomanagers-and-you-the-growing-intimacy-of-technology

Cronin, K. and McLaren, I. 2018. Conceptualising OEP: a review of the theoretical and empirical literature in open educational practices. *Open Praxis* 10(2), 127–143.

Cullen, C. 1996. *Astronomy and Mathematics in Ancient China: The 'Zhou bi suan jing.* Cambridge, UK: Cambridge University Press.

Czerniewicz, L. 2013. Inequitable power dynamics of global knowledge production and exchange must be confronted head-on. *London School of Economics Impact Blog* http://blogs.lse.ac.uk/impactofsocialsciences/2013/04/29/redrawing-the-map-from-access-to-participation/#more-10331

Czerniewicz, L. and Naidoo, U. 2013. MOOC-less in Africa. *OpenUCT Initiative Blog* https://open.uct.ac.za/bitstream/handle/11427/2373/OpenUCT_Czerniewicz_ MOOCAfrica_2013.pdf?sequence=1

Dahaner, J. 2015. How might algorithms rule our lives? Mapping the social space of algocracy. *Philosophical Disquisitions* https://philosophicaldisquisitions.blogspot.com/2015/06/how-might-algorithms-rule-our-lives.html [Accessed 29 January 2016]

Dahaner, J. 2016. The logical space of algocracy (redux). *Philosophical Disquisitions* https://philosophicaldisquisitions.blogspot.com/2016/11/the-logical-space-of-algocracy-redux.html [Accessed 29 January 2016]

Dall 'Alba, G. and Barnacle, R. 2007. An ontological turn for higher education. *Studies in Higher Education* 32: 671–691.

Davies, T. 2008. *Humanism*. Abingdon: Routledge.

de Certeau, M. 1981. *The Practice of Everyday Life*. Translated by Steven F. Rendall. Berkeley, CA: University of California Press.

Deleuze, G. and Guattari, F. 2004. *A Thousand Plateaus: Capitalism and Schizophrenia*. (Trans Massumi, B.) London, UK: Continuum.

Deleuze, G. and Guattari, F. 1987. *A Thousand Plateaus: Capitalism and Schizophrenia*. Minneapolis, MI: University of Minnesota Press.

Diakapolous, N. 2015. Algorithmic accountability: journalistic investigation of computational power structures *Digital Journalism* 3(3), 398–415.

Dinker, K. and Pedersen, H. 2016. Critical Animal Pedagogies: re-learning our relations with animal others. In Lees, N. and Noddings, N. (Eds.) *The Palgrave International Handbook of Alternative Education*. London: Palgrave Macmillan.

Dolphijn, R and van der Tuin, I. 2011. Pushing dualism to an extreme: on the philosophical impetus of a new materialism. *Continental Philosophy Review* 44(4), 383–400.

Dolphijn, R and van der Tuin, I. (Eds) 2012. *New Materialism: Interviews and Cartographies*. Ann Arbor, MI: Open Humanities Press.

Dourish, P. 2016. Algorithms and their others: algorithmic culture in context. *Big Data and Society* 3(2), 1–11.

Downes, S. 2011. *Free Learning: Essays on Open Educational Resources and Copyright* https://www.downes.ca/files/FreeLearning.pdf

Dreyfus, H. and Spinosa, C. 2003. Further reflections on Heidegger, technology, and the everyday. *Bulletin of Science, Technology and Society* 23(5), 339–349.

Dunne, E. and Owen, D. 2013. *The Student Engagement Handbook: Practice in Higher Education*. Bingley, UK: Emerald.

Dyjkstra, E. 1985. On anthropomorphism in science. https://www.cs.utexas.edu/users/ EWD/transcriptions/EWD09xx/EWD936.html [Accessed 29 January 2020]

EdX. 2019. The University of Queensland 2019 *Philosophy and Critical Thinking META101x*. EdX https://www.edx.org/course/philosophy-and-critical-thinking

Emerson, L, 2014. *Reading Writing Interfaces: From the Digital to the Bookbound.* Minneapolis, MN: University of Minnesota Press.

Enfield, J. 2013. Looking at the impact of the flipped classroom model of instruction on undergraduate multimedia students at CSUN. *TechTrends* 57(6), 14–27.

Fairclough, N. 1992. *Discourse and Social Change.* Cambridge, UK: Polity.

Fairclough, N. 1995. *Critical Discourse Analysis: The Critical Study of Language.* London, UK: Longman.

Fenwick, T. and Edwards, R. 2011. Considering materiality in educational policy: messy objects and multiple reals. *Educational Theory* 61(6), 709–726.

Fenwick, T., R. Edwards, and P. Sawchuk 2011. *Emerging Approaches to Educational Research: Tracing the Sociomaterial.* London, UK: Routledge.

Ferguson, S. 2012. Learner analytics: drivers, developments and challenges. *International Journal of Technology Enhanced Learning* 4(5–6): 304–317.

Ferrando, F. 2013. Posthumanism, transhumanism, antihumanism, metahumanism, and new materialisms: differences and relations. *Existenz* 8(2), 26–32.

Foucault, M. 1988. In Martin, L., Gutman, H. and Hutton, P. (Eds) *Technologies of the Self: a Seminar with Michel Foucault.* Amherst, MA: University of Massachusetts Press, 16–49.

Fichte, J. 1993. Concerning the difference between the spirit and the letter in philosophy. In Breazeale, D. (Ed.) *Fichte: Early Philosophical Writings.* Ithaca, NY: Cornell University Press, 185–216.

Fraser, M., Kember, S. and Lury, C. 2005. Inventive life: approaches to the New Vitalism. *Theory, Culture and Society* 22(1), 1–14.

Fredericks, J., Blumenfeld, P. and Paris, A. 2004. School engagement: potential of the concept, state of the evidence. *Review of Educational Research* 74: 59–109.

Friesen, N. 2014. Old literacies and the 'new' literacy studies: revisiting reading and writing. *Seminar.net: International Journal of Media, Technology and Lifelong Learning* 10(2)

Friesen, N. 2017. *The Textbook and the Lecture: Education in the Age of New Media.* Baltimore: Johns Hopkins.

Friesen, N. 2018. Posthumanism=posteducation. A reply to Sian Bayne's Posthumanism: A navigation aid for educators. *On Education: A Journal for Research and Debate* 1(2).

Frohmann, B. 2004. Documentation redux: prolegomenon to (another) philosophy of information. *Library Trends* 54: 387–407.

Frohman, B. 2007. Multiplicity, materiality, and autonomous agency of documentation. In Skare, R., Windfeld Lund N., and Varheim, A. (Eds.) *A Document (Re)turn.* Frankfurt am Main: Laing.

Gitelman, L. 2014. *Paper Knowledge: Towards a Media History of Documents.* London, UK: Duke University Press.

Goffman, E. 1969. *The Presentation of the Self in Everyday Life*. London, UK: Penguin (First edition published in in the USA by Anchor Books, 1959).

Goffman, E. 1974. *Frame Analysis*. New York, NY: Harper and Row.

Goffman, E. 1981. *Forms of Talk*. Oxford, UK: Blackwell.

Goodfellow, R. 2011. Literacy, literacies and the digital in higher education. *Teaching in Higher Education*, 16(1), 131–144.

Gourlay, L. 2012. Cyborg ontologies and the lecturer's voice: a posthuman reading of the 'face-to-face'. *Learning, Media and Technology* 37(2), 198–211.

Gourlay, L. 2014. Creating time: students, technologies and temporal practices in higher education. *Elearning and Digital Media* 11(2), 141–153.

Gourlay, L. 2015a. Open education as a 'heterotopia of desire'. *Learning, Media and Technology* 40(3), 310–327.

Gourlay, L. 2015b. Posthuman texts: nonhuman actors, mediators and the digital university. *Social Semiotics* 25 (4), 484–500.

Gourlay, L. 2015c. Student engagement and the tyranny of participation. *Teaching in Higher Education* 20(4): 402–411.

Gourlay, L. 2017. Student engagement, 'learnification' and the sociomaterial: critical perspectives on higher education policy. *Higher Education Policy* 30(1), 23–34.

Gourlay, L. 2019. Textual practices as already-posthuman: re-imagining text, authorship and meaning-making in higher education. In Taylor, C. and Bailey, A. (Eds) *Posthumanism and Higher Education: Reimagining Policy, Practice and Research*. London, UK: Palgrave Macmillan.

Gourlay, L. and Deane, J. 2009. Loss, responsibility, blame? Staff discourses of student plagiarism. *Innovations in Education and Teaching International* 49(1) 19–29.

Gourlay, L. and Oliver, M. 2013. Beyond 'the social': digital literacies and sociomaterial practice. In Goodfellow, R. and Lea, M. (Eds.) *Literacy in the Digital University: Critical Perspectives on Learning, Scholarship and Technology*. London: Routledge.

Gourlay, L. and Oliver, M. 2016a. Students' digital and physical sites of study: making, marking and breaking boundaries. In L. Carvahlo, P. Goodyear, and M. de Laat (Eds) *Place-Based Spaces for Networked Learning*. New York, NY: Routledge, 73–86.

Gourlay, L. and Oliver, M. 2016b. It's not all about the learner: reframing students' digital literacy and sociomaterial practice. In T. Ryberg, C. Sinclair, S. Bayne, and M. de Laat, (Eds) *Research, Boundaries and Policy in Networked Learning*. Switzerland: Springer, 77–92.

Gourlay, L. and Oliver, M. 2018. *Student Engagement in the Digital University: Sociomaterial Assemblages*. London, UK: Routledge.

Gourlay, L., Hamilton, M. and Lea, M. 2013. Textual practices in the new media landscape: messing with digital literacies. *Research in Learning Technology* 21.

Greiner, C. and Sakdapolrak, P. 2013. Translocality: concepts, applications and emerging research perspectives. *Geography Compass* 7(5), 373–384.

Gramsci, A. 1971. *Selection from the Prison Notebooks*. London, UK: Lawrence and Wishart.

Grice, H. 1975. Logic and conversation. In Cole, P. and Morgan, J. (Eds) *Syntax and Semantics 3: Speech Acts.* New York, NY: Academic, 41–48.

Gross, D. 2017. Why artificial intelligence needs some emotional intelligence. *Harvard Business Review* 9 March https://www.strategy-business.com/blog/Why-Artificial-Intelligence-Needs-Some-Emotional-Intelligence?gko=52d91 [Accessed 29 January 2020]

Guardian. 2019. Pearson shifts to Netflix-style subscription model for textbooks. https://www.theguardian.com/media/2019/jul/16/pearson-netflix-style-rental-academic-textbooks

Halliday, M. 1978. *Language as Social Semiotic.* London, UK: Arnold.

Hamilton, M. 2001. Privileged literacies: policy, institutional process and the life of IALS. *Language and Education* 15(2), 178–96.

Haraway, D. 1985. A Manifesto for Cyborgs: Science, Technology and Socialist Feminism in the 1980s. *Socialist Review* 15(2), 65–107.

Haraway, D. 1991. A cyborg manifesto: science, technology, and socialist-feminism in the late twentieth century. In Haraway, D. (Ed.) *Simians, Cyborgs and Women: The Reinvention of Nature.* New York, NY: Routledge, 149–181.

Harman, G. 2002. *Tool-Being: Heidegger and the Metaphysics of Objects.* Chicago, IL: Open Court.

Harris, R. 1996. *Signs, Language and Communication.* London, UK: Routledge.

Hassan, I. 1977. Prometheus as performer: towards a posthumanist culture? *The Georgia Review* 314, 830–850.

Havelock, E. 1982. *The Literate Revolution in Greece and its Cultural Consequences.* Princeton, NJ: Princeton University Press.

Hayles, K. 1999. *How We Became Posthuman: Virtual Bodies in Cybernetics, Literature and Informatics.* Chicago, IL: University of Chicago Press.

Hayles, K. 2002. *Writing Machines.* Cambridge, Mass: MIT University Press.

Hayles, K. 2005. *My Mother was a Computer: Digital Subjects and Literary Texts.* Chicago, IL: University of Chicago Press.

Hayles, K. 2006. Unfinished work: from cyborg to cognisphere. *Theory, Culture and Society* 23(7–8), 159–166.

Hayles, K. 2012. *How We Think: Digital Media and Contemporary Technogenesis.* Chicago, IL: University of Chicago Press.

Heath, S. 1982a. Protean shapes in literacy events: ever shifting oral and literate traditions. In Tannen, D. (Ed.) *Spoken and Written Language: Exploring Literacy and Orality.* Norwood, NJ: Ablex.

Heath, S. 1982b. What no Bedtime Story Means: Narrative Skills at Home and School. *Language in Society* 11(1), 49–76.

Heath, S. 1983. *Ways with Words.* Cambridge, UK: Cambridge University Press.

Heath, T. 2013. *The Thirteen Books of Euclid's Elements.* Cambridge, UK: Cambridge University Press.

Heidegger, M. 1971a. Building Dwelling Thinking. In *Poetry, Language and Thought* (Hofstader, A. trans.) New York, NY: Harper and Row, 145–161.

Heidegger, M. 1971b. The Thing. In *Poetry, Language and Thought* (Hofstader, A. trans.) New York, NY: Harper and Row, 163–186.

Heidegger, M. 1962. *Being and Time*. Trans J. Macquarie and E. Robinson. New York, NY: Harper and Row.

Higher Education Academy 2011. *The UK Professional Standards Framework for Teaching and Supporting Learning*. https://www.heacademy.ac.uk/system/files/downloads/ukpsf_2011_english.pdf [Accessed 12 December 2016]

Howells, K. 2007. PowerPoint: Friend or foe? In Green, V. and Sigafoos, J. (Eds) *Technology and Teaching: A Casebook for Editors*. New York, NY: Nova Science Publishers, 137–145.

Hjorland, B. 2000. Documents, memory institutions, and information. *Journal of Documentation* 56(1), 27–41.

Hurley, S. 1998. *Consciousness in Action*. Cambridge, MA: Harvard University Press.

Hymes, D. 1977/1994. Towards ethnographies of communication. In Maybin, J. (Ed.) *Language and Literacy in Social Practice*. Clevedon, UK: The Open University.

Iedema, R. 1999. Formalising organizational meaning. *Discourse and Society* 10(1), 49–65.

Iedema, R. 2001. Resemiotisation. *Semiotica* 137 (1–4), 23–39.

Iedema, R. 2003. Multimodality, resemiotisation: extending the analysis of discourse as multi-semiotic practice. *Visual Communication* 2(1), 29–57.

Ihde, D. 1990. *Technology and the Lifeworld: From Garden to Earth*. Bloomington: Indiana University Press.

Illich, I. 1996. Philosophy … artifacts … friendship – and the history of the gaze. In Duart, T. (Ed.) *Philosophy of Technology: Proceedings of the American Catholic Philosophical Association* 70. Washington, DC: National Office of the American Catholic Philosophical Association, Catholic University of America, 61–82.

Ingold, T. 2000. *The Perception of the Environment: Essays in Livelihood, Dwelling and Skill*. London, UK: Routledge.

Ingold, T. 2005. Up, across and along. http://spacesyntax.tudelft.nl/media/Long%20papers%20I/tim%20ingold.pdf

Ingold, T. 2007. *Lines: A Brief History*. Routledge: Oxford.

Ingold, T. 2007a. Materials against materiality. *Archeological Dialogues* 14(1), 1–16.

Ingold, T. 2007b. Writing texts, reading materials. A response to my critics. *Archeological Dialogues* 14(1), 31–38.

Ingold, T. 2008. Bindings against boundaries: entanglements of life in an open world. *Environment and Planning A* 40(8), 1796.

Ingold, T. 2012a. Looking for lines in nature. *Earthlines* 3, 48–51.

Ingold, T. 2012b. Toward an ecology of materials. *Annual Review of Sociology* 41, 427–442.

Ingold, T. 2013. *Making: Anthropology, Archeology, Art and Architecture*. London, UK: Routledge. anal

Ingold, T. 2015. *The Life of Lines*. London, UK: Routledge.

Ingold, T. 2016. *Lines*. London, UK: Routledge.

Introna, L. 2011. The enframing of code: agency, originality, and the plagiarist. *Theory, Culture and Society* 28(6), 113–141.

Jackson, P. 1968. *Life in Classrooms*. New York, NY: Teachers' College Press.

Jandric, P., Knox, J., Maceod, H., and Sinclair, C. 2017. Learning in the age of algorithmic cultures. *Elearning and Digital Media* 14(3), 101–104.

Jasanoff, S. 2015. Future imperfect: science, technology and the imaginations of modernity. In Jasanoff, S. and Kim, S. (Eds) *Dreamscapes of Modernity: Sociotechnical Imaginaries and the Fabrication of Power*. London, UK: University of Chicago Press.

Jimerson, S., Campos, E. and Greif, J. 2003. Toward and understanding of definitions and measures of school engagement and related terms. *California School Psychologist* 8, 7–27.

Joint Information Services Committee (JISC) 2000. Circular 7/100: *MLEs in Further Education: Progress Report*. JISC.

Kahn, P. 2013. Theorising Student Engagement in Higher Education. *British Educational Research Journal* 40(6): 1005–1018.

Kahu, E. 2013. Framing student engagement in higher education. *Studies in Higher Education* 38(5), 758–773.

Kell, C. 2006. Crossing the margins: literacy, semiotics and the recontextualisaiton of meanings. In Pahl, K. and Rowsell, J. (Eds) *Travel Notes from the New Literacy Studies: Instances of Practice*. Clevedon, UK: Multilingual Matters, 147–172.

Kell, C. 2009. Literacy Practices, Text/s and Meaning making Across Time and Space. In *The Future of Literacy Studies*, Prinsloo, M. and Baynham, M. (Eds) New York, NY: Palgrave, 75–99.

Kell, C. 2015. 'Making people happen': materiality and movement in meaning-making trajectories. *Social Semiotics* 25(4), 423–445.

Kell, C. 2015. Ariadne's Thread: Literacy, Scale and Meaning-Making Across Time and Space. In *Language, Literacy and Diversity: Moving Words,* Christopher, S and Prinsloo, M. (Eds) 72–91. London, UK: Routledge.

Kell, C. 2017. Tracing trajectories as units of analysis for the study of social processes: addressing mobility and complexity in sociolinguistics. *Text and Talk* 37(4), 531–551.

Kell, C. 2017. Travelling texts, translocal/transnational literacies, and transcontextual analysis. In Canagarajah, S. (Ed.) *The Routledge Handbook of Migration and Language*. London, UK: Routledge.

King, A. 1993. From sage on the stage to guide on the side. *College Teaching* 41(1), 30–35.

Kirchenbaum, M. 2012. *Mechanisms: New Media and the Forensic Imagination*. Cambridge, Mass: MIT University Press.

Kitchen, R. 2014. *The Data Revolution: Big Data, Open Data, Data Infrastructures and Their Consequences.* London, UK: SAGE.

Kittler, F. 2004. Universities: Wet, Hard, Soft, and Harder. *Critical Inquiry* 31(1), 244–255.

Knorr-Cetina, K. 2001. Objectual practice. In Schatzki, Theodore, Karin Knorr-Cetina, and Eike von Savigny, (Eds) *The Practice Turn in Contemporary Theory.* London, UK: Routledge and Taylor and Francis, 175–188.

Knorr-Cetina, K. 2010. The epistemics of information: a consumption model. *Journal of Consumer Culture* 10(2), 171–201.

Knox, J. 2010. Spies in the house of learning: a typology of surveillance in online learning environments. In Proceedings from *e-learning: The Horizon and Beyond* conference, St Johns, Newfoundland, Canada.

Knox, J. 2016. *Posthumanism and the Massive Online Course: Contaminating the Subject of Global Higher Education.* London, UK: Routledge.

Knox, J. 2016. Posthumanism and the MOOC: Opening the subject of digital education. *Studies in Philosophy and Education.*

Kosciejew, M. 2017. A material-documentary literacy: documents, practices and the materialization of information. *Minnesota Review* 88, 96–111.

Kress, G. and van Leeuwen, T. 1996. *Reading Images: The Grammar of Visual Design.* London, UK: Routledge.

Kuby, C., Spector, K. and Johnson Thiel, J. (Eds) 2019. *Posthumanism and Literacy Education: Knowing / Becoming / Doing Literacies.* London, UK: Routledge.

Kuh, G. 2001. *The National Survey of Student Engagement: Conceptual Framework and Overview of Psychometric Properties.* Bloomington, IN: Indiana University Centre for Postsecondary Research and Planning.

Kuh, G. 2009a. *The National Survey of Student Engagement: Conceptual and Empirical* Foundations, New Directions for Institutional Research 2009 (141): 5–20.

Kuh, G. 2009b. What student affairs professionals need to know about student engagement. *Journal of College Student Development* 50: 683–706.

Kuhn, T. 1962. *The Structure of Scientific Revolutions.* Chicago, IL: University of Chicago Press.

Lage, M., Platt, G. and Treglia, M. 2000. Inverting the classroom: a gateway to creating n inclusive learning environment. *The Journal of Economic Education* 31(1), 30–43.

Lane, A. 2009. The impact of openness on bridging educational digital divides. *The International Review of Research in Open and Distance Learning* 10(5) http://www.irrodl.org/index.php/irrodl/article/view/637/1408

Latour, B. 1987. *Science in Action.* Cambridge, Mass: Harvard University Press.

Latour, B. 1990. Drawing things together. In Lynch, M. and Woolgar, S. (Eds) *Representation and Scientific Practice.* Cambridge, Mass: MIT Press, 19–68.

Latour, B. 2005. *Reassembling the Social: An Introduction to Actor-Network Theory.* Oxford, UK: Oxford University Press.

Latour, B. 2012. Love your monsters. Why we must care for our technologies as we do for our children. *The Breakthrough* 2 https://thebreakthrough.org/journal/issue-2/love-your-monsters [Accessed 29 January 2020]

Latour, B. 2014. How to talk about the body? The normative dimension of science studies. *Body and Society* 10 (2–3), 202–229.

Laurillard, D. 2001. *Rethinking University Teaching: A Conversational Framework for the Effective Use of Learning Technologies* (2nd Ed.) London, UK: Routledge.

Law, J. and Singleton, V. 2013. ANT and politics: working in and on the world. *Qualitative Sociology* 36(4), 485–502.

Lea, M. and Street, B. 1998. Student writing in higher education: an academic literacies approach. *Studies in Higher Education* 23(2), 157–

Leander, K. and Boldt, G. 2012. Rereading 'a pedagogy of multiliteracies': bodies, texts and emergence. *Journal of Literacy Research* 45(1), 22–46.

Leander, K. and de Haan, M. (Eds) 2014. Media and migration: learning in a globalized world. Special Issue, *Learning, Media and Technology* 39(4), 405–535.

Leander, K. and Lovorn, J. 2006. Literacy networks: following the circulation of texts, bodies and objects in the schooling and online gaming of one youth. *Cognition and Instruction*, 2(3), 291–340.

Leclerq, J. 1961. *The Love of Learning and the Desire of God*, trans C. Mrahi, New York: Fordham University Press.

Lehmann, A. 2016. *A cube of wood: material literacy for art history*. Inaugural lecture University of Groningen, Groningen, Netherlands April 12 https://www.rug.nl/about-us/news-and-events/events/inauguration/2016/0412-lehmann bluhm?lang=en

Lenters, K. 2014. Reassembling the literacy event in Shirley Brice-Heath's 'Ways with Words'. In Prinsloo, M. and Stroud, C. (Eds) *Educating for Language and Literacy Diversity: Mobile Selves*. London, UK: Routledge, 153–172.

Levy, D. 2001. *Scrolling Forward: Making Sense of Documents in the Digital Age*. New York, NY: Arcade Publishing.

Lexico 2019. *Online Dictionary*. Oxford English Dictionary. https://www.lexico.com

Locke, J. 1700. *Essay Concerning Human Understanding*. London, UK: Awnsham and John Churchill.

Lund, N. 2007. Building a discipline: creating a profession: an essay on the childhood of 'Dovcit'. In Skare, R., Winfeld Lund, N. and Varheim, A. (Eds) *A Document (Re)turn*. Frankfurt am Main: Laing.

Lyotard, J. 1984. *The Postmodern Condition: A Report on Knowledge*. (Translated by Geoff Bennington and Brian Massumi) Minneapolis, MI: University of Minnesota Press.

Macfarlane, B. 2017. *Freedom to Learn: The Threat to Academic Freedom and Why it Needs to be Reclaimed*. London, UK: Routledge.

Macfarlane, B. and Gourlay, L. 2009. The reflection game: enacting the penitent self. *Teaching in Higher Education* 14(4): 455–459.

Mak, B. 2011. *How the Page Matters*. Toronto, Canada: University of Toronto Press.

Mann, S. 2001. Alternative perspectives on the student experience: alienation and engagement. *Studies in Higher Education* 26: 7–19.

Massey, D. 2005. *For Space*. London, UK: Sage.

Massumi, B. 2002. *Parables for the Virtual: Movement, Affect, Sensation*. Chicago, IL: Duke University Press.

Maturana, H. and Varela, F. 1992. *The Tree of Knowledge: The Biological Roots of Human Understanding*. Boston, Mass: Shambala.

Maybin, J. 2017. Textual trajectories: theoretical roots and institutional consequences. *Text and Talk* 37,(4): 415–435.

McGill, L. Falconer, I., Dempster, J., Littlejohn, A. and Beetham, H. 2013. *Journeys to open educational practice: UKOER/SCORE review final report*. https://oersynth. pbworks.com/w/page/60338879/HEFCE-OER-Review-Final-Report

McLaren, P. 1993. *Schooling as Ritual Performance: Towards a Political Economy of Educational Symbols and Gestures*. London: Routledge.

McLuhan, M. 1964/2003. *Understanding Media: The Extensions of Man*. Gordon, I. (Ed.) Corte Madera: Ginko Press.

McLuhan, M. 1971. *Letters of Marshall McLuhan*. Edited by Molinaro, M., McLuhan, C. and Toye, W. Toronto: University of Toronto Press.

McLuhan, M. and McLuhan, E. 1988. *Laws of Media: The New Science*. Toronto, ON: University of Toronto Press.

Micciche, L. 2014. Writing material. *College English* 76 (6), 488–505.

Michaels, S. and Somer, R. 2000. Narratives and inscriptions: cultural tools, power and powerful sense-making In Cope, B. and Kalantzis, M. (Eds) *Multiliteracies: Literacy Learning and the Design of Social Futures*. New York, NY: Routledge.

Milman, N. 2012. The flipped classroom strategy: what is it and how can it be used? *Distance Learning* 9(3), 85–87.

Milton, J. 1644. *Areopagitica: A Speech of Mr John Milton for the Liberty of Unlicensed Printing to the Parliament of England*. London, UK.

Mulcahy, D. 2012. Thinking teacher professional learning performatively: a sociomaterial account. *Journal of Education and Work* 25(1), 121–139.

Mulcahy, D. 2013. Turning around the question of 'transfer' in education: tracing the sociomaterial. *Educational Philosophy and Theory* 45(12), 1276–1289.

New London Group 1996. *A Pedagogy of Multiliteracies*. Harvard Educational Review, 66(1), 60–92.

Nietzsche, F. 2016. *Anti-Education: On the Future of our Educational Institutions*. Translated by Damion Searls. New York, NY: New York Review of Books.

Nichols, S. 2006. From boardroom to classroom: teaching a globalized discourse on thinking through internet texts and teaching practices. In Pahl, K. and Rowsell, J. (Eds) *Travel Notes from the New Literacy Studies: Instances of Practice*. Clevedon, UK: Multilingual Matters.

Olson, D. 1994. *The World on Paper: The Conceptual and Cognitive Implications of Writing and Reading*. Cambridge, UK: Cambridge University Press.

Ong, W. 2005. *Orality and Literacy: The Technologising of the Word*. London, UK: Routledge.

Onishi, B. 2011. Information, bodies and Heidegger: tracing visions of the posthuman. *Sophia* 50(1), 101–112.

Oxford English Dictionary Online. 2019. https://www.oed.com

Orom, A. 2007. The concept of information versus the concept of document. In In Skare, R., Winfeld Lund, N. and Varheim, A. (Eds) *A Document (Re)turn*. Frankfurt am Main: Laing.

Pahl, K. and Rowsell, J. 2006. *Travel Notes for the New Literacy Studies: Instances of Practice*. Clevedon, UK: Multilingual Matters.

Pahl, K. and Rowsell, J. 2010. *Artifactual Literacies: Every Object Tells a Story*. New York, NY: Teachers College Press.

Pasquale, F. 2015. The algorithmic self. *The Hedgehog Review* 17(1)

Pennycook, A. 2010. *Language as a Local Practice*. London, UK: Routledge.

Pennycook, A. 2016. Posthumanist Applied Linguistics. *Applied Linguistics* 39(4), 445–461.

Pennycook, A. 2017. Translanguaging and semiotic assemblages. *International Journal of Multilingualism* 14(3), 269–282.

Pennycook, A. 2018. *Posthumanist Applied Linguistics*. London, UK: Routledge.

Pennycook, A. and Otsuji, E. 2014a. Metrolingual multitasking and spatial repertoires: 'Pizza mo two minutes coming.' *Journal of Sociolinguistics* 18(2), 161–184.

Pennycook, A. and Otsoji, E. 2014b. Market lingos and metrolingual francas. *International Multilingual Research Journal* 8(4), 255–270.

Pennycook, A. and Otsuji, E. 2017. Fish, phone cards and semiotic assemblages in two Bangladeshi shops in Sydney and Tokyo. *Social Semiotics* 27(4), 434–450.

Pestalozzi, J. 1889. *How Gertrude Teaches her Children*. Syracuse, NY: C.W. Bardeen.

Pickering, A. 2001. Practice and posthumanism: social theory and a history of agency. In Schatzki, Theodore, Karin Knorr-Cetina, and Eike von Savigny, (Eds) *The Practice Turn in Contemporary Theory*. London, UK: Routledge and Taylor and Francis, 163–174.

Power, M. 1994. *The Audit Explosion*. London, UK: Demos.

Power, M. 1997. *The Audit Society: Rituals of Verification*. Oxford, UK: Oxford University Press.

Prensky, M. 2001. Digital natives, digital immigrants. *On the Horizon*, MCB University Press 9(5) https://www.marcprensky.com/writing/Prensky%20-%20Digital%20 Natives,%20Digital%20Immigrants%20-%20Part1.pdf

Prinsloo, P. 2015. Algorithmic decision-making in higher education: there be dragons there . . . 14 December. [Blog post] *Opendistanceteachingandlearning*. https:// opendistanceteachingandlearning.wordpress.com/2015/12/14/algorithmic-decision-making-in-higher-education-there-be-dragons-there/ [Accessed 29 January 2020]

Prinsloo, P. 2017. Fleeing from Frankenstein's monster and meeting Kafka on the way: algorithmic decision-making in higher education. *Elearning and Digital Media* 14(3), 138–163.

Quaye, J. and Harper, J. (Eds) 2015. *Student Engagement in Higher Education: Theoretical Perspectives and Practical Approaches for Diverse Populations* (2nd edn), New York, NY: Routledge.

Reder, S. and Davila, E. 2005. Context and literacy practices. *Annual Review of Applied Linguistics* 25: 170–187.

Rheinberger, H. 1997. *Towards a History of Epistemic Things: Synthesising Proteins in the Test Tube.* Stanford: Stanford University Press.

Roehl, A., Linga Reddy, S. and Jett Shannon, G. 2013. The flipped classroom: an opportunity to engage millennial students through active learning strategies. *Journal of Family and Consumer Sciences* 105(2), 44–49.

Rohl, T. 2015. Transsituating education: educational artefacts in the classroom and beyond. In Bollig, S., Honig, M-S, Neumann, S., Seele, C. (Eds) *MultiPluriTrans in Educational Ethnography: Approaching the Multimodality, Plurality and Translocality of Educational Realities.* Beilefield, Germany: Transcript, 143–161.

Sclater, N., Peasgood, A. and Mullan, J. 2016. *Learning Analytics in Higher Education: A Review of UK and International Practice.* Bristol, UK: JISC.

Sclater, N. and Peasgood, A. 2017. *JISC Briefing: Learning Analytics and Student Success - Assessing the Evidence.* Bristol, UK: JISC.

Scollon, R. 2001. *Mediated Discourse: The Nexus of Practice.* London, UK: Routledge.

Scollon, R. and Scollon, S. 2003. *Discourses in Place: Languages in the Material World.* London, UK: Routledge.

Scollon, R. and Scollon, S. W. 2004. Nexus Analysis: Discourse and the Emerging Internet. New York, NY: Routledge.

Scollon, R. and Scollon, S. W. 2007. Nexus analysis: refocusing ethnography on action. *Journal of Sociolinguistics* 11(5), 608–625.

Schivelbusch, W. 1986. *The Railway Journey: The Industrialisation of Time and Space in the 19th Century.* Berkeley, CA: University of California Press.

Searle, J. 1969. *Speech Acts.* Cambridge, UK: Cambridge University Press.

Searle, J. 1976. A classification of illocutionary acts. *Language in Society* 5, 1–23.

Searle, J. 1979. *Expression and Meaning.* Cambridge, UK: Cambridge University Press.

Sellen, A. and Harper, R. 2002. *The Myth of the Paperless Office.* Cambridge MA: MIT Press.

Shuttleworth Foundation and Open Society Foundations. 2007. *Cape Town Open Education Declaration.* https://www.capetowndeclaration.org/read-the-declaration

Silverstein, M. 1979. Language, structure and linguistic ideology. In Clyne, P., Hanks, W. and Hofbauer, C. (Eds) *The Elements: A Parasession on Linguistic Units and Levels.* Chicago, IL: Chicago Linguistics Society.

Silverstein, M., and Urban, G. (Eds) 1996. *Natural Histories of Discourse*. Chicago, IL: University of Chicago Press. Y1.4 SIL

Smith, R. 2007. An overview of research on student support: helping students to achieve or achieving institutional targets? Nurture or de-nature? *Teaching in Higher Education* 12: 683–695.

Siemens, G. 2005. Connectivism: A Learning Theory for the Digital Age. *International Journal of Instructional Technology and Distance Learning* 2(1), 3–10. http://www. itdl.org/Journal/Jan_05/article01.htm [Accessed 10 August 2017]

Stark, W. 2017. Assembled bodies: reconfiguring quantum identities. *Minnesota Review* 88, 69–82

Street, B. 1984. *Literacy in Theory and Practice*. Cambridge, UK: Cambridge University Press.

Street, B. 1993. Introduction: the new literacy studies. In Street, B. (Ed.) *Cross-Cultural Approaches to Literacy*. Cambridge, UK: Cambridge University Press, 1–21.

Swales, J. 1990. *Genre Analysis: English in Academic and Research Settings*. Cambridge, UK: Cambridge University Press.

Thesen, L. 2009. Researching 'ideological becoming' in lectures: challenges for knowing differently. *Studies in Higher Education* 34(4), 391–402.

Thesen, L. 2007. Breaking the frame: lecture, rituals and academic literacies. *Journal of Applied Linguistics* 4(1), 33–53.

Thomas, L. 2002. Student retention in higher education: the role of institutional habitus. *Journal of Educational Policy* 17: 423–442.

Thompson, T. L. 2012a. I'm deleting as fast as I can: negotiating learning practices in cyberspace. *Pedagogy, Culture and Society* 20(1), 91–110.

Thompson, T. L. 2012b. (Re/Dis)assembling learning practices online with fluid object and spaces. *Studies in Continuing Education* 34(3), 251–266.

Thompson, T. L. 2016. Digital doings: curating work-learning practices and ecologies. *Learning, Media and Technology* 41(3), 480–500.

Thompson, T. L. 2018. The making of mobilities in online work-learning practices. *New Media and Society* 20(3), 1031–1046.

Thorsteinsson, G. and Page, T. 2014. Speaking with things: encoded researchers, social data, and other posthuman concoctions. *Distinktion: Scandinavian Journal of Social Theory* 14(3), 342–361.

Thibodeau, K. 2002. Overview of technical approaches to digital preservation and challenges in the coming years. *The State of Digital Preservation: An International Perspective*. Council on Library and Information Resources Pub107 https://www.clir. org/pubs/reports/pub107/thibodeau/

Thrift, N. 2007. *Non-Representational Theory: Space/Politics/Affect*. London, UK: Routledge.

Trowler, V. 2010. *Student Engagement Literature Review*. York, UK: The Higher Education Academy.

Tucker, B. 2012. The flipped classroom: online instruction at home frees class time for learning. *Education Next* 12(1): 82–83.

Tufte, E. 2003. PowerPoint is evil: power corrupts. PowerPoint corrupts absolutely. *Wired* 11(9), available online https://www.wired.com/2003/09/ppt2/ [Accessed 28 October 2019]

Turkle, S. 2004. The fellowship of the microchip: global technologies as evocative objects. In Suarez-Orozco, M. and Qin-Hilliard, D. (Eds) *Globalization: Culture and Education in the New Millenium*. Berkeley, CA: University of California Press, 97–113.

Turner, V. 1974. Liminal to limanoid in play, flow, and ritual. *Rice University Studies* 60, 53–92. Reprinted in V. Turner 1982. *From Ritual to Theatre: The Human Seriousness of Play*. New York, NY: PAJ, 20–60

UNESCO 2012. What is the Paris OER Declaration? https://en.unesco.org/themes/building-knowledge-societies/oer

Usher, R. and Edwards, R. 1994. *Postmodernism and Education: Different Voices, Different Worlds*. London, UK: Routledge.

van Lennep, D. 1987. The psychology of driving a car. In Kockelmans, J. (Ed.) *Phenomenonological Psychology: The Dutch School*. Dordrecht: Martinus Nijhoff Publishers, 217–227.

van Manen, M. 1990/1997. *Researching Lived Experience: Human Science for an Action-Sensitive Pedagogy*. State University of New York: New York.

van Oenen, G. 2006. A machine that would go of itself: interpassivity and its impact of political life. *Theory & Event* 9(2)

Veletsianos, G. and Kimmons, R. 2012. Networked participatory scholarship: emergent techno-cultural pressures toward open and digital scholarship in online networks. *Computers and Education* 58(2), 766–774. https://www.sciencedirect.com/science/article/pii/S0360131511002454?via%3Dihub

Webopedia. 2005. *Online Tech Dictionary for IT Professionals*. https://www.webopedia.com

Weller, M. 2007. *Virtual Learning Environments: Using, Choosing, and Developing your VLE*. London, UK: Routledge.

Weller, M. 2015. MOOCs and the silicon valley narrative. *Journal of Interactive Media in Education*, 1(5), 107.

White, M. 2008. The hand blocks the screen: a consideration of how the ways of the interface is raced. In HASTAC (Ed.) *Electronic Tectonics: Thinking at the Interface*, 117–128.

Whitehead, D. 2001. Quantum literacy. *Teaching in Higher Education* 6(4), 519–526.

Williamson, B., Knox, J. and Doyle, S. 2014. Education as a calculated public. [blog post] *Code Acts in Education*, 30 May. https://codeactsineducation.wordpress.com/2014/05/30/ [Accessed 29 January 2020]

Williamson, B. 2017. Who owns educational theory? Big data, algorithms and expert power of education data science. *Elearning and Digital Media* 14(3), 105–122

Wolfe, C. 2010. *What is Posthumanism?* University of Minnesota Press MI: Minnesota.

Woydack, J. and Rampton, B. 2016. Text trajectories in a multilingual call centre: the linguistics ethnography of a calling script. *Language in Society* 45, 709–732.

Zepke, N., Leach, L. and Butler, P. 2010. Engagement in post-compulsory education: students' motivation and action. *Research in Post-Compulsory Education* 15: 1–18.

Zizek, S. 1998. The interpassive subject. http://www.lacan.com/zizek-pompidou.htm

Index

Moodle 112–14, 136–7
PowerPoint 104–8, **106**
as proxy for student engagement 155–6
slideshow applications 104, 109
uses of 103, 109, 124
vitalism 14
vitality 48

wayfaring 126, 128, 130, 134–5
Weller, M. 102–3
White, M. 123
Whitehead, D. 139–40

Williamson, B. 156, 157
Wolfe, C. 13
writing
by hand 127
in higher education 42
hyperwriting 129–37
micro-practices of 49–53
as process 130
teaching of 98

Zepke, N. 59
Zhou Bi Suan Jing 100–1